T0406178

# Celebrity, Social Media Influencers and Brand Performance

Saloomeh Tabari • Qing Shan Ding
Editors

# Celebrity, Social Media Influencers and Brand Performance

Exploring New Dynamics and Future Trends in Marketing

palgrave
macmillan

*Editors*
Saloomeh Tabari
Cardiff Business School
Cardiff University
Cardiff, UK

Qing Shan Ding
Huddersfield Business School
University of Huddersfield
Huddersfield, UK

ISBN 978-3-031-63515-1      ISBN 978-3-031-63516-8   (eBook)
https://doi.org/10.1007/978-3-031-63516-8

© The Editor(s) (if applicable) and The Author(s), under exclusive license to Springer Nature Switzerland AG 2024

This work is subject to copyright. All rights are solely and exclusively licensed by the Publisher, whether the whole or part of the material is concerned, specifically the rights of translation, reprinting, reuse of illustrations, recitation, broadcasting, reproduction on microfilms or in any other physical way, and transmission or information storage and retrieval, electronic adaptation, computer software, or by similar or dissimilar methodology now known or hereafter developed.
The use of general descriptive names, registered names, trademarks, service marks, etc. in this publication does not imply, even in the absence of a specific statement, that such names are exempt from the relevant protective laws and regulations and therefore free for general use.
The publisher, the authors and the editors are safe to assume that the advice and information in this book are believed to be true and accurate at the date of publication. Neither the publisher nor the authors or the editors give a warranty, expressed or implied, with respect to the material contained herein or for any errors or omissions that may have been made. The publisher remains neutral with regard to jurisdictional claims in published maps and institutional affiliations.

This Palgrave Macmillan imprint is published by the registered company Springer Nature Switzerland AG.
The registered company address is: Gewerbestrasse 11, 6330 Cham, Switzerland

If disposing of this product, please recycle the paper.

*This book is dedicated with love to my parents, and my first friends Sarah and Mohsen. Thank you for telling me what I am capable of, for giving me the possibility to dream and for believing in me. To Jolanta and Dariusz for being you, love you so much.*
*To my best friend, my love, and my greatest support, Dr Daniel Prokop, who always pushes me to be my best version and looks at the moon with me. Thank you for changing our coffee to decaf and listening to all my moaning.*
*Saloomeh*
*I would like to dedicate this edited book to my loving family, for all the times we spent together and for cherished memories.*
*Qing Shan*

# Preface

This collection is designed with researchers whose expertise is aligned with marketing and consumer behaviour, including research students with a doctorate in these areas who would like to understand the world of celebrities, social media influencers, and brands. The book is structured to discuss not only the changes in consumption behaviour but also broader considerations of the current impact of influencers on marketing strategies and brands. All chapters have been prepared by active researchers in the field and provide a holistic view of current literature and present robust discussion.

The book included ten chapters covering a range of topics within the impact of celebrities and social media influencers on brand performance. The book starts with Chap. 1, introduction. In Chap. 2, Jonathan Wilson, Lika Baghdasaryan, and Laura Arroyo introduce conceptualising influencer, brand, and audience relationships on social media platforms. In Chap. 3, Li Ding explores the effect of social media influencers on customers' perceived brand value, brand-influencer, and purchase intention: a perspective of Gen Z. In Chap. 4, Aafiya Mundakappadath Firose, Wei Chen, and Saloomeh Tabari discuss the impact of social media influencers on choosing a travel destination. In Chap. 5, Eleonora Cattaneo and Yan Sun explore the advantages and disadvantages of using social media influencers for brands. In Chap. 6, Guangjin Su discusses the research on the effect of virtual influencers' endorsement on consumer purchase

vii

intention. In Chap. 7, Ruitong Cui explains the play or attack: exploring identity in the virtual world. In Chap. 8, Saloomeh Tabari and Qing Shin Dang introduce the virtual world, fear of missing out, and its impact on impulsive buying. In Chap. 9, Yan Sun and Chen Yang explore virtual influencers, the future of marketing and branding. The book ends with Chap. 10, Qing Shan Ding and Saloomeh Tabari discuss influencers, materialism, mental health, and sustainability.

Cardiff, UK Saloomeh Tabari
Huddersfield, UK Qing Shan Ding

# Acknowledgements

We would like to thank the contributors to the book for their forbearance in the face of a protracted editorial process, special thanks to the reviewers for their positive and encouraging comments, and the support of the Palgrave Macmillan group.

*Saloomeh and Qing*

# Contents

**1 Introduction**    1
*Saloomeh Tabari and Qing Shan Ding*

**2 Conceptualising Influencer, Brand, and Audience Relationships on Social Media Platforms**    9
*Jonathan A. J. Wilson, Laura Arroyo, and Lika Baghdasaryan*

**3 The Effect of Social Media Influencers' Trustworthiness on Customers' Perceived Brand Value, and Purchase Intention: A Perspective of Gen Z**    39
*Li Ding*

**4 Impact of Social Media Influencers (SMIs) on Millennials Choosing a Travel Destination**    63
*Aafiya Mundakappadath Firose, Wei Chen, and Saloomeh Tabari*

**5 Advantages and Disadvantages for Brands of Using Social Media Influencers**    79
*Eleonora Cattaneo and Yan Sun*

xi

# Contents

**6 Research on the Effect of Brand Virtual Influencers on Consumers' Purchase Intention**     105
*Guangjin Su*

**7 Play or Attack? Navigating Identity in the Virtual World, a Conceptual Perspective on Virtual Influencers and Influencer Marketing**     133
*Esther Ruitong Cui*

**8 Virtual World, Fear of Missing Out and Its Impact on Impulsive Buying**     159
*Saloomeh Tabari and Qing Shan Ding*

**9 Virtual Influencers: The Future of Marketing and Branding?**     175
*Chen Yang and Yan Sun*

**10 Influencers, Materialism, Mental Health and Sustainability**     197
*Qing Shan Ding and Saloomeh Tabari*

**Index**     213

# Notes on Contributors

**Laura Arroyo** is a Digital Marketing Strategist with a career and study that has led her to Puerto Rico, the USA, and the UK. She has worked in several marketing roles, specialising in analytics, social media engagement, influencer brand activation, content creation, fashion, and fitness—in addition to being a micro-influencer in her own right. She received her Bachelor's degree in Public Relations, Advertising and Applied Communication from James Madison University, Virginia, USA, and MSc in Digital Marketing from Loughborough University London, UK. She is also an avid kite surfer and surfer.

**Lika Baghdasaryan** is Assistant Professor of Marketing and Brand Management. She holds a BSc (Hons) in Linguistics and Philology and an MA in International Business and Management, and her doctorate explores iconography, symbolic power, visual culture, and consumption in advertising. Lika regularly chairs industry brand forums and consults businesses on social media, image, and identity strategies.

**Eleonora Cattaneo** is Professor of Marketing and Director of the MSc and Executive Master's in Luxury Brand Management at the Glion Institute of Higher Education in Switzerland. Her research interests are focused on brand revival, brand collaborations, and sustainable luxury. Her areas of luxury research are rebranding, heritage branding, and sustainable buying behaviour. Her work has been published in *Journal of*

xiii

xiv  **Notes on Contributors**

*Brand Management, Long Range Planning,* and *Strategic Change,* among others. She is a senior fellow of the UK Chartered Management Institute and fellow of the Swiss Center for Luxury Research.

**Wei Chen** is Senior Lecturer in Strategic Management at Sheffield Hallam University. He has wide experience in cross-culture management in the hospitality and tourism industry. His book *International Hospitality Management* with Professor Alan Clarke has been published in English, French, and Portuguese, and he has translated books such as *Trade Show and Event Marketing* into different languages. He is the chief overseas editor for *Finance and Economy*, a business magazine in China. Wei Chen is also a senior business advisor of a renowned sports company in England.

**Esther Ruitong Cui** is a postgraduate researcher who is pursuing studies in the field of Fashion Business and Technology at the Department of Materials, University of Manchester. As a graduating teaching assistant at the University of Manchester and a fellow of Advance Higher Education, Ruitong combines academic curiosity with a drive to guide others on their scholarly journeys. Her research pursuits centre on the compelling interplay between fashion and technology, as well as mapping domains within the ever-evolving landscape of management and marketing. In her PhD research, Ruitong utilises qualitative research methodologies to examine two distinct and growing domains: fashion rental and block-chain technology. Underpinning her work is a profound interest in exploring the potential of emerging technologies to facilitate notable advancements in social change within the context of fashion businesses and consumer interactions. Her academic prowess and passion for work have earned her recognition at prestigious conferences and workshops. She was awarded the Best Innovation Research Award at the Global Fashion Conference 2022. She has also been nominated for Best Graduating Teaching Assistant at the University of Manchester for her commitment to teaching and mentorship. Ruitong displays a keen interest in pursuing and cultivating international partnerships with commercial enterprises and scholarly organisations.

**Li Ding** is an assistant professor at Institut Paul Bocuse, France. She graduated from Oklahoma State University in 2018 with a doctoral degree in Hospitality Management. Her research concentrates on hospitality strategic management and financial management. She has published research papers in the *International Journal of Hospitality Management*, *International Journal of Contemporary Hospitality Management*, *International Hospitality Review*, *International Journal of Tourism Sciences*, and *Global Business and Financial Review* and presented research papers at over twenty international academic conferences. She serves as the editorial advisory board member of *Leisure Studies* and review board member of the *International Journal of Business Events and Legacies*.

**Qing Shan Ding** is Senior Lecturer in Marketing at Huddersfield Business School, University of Huddersfield. His primary research interest is consumer behaviour, exploring how various cultural and identity factors influence brand preferences and purchase intentions. He is interested in strategic marketing, examined how FMCG firms adjust their tactics during a crisis such as COVID and investigated how typographic design and transparency information could be utilised to enhance brand authenticity. His research has been published in a few leading international journals and presented in prestigious international conferences. He taught digital and social media marketing in the past and is an active user of social media platforms, including Twitter and LinkedIn, as well as a few influential Chinese social media apps.

**Aafiya Mundakappadath Firose** has completed her Master's degree in Hospitality Management at Sheffield Hallam University.

**Guangjin Su** obtained her PhD in Marketing from Northumbria University, UK, in 2022 and participated in several high-profile conferences. Her doctoral work explores the factors that affect the mobile payments' continuance use in China under different constructs, both habit-related and product-related factors.

**Yan Sun** is Senior Lecturer in Marketing at Oxford Brookes Business School, UK. She is leading specialist modules for MSc International Luxury Marketing at Oxford Brookes University. Yan Sun has published with ABS 3*, 2* and 1* journals, including *Information Technology & People*; *International Journal of Hospitality Management*; *Strategic Change*;

*Journal of Fashion Marketing and Management*; and *Information Management and Computer Security*. Her research interests are luxury marketing, ageing society, digitalisation, and sustainable consumption. She also contributed teaching cases on luxury retailing and international tourists to Bloomsbury Fashion Central.

**Saloomeh Tabari** is Lecturer in Marketing and Strategy at Cardiff Business School, Cardiff University. Her research centres on customer experience in particular intercultural communication and sensitivity in service and marketing. She has a special interest in issues relating to 'cultural differences', 'cross-cultural', and 'cultural centrism' and the provision of service and marketing to different customers to enhance their experiences and perceptions by adopting strategies based upon changes in consumer behaviour. She published my research in various leading international academic journals and books and presented at international conferences. She has co-edited the *Global Strategic Management in the Service Industry: A Perspective of the New Era* book. She is on the editorial board of international journals and associate editor of the *Journal of Islamic Marketing*.

**Jonathan A. J. Wilson** has two doctorates and specialises in what he calls the ABCDs of business: advertising, branding, communications, and digital. He started his career in the late 1990s, working in advertising management roles in London, alongside being a professional musician, with international performances and recording credits. His chair is in Brand Strategy and Culture, with over 200 published pieces of work, 100 listed conference talks across the globe, and travel to 40 countries. He consults brands, governments, and influencers on branding, marketing communications, and consumer behaviour. He has been listed in LinkedIn's annual Top Voices awards for several years.

**Chen Yang** is Lecturer in Digital Marketing at Greenwich University, UK. She holds a PhD in Media Studies (2022) from the University of Westminster. Her research interests include influencer culture, attention economy, self-branding, and online representation. Chen is also the founder of a TikTok-partnered agency in the UK and the top-ranked lifestyle and fitness creator on TikTok UK with more than 250,000 followers.

# List of Figures

| | | |
|---|---|---|
| Fig. 2.1 | The magic marketing triangle (Wilson & Arroyo, 2022) | 12 |
| Fig. 2.2 | Stakeholder typology (Mitchell et al., 1997) | 21 |
| Fig. 2.3 | Brand stakeholder relations model (Wilson, 2011) | 26 |
| Fig. 2.4 | Influencer dual-process mediation model (Wilson & Arroyo, 2022) | 27 |
| Fig. 3.1 | Average time spent per day on social media | 40 |
| Fig. 3.2 | Social media platforms | 41 |
| Fig. 3.3 | US social media buyers by generations | 42 |
| Fig. 3.4 | Proposed research framework | 46 |
| Fig. 3.5 | Frequency of using social media in daily life | 51 |
| Fig. 3.6 | Basic structural model path coefficients | 55 |
| Fig. 4.1 | Conceptual framework. Source: Authors | 71 |
| Fig. 6.1 | Research model. Source: Author | 111 |
| Fig. 6.2 | Research result of hypotheses testing. Note: ***Significant at $p < 0.001$; **Significant at $p < 0.01$; *Significant at $p < 0.05$ | 122 |
| Fig. 8.1 | Conceptual framework, SMIs' influence on UTB because of FOMO and peer pressure of followers. Source: Authors | 166 |

# List of Tables

| | | |
|---|---|---|
| Table 2.1 | Classifying and ranking influencer reach and audience engagement (Wilson & Arroyo, 2022) | 17 |
| Table 2.2 | Brand stakeholders (Wilson, 2011) | 22 |
| Table 3.1 | Demographic information ($n$ = 312) | 50 |
| Table 3.2 | Correlation table ($n$ = 312) | 51 |
| Table 3.3 | Summary of the measurement model | 53 |
| Table 3.4 | PLS-SEM bootstrapping results (5000 subsamples) | 54 |
| Table 3.5 | PLS-SEM bootstrapping MGA results (5000 subsamples) | 55 |
| Table 6.1 | Demographic details of the respondents ($N$ = 486) | 117 |
| Table 6.2 | Construct measures, factor loadings, and reliability and validity measures | 118 |
| Table 6.3 | Correlations and discriminant validity | 120 |
| Table 6.4 | Results of path analysis | 121 |

# 1

# Introduction

### Saloomeh Tabari and Qing Shan Ding

The celebrity endorsement technique has been employed by many brands as their main technique of advertising (Wei & Lu, 2013). By choosing the appropriate endorser, the marketer may enhance attitudes and reinforce behavioural intentions (Knoll & Matthes, 2017) and shape brand perceptions (Erdogan et al., 2001). Companies devoted a lot to celebrity endorsement to exploit emotional bonds between consumers and brands to accomplish higher brand image, brand awareness, differentiation, and brand loyalty (Thomson, 2006). Recent studies have indicated that celebrity endorsement contributes to the perceived quality of the brand, but the direct and indirect effects of celebrity attachment on brand attachment and brand loyalty have not been fully investigated (Um &

---

S. Tabari (✉)
Cardiff Business School, Cardiff University, Cardiff, UK
e-mail: tabaris@cardiff.ac.uk

Q. S. Ding
Huddersfield Business School, University of Huddersfield, Huddersfield, UK
e-mail: Q.s.ding@hud.ac.uk

© The Author(s), under exclusive license to Springer Nature Switzerland AG 2024
S. Tabari, Q. S. Ding (eds.), *Celebrity, Social Media Influencers and Brand Performance*,
https://doi.org/10.1007/978-3-031-63516-8_1

Jang, 2020; Özer et al., 2022). The number of celebrity endorsement strategies has increased over the past few years by brands. While in Western countries the contribution of celebrity endorsement is around 15% (Schimmelpfennig & Hunt, 2020), this has reached 60% in some Asian countries (Chung & Cho, 2017). Jain and Roy (2016) stated that the celebrity endorsement process not only transfers the meanings from celebrities to the endorsed brand as well as emotions. In addition, celebrities can foster brand-related attitudes such as self-concept and brand quality as well as behavioural intention in a celebrity endorsement process. Consumers set personal goals based on reference points of their celebrities (Choi & Rifon, 2012). Studies by Erdogan (1999) and Spry et al. (2011) suggested that celebrities enhance the success of the celebrity endorsement strategy because consumers trust their favourite celebrity and the recommendation made by them. Brands endorsed by a favourite celebrity become more credible and trustworthy.

Considering the growing popularity of social media advertising using celebrities and influencers to endorse the brand is more than ever gaining attention from marketers and brands. The popularity of social media personalities provided opportunities for social media influencers (SMI), who help to shape consumer attitudes towards a brand (Freberg et al., 2011). Studies have shown that collaborating with a YouTube influencer can give a brand four times more lift in brand familiarity than collaborating with a celebrity (Newberry, 2018).

Schouten et al. (2020) stated that influencers have a more constructive and positive impact because consumers find it easier to trust and identify with the brand. Therefore, SMIs have the power to influence a wider audience's purchase decisions, by developing deeper and more meaningful relationships and also being seen as more trustworthy with their followers (Belanche et al., 2021; Djafarova & Rushworth, 2017). Influencers are frequently linked with millennials in different areas like fashion, luxury travel, and cosmetics, but recently they have appeared across a broad range of age groups and products (Campbell & Farrell, 2020). SMIs try to create a connection, engagement, and trust with their followers through self-disclosure, whereas the audience engages with them through their comments, likes, or sharing (Gómez, 2019).

Furthermore, followers of SMIs have shown impulsive purchases of fashion and cosmetic products (Prihana Gunawan & Permadi Iskandar, 2020). The trust gained by SMIs has a significant role in enhancing the urge-to-buy (UTB) impulsively on social networking sites (Shamim & Islam, 2022). On the other hand, SMIs are considered role models with a high impact on their follower's behaviour, and who also are responsible for any ethical and unethical behaviour they exhibit on their platform. For instance, some SMIs end up using fake authenticity campaigns or unsustainable consumption which leads to fast fashion.

Comparisons between traditional celebrities and influencers are specific interests of the brands. The research on influencer marketing for advertising practice is still growing days, and the pandemic has not only increased social media usage among all generations (Insider Intelligence, 2020) but also suggested the need for a better understanding of influencer marketing as a key advertising tool (Hudders et al., 2021; Taylor, 2020). However, the rise of SMIs implements social pressures on all generations specifically on the young generation for urge-to-buy (UTB) and impulsive consumption to feel part of the group due to Fear of Missing Out (FoMO). Furthermore, the increased usage of AI and the three-dimensional virtual world (metaverse) has provided many opportunities for brands to leverage virtual influences. The metaverse offers experiences around play, work, connection with groups, and consumption. Virtual influencers extend higher engagement and gain attention among young consumers especially Gen Z's compared to human influencers. However, still social media's dark side, the negative effects of self-evaluation, body image, unrealistic expectations, fear of missing out and unsustainable consumption need to be explore and discuss further, along with the topic of, how brands employ celebrities, and SMIs as key opinion leaders or virtual influencers (metaverse) for endorsement.

This edited book addresses the need to examine the new era of marketing by focusing on the impact of employing celebrities, SMIs, and virtual influencers to endorse the brand as a key advertising tactic for companies. The contributors focus on the rise of social media usage and the change in advertising strategies in the digital era. Below we have highlighted each chapter's significance and how it adds to our understanding of the changing nature of brand marketing via social media and influencers. To begin with, Chap. 2, by Jonathan Wilson, Lika Baghdasaryan, and Laura Arroyo, opens up the discussion on the effect of influencers on emotion, lifestyle choices, and purchase intention.

In Chap. 3, Li Ding investigates the social media influencer's trustworthiness in Gen Z's buying intention, by looking at 312 Gen Z restaurant-goers in the United States and their impact on the decision-making process of them. Chapter 4, by Aafiya Mundakappadath Firose, Wei Chen, and Saloomeh Tabari, turns to the decision-making process of millennials on travel destinations through the social media influencer's comments. The study demonstrates the importance of transparency and authenticity of influencers and the impact of their recommendations on destination branding.

In Chap. 5, Eleanora Cattaneo and Yan Sun focus on the advantages and disadvantages of using social media influencers by brands by interviewing two social media influencers. In Chap. 6, Guangjin Su draws on the effect of using virtual influencers by brand on purchase intention, the importance of influencers' characteristics, and how their interactivity and popularity can increase the purchase intention of customers. In Chap. 7, Ruitong Cui investigates the use of the concept of the virtual influencer within the marketing and use of avatars and the negative impact on individuals' self-esteem and overall well-being. In Chap. 8, Saloomeh Tabari and Qing Shan Ding address the fear of missing out on an urge to buy within the virtual world by providing a conceptual framework to show these relationships. Chapter 9, by Chen Yang and Yan Sun, on the future of brand marketing and using virtual influencers, looks at different case studies from Chinese virtual influencers. In Chap. 10, Qing Shan Ding discusses the mental health and sustainability of influencer and looking at the materialism issues and negative aspects of it on influencers and their followers.

## The Origins of This Book

This book is the result of a series of truly collaborative endeavours that in many ways has resulted in the emergence of social media influences and brand performance with an interest in the book's subject matter. Most of the contributors to the volume are established researchers in this area, and as editors, we are grateful for all the fresh and novel chapters they have provided. Taken as a whole, they result in a wealth of new insights on the increased use of influencers and virtual influencers on brand performance while looking at both the negative and positive sides of these concepts on both customer influencers and brands. We hope that this book will give readers a lot to consider when considering how social media influencers affect brand performance.

# References

Belanche, D., Flavián, M., & Ibáñez-Sánchez, S. (2021). Followers' reactions to influencers' Instagram posts. *Spanish Journal of Marketing-ESIC.*

Campbell, C., & Farrell, J. R. (2020). More than meets the eye: The functional components underlying influencer marketing. *Business Horizons, 63*(4), 469–479.

Choi, S. M., & Rifon, N. (2012). It is a match: The impact of congruence between celebrity image and consumer ideal self on endorsement effectiveness. *Psychology and Marketing, 29*(9), 639–650.

Chung, S., & Cho, H. (2017). Fostering parasocial relationships with celebrities on social media: Implications for celebrity endorsement. *Psychology and Marketing, 34*(4), 481–495.

Djafarova, E., & Rushworth, C. (2017). Exploring the credibility of online celebrities' Instagram profiles in influencing the purchase decisions of young female users. *Computers in Human Behavior, 68*, 1–7.

Erdogan, B. Z. (1999). Celebrity endorsement: A literature review. *Journal of Marketing Management, 15*(4), 291–314.

Erdogan, B. Z., Baker, M. J., & Tagg, S. (2001). Selecting celebrity endorsers: The practitioner's perspective. *Journal of Advertising Research, 41*(3), 39–48.

Freberg, K., Graham, K., McGaughey, K., & Freberg, L. (2011). Who are SMIs? A study of public perceptions. *Public Relations Review, 37*, 90–92. https://doi.org/10.1016/j.pubrev.2010.11.001

Gómez, A. R. (2019). Digital fame and fortune in the age of social media: A classification of social media influencers. *aDResearch: Revista Internacional de Investigación en Comunicación*, (19), 8–29.

Gunawan, P., & Iskandar, P. (2020). Analyzing the impact of fashion influencer on online impulsive buying behavior. In *International conference on economics, business and economic education 2019, KnE social sciences* (pp. 350–363). https://doi.org/10.18502/kss.v4i6.6611

Hudders, L., De Jans, S., & De Veirman, M. (2021). The commercialization of social media stars: A literature review and conceptual framework on the strategic use of social media influencers. *International Journal of Advertising, 40*(3), 327–375. https://doi.org/10.1080/02650487.2020.1836925

Insider Intelligence. (2020). *Global Instagram users 2020.* Accessed June 2023, from https://www.emarketer.com/content/global-instagram-users-2020

Jain, V., & Roy, S. (2016). Understanding meaning transfer in celebrity endorsements: A qualitative exploration. *Qualitative Market Research: An International Journal, 19*(3), 266–286.

Knoll, J., & Matthes, J. (2017). The effectiveness of celebrity endorsements: A meta-analysis. *Journal of Academy of Market Science, 45*(1), 55–75. https://doi.org/10.1007/s11747-016-0503-8

Newberry, C. (2018, May 2). *23 Benefits of social media for business.* Accessed August 20, 2022, from https://blog.hootsuite.com/social-media-for-business

Özer, M., Özer, A., Ekinci, Y., & Koçak, A. (2022). Does celebrity attachment influence brand attachment and brand loyalty in celebrity endorsement? A mixed methods study. *Psychology & Marketing*, 1–17. https://doi.org/10.1002/mar.21742

Schimmelpfennig, C., & Hunt, J. B. (2020). Fifty years of celebrity endorser research: Support for a comprehensive celebrity endorsement strategy framework. *Psychology & Marketing, 37*(3), 488–505.

Schouten, A. P., Janssen, L., & Verspaget, M. (2020). Celebrity vs. influencer endorsements in advertising: The role of identification, credibility, and product-endorser fit. *International Journal of Advertising, 39*(2), 258–281.

Shamim, K., & Islam, T. (2022). Digital influencer marketing: How message credibility and media credibility affect trust and impulsive buying. *Journal of Global Scholars of Marketing Science, 32*(4), 601–626. https://doi.org/10.1080/21639159.2022.2052342

Spry, A., Pappu, R., & Bettina Cornwell, T. (2011). Celebrity endorsement, brand credibility and brand equity. *European Journal of Marketing, 45*(6), 882–909.

Taylor, D. G. (2020). *Social media usage, FOMO, and conspicuous consumption: An exploratory study: An abstract* (pp. 857–858). Springer International Publishing.

Thomson, M. (2006). Human brands: Investigating antecedents to consumers' strong attachments to celebrities. *Journal of Marketing, 70*(3), 104–119.

Um, N. H., & Jang, A. (2020). Impact of celebrity endorsement type on consumers' brand and advertisement perception and purchase intention. *Social Behavior and Personality: An International Journal, 48*(4), 1–10.

Wei, P. S., & Lu, H. P. (2013). An examination of the celebrity endorsements and online customer reviews influence female consumers' shopping behavior. *Computers in Human Behavior, 29*(1), 193–201.

# 2

# Conceptualising Influencer, Brand, and Audience Relationships on Social Media Platforms

### Jonathan A. J. Wilson, Laura Arroyo, and Lika Baghdasaryan

## Introduction

In an increasingly mobile-first integrated marketing communications brandscape, how marketers are attempting to find ways of grabbing attention and engineering engagement has never been more accessible and at the same time challenging. With added noise and choice, consumer attention spans are becoming shorter; and being marketed to, most of the time, is viewed as an unwanted intrusion.

The growth of influencer marketing has transformed more traditional online marketing approaches: in redefining what constitutes an advertisement according to designated media spaces; blurring the lines between

J. A. J. Wilson (✉) • L. Baghdasaryan
International Business, Regent's University London, London, UK
e-mail: WilsonJ@regents.ac.uk; Lilit.Baghdasaryan@regents.ac.uk

L. Arroyo
Loughborough University, London, UK
e-mail: laura.arroyo439@gmail.com

© The Author(s), under exclusive license to Springer Nature Switzerland AG 2024
S. Tabari, Q. S. Ding (eds.), *Celebrity, Social Media Influencers and Brand Performance*,
https://doi.org/10.1007/978-3-031-63516-8_2

marketing communications channels; increasing customer intimacy; expanding classical definitions as to what constitutes an influencer or celebrity; and eliciting greater consumer reciprocity and interactivity.

From marketing activities that incorporate high-profile celebrity endorsement, right down to micro-influencers who are consumers active on social media where they share their views, preferences, and purchases publicly, companies are turning to this tactic increasingly for branded product and service recommendations—as an augmented approach to advertising via social media.

While classic advertising is defined as a promotional activity that exists in a designated media space only for advertising, these social media posts that are native among other regular posts now also have evolved into being classified as advertising. This is due to the contractual obligations which are drawn up between parties where in return celebrities and influencers are paid for their social media posts; and legislation necessitating that such content is labelled with hashtags happens, to indicate that they are forms of paid advertising promotional activities.

With this, traditional forms of advertising are being disrupted also by rich social media content that is both dynamic and long-tailed—due to search and reshares. Furthermore, the ability to access a broader reach at lower costs, target audiences more precisely, improve customer relationships, and the opportunity to obtain big and thick consumer data behaviour are some of the reasons why social media marketing is becoming one of the most effective and preferred marketing promotional strategies.

Social media influencers can be categorised according to platform, reach, audiences, and influence. In particular, micro-influencers are becoming one of the most requested types of social media influencers, despite the larger levels of reach comparably that celebrities and macro-influencers have—due to studies that point to micro-influencers having more effective levels of engagement and influence among followers, relative to metrics and resources.

Micro-influencer marketing started off as online word-of-mouth marketing (Wong, 2014). However, as it gained popularity, brands started collaborating with micro-influencers, moving the industry towards online sponsored endorsements or user-generated advertorial models. Some of the most common forms of social media marketing are through sponsored posts and paid collaborations. This switch from word-of-mouth marketing to online sponsored advertising has played an important role in shaping how consumers perceive social media micro-influencers.

With these in mind, this chapter investigates the categories and differences between influencers in more detail, people's perceptions and purchasing behaviour linked to influencers, and how performance is measured. Furthermore, as the micro-influencer industry has evolved rapidly during the past decade in response to diminishing returns, which is raising questions about the future of the industry, we are interested also in how greater understanding of benchmarking possibly could help address stakeholder concerns.

# Understanding the Performative and Collaborative Nature of Marketing Communications

## The Advertising Hydra

Online platforms facilitate a form of consumption, with associated rituals, interactions, and emotional transactions within communities that exhibit tribalism (Kozinets, 1999; Cova & Cova, 2002; Kozinets, 2006; Cova et al., 2007; Kozinets et al., 2017). In addition, social media tribalism is becoming commoditised and commercialised in innovative and entrepreneurial ways, through advertising and brand endorsement agreements where "[t]ribal entrepreneurship is distinct from conventional entrepreneurship since it involves managing and commercializing existing emotional bonds" (Mardon et al., 2018, p. 451).

Furthermore, influencers are perceived to betray their fellow tribe members where "they appear to prioritize their own financial interests over the interests of the tribe. Recurring moral betrayals included a lack of transparency surrounding sponsorship, the production of sub-standard content or merchandise, and declining interaction with non-Guru tribe members" (Mardon et al., 2018, p. 448).

Therefore, with these developments, existing social tensions and obligations are being contested and mediated by a broad range of stakeholders—in the theatre of social media platforms, and the presence of an advertising hydra seeking to increase its influence.

## The Magic Marketing Triangle

The emergence of influencers on social media has gained significant attention from businesses and is currently the most popular strategy used by marketing professionals (Dinesh, 2017). According to a survey by the Association of National Advertisers (2018), "75% of companies currently employ influencer marketing and almost half plan to increase their spending in the next year. However, the majority aren't sure about the effectiveness of their influencer marketing strategies (44% neutral, 19% said it's ineffective, 36% said it's effective)."

With arguments for the rise in significance of influencers and social media areas, we observe how in a digital, increasingly mobile first environment, where social media permeates and punctuates many of our everyday behaviours, three domains have emerged as the engines driving marketing communications today (Wilson & Arroyo, 2022; Fig. 2.1). Here, advertising, branding, and consumption feed each other in a perceived virtuous cycle, generating laddered transactions and social currency (Enke & Borchers, 2019; Wilson, 2011).

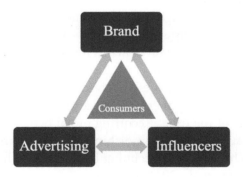

**Fig. 2.1** The magic marketing triangle (Wilson & Arroyo, 2022)

Consumer brand experience is the foundation of consumers' branded preferences. In addition, perceptions of different brand meanings help to build such preferences (Ebrahim et al., 2016). Amos et al. (2008) and Lou and Yuan (2019) find that celebrity endorsers are most effective at influencing purchase intentions, brand attitudes, and attitudes towards advertisements when their credibility has been ratified—and this is according to trustworthiness, celebrity expertise, and attractiveness. More recently, with the increase in rich multimedia user-generated content creation, Xiao et al. (2018) also cite quality of argument and content as being essential components in establishing credibility.

Celebrity and Influencer endorsements, whether sponsored or not, where their perceived authenticity and attractiveness is positively related to the images and content that they post, do yield more favourable perceptions. However, favourability does diminish with sponsored content, especially where the perceived fit of the endorser or their relevant expertise is not aligned sufficiently and there is insufficient transparency (De Veirman & Hudders, 2020; De Cicco et al., 2020; Martínez-López et al., 2020a, b; Shan et al., 2020; Trivedi & Sama, 2020).

One way of bridging these gaps is through a blending process, drawing on Word Of Mouth (WOM) and peer endorsements (Jin & Phua, 2014; Kwon et al., 2014; Chu et al., 2016; Pöyry et al., 2019; Martínez-López et al., 2020a, b). Nevertheless, having made this observation: Lou et al. (2019) argue that consumers express much more positive sentiments towards influencer-promoted advertisements over brand-promoted advertisements.

Furthermore, heavy social media users demonstrate cultlike appreciation for influencers' product sharing and show high involvement in their influencer-promoted advertisements and products. Hayes and Carr (2020) report on how peer-generated snark and schadenfreude towards competitor brands were effective among in-group communities, who exhibit preferences towards brands they identify with and reinforce their self-identity. Bennett et al. (2020) also highlight how a bad-boy influencer image and celebrity scandals create hedonic fantasy relationships, which allow consumers an escape from everyday life—enhancing endorser effectiveness.

**14**     J. A. J. Wilson et al.

It is these activities that point towards an evolving and augmented approach to integrated marketing communications and advertising, where experiential consumer intimacy, collaborative personalisation, dialogue, and validation are crucial (Wilson, 2011; Colliander et al., 2015). But Childers et al. (2019) also find from their study that still advertising agency professionals feel that this billion-dollar influencer marketing industry is largely uncharted territory.

## Celebrities, Endorsers, and Influencers

Increasingly, these terms are being used interchangeably. McCracken (1989) defines a celebrity endorser "as any individual who enjoys public recognition and who uses this recognition on behalf of a consumer good by appearing with it in an advertisement" (p. 310). The creation of celebrity is viewed as a competitive weapon in mature and saturated markets, filled with advertising clutter and almost no room for actual product differentiation (Erdogan, 1999).

Over the past two decades, an approach to the digital branded self has mushroomed into an economy, encompassing personal consumption and the individual identities of professionals—as a means to amplify a personal identity and possible vehicle for monetisation. "The productive identity work for the creation of a professional self in the digital economy cannot but be a social process embedded in a web of ties where collaboration mingles with competition and cooperation in a unique domain" (Gandini, 2016, p. 136).

Beyond this form of self-expression intended to contribute towards identity construction and presentation (Belk, 1988; Sirgy, 1982; Eckhardt et al., 2015; Ma et al., 2017), Sung et al. (2018) find that "[r]egardless of the reasons, those who post brand-selfies aim to associate themselves with those brands, and they expect to benefit from such associations" (p. 17). Brands are viewed as effective means of self-expression and, furthermore, those that post selfies are more receptive to brand/product messages on social networking sites (Sung et al., 2018).

Social media influencers have risen as phoenixes in a world tired of marketing propaganda. With such suspicion, consumers turn to real people, who dedicate their time for free, offering real personal views that are authentically their own, with values and principles. However, this channel relationship did not last long, before marketers saw a hack, and influencers found a side-hustle and potential new career path.

According to Freberg et al. (2011), "Social media Influencers (SMIs) are independent third-party endorsers, who through posts on blogs, Twitter, Instagram, and other social media, express their experience and opinions, shaping the public attitude towards brands, causes, and such other matters" (p. 90). As such, social media influencers have become one of the most important and effective components of today's online marketing platforms.

Do Nascimento et al. (2020) highlight how endorsement deals fulfil several functions for influencers: "Acting as providers and partners, instead of offering only financial returns, brands create value for digital endorsers by enabling experiences, connections with other actors and recognition within the marketing system on social media. For smaller bloggers, brand endorsement will come from activities that help progress the influencer's career, seeding goodwill and therefore generating spontaneous praise and reviews for the brand" (p. 16). Findings from Kay et al. (2020) reinforce the argument for micro-influencers increasing in importance as consumers demonstrate higher levels of purchase intentions from their sponsored posts compared with macro-influencers, due to held perceptions that micro-influencers have greater product knowledge.

As the world, communications, and consumption become more digital and mobile-first, this relatively new marketing strategy has outgrown traditional forms of advertising such as print media and television commercials. Some of the benefits social media influencers possess are their agility, the way with which they are able to align themselves with sectors and product categories, offering a higher return on investment relative to other marketing communications channels, and their high degree of influence on a customer's purchasing decision (Brown & Hayes, 2008, p. 50).

## Does Size of Following Matter?

Brown and Fiorella (2013) define macro-influencers as "[i]ndividuals with a large active social following comprised of people with whom they have a loosely defined or unknown relationship" (p. 122). Macro-influencers mostly consist of celebrities who get paid for sponsoring products and/or services on their social media platforms. On the other hand, Brown and Fiorella (2013) define micro-influencers as individuals within a consumer's social graph who have a direct impact on their followers' behaviour, based upon the nature of their relationship—forged through social media interactions and personalised communications.

The banding of influencer categories is still yet to be formalised. However, there are similarities between the grouping of followers outlined in reports by Gibs (2017), Ismail (2018), Statista (2019), and Griffin (2020). Gibs (2017), from L2 Inc., presents the following classification:

Mega: over 1 million (2–5% Audience Engagement [AE])
Macro: 100K–1 million (5–25% AE)
Micro: 1–100K (25–50% AE)
Nano: less than 1K (50% AE)

Their findings measure the efficacy of influencers, where L2 Inc. determined the average lift in engagement associated with brand mentions of influencers of 10 different community sizes, ranging from fewer than 20,000 followers to over 7 million. Their sample included 5038 influencers partnered with 875 brands across 16 sectors.

Gibs (2017) presents results that reveal a U-shaped curve where:

Micro-influencers (under 70,000 followers) and macro-influencers (over 2.5M followers) provide brands with engagement lifts above 10%, with mega-influencers (over 7M followers) yielding outsized lifts in engagement.

Middling influencers (70,000–2.5M followers), however, generate disappointingly low lifts under 10%.

## 2 Conceptualising Influencer, Brand, and Audience... 17

The main differences between macro-influencers and micro-influencers are their audiences, reach level, and engagement. When compared to micro-influencers, macro-influencers have a larger audience and broader reach than micro-influencers—however, micro-influencers have higher levels of engagement (Zinck, 2018; Markerly, 2020). Markerly (2020) also state that influencers in the 10K–1000K follower range "offer the best combination of engagement and broad reach, with like and comment rates that exceed influencers with a higher number of followers."

The reality is that if influencers have millions of followers, then the numbers are so big that they get sizeable engagement. However, micro-influencers also offer an attractive marketing proposition—as they are much cheaper, tend to know most of their followers, and therefore drive engagement through responding to comments.

Gibs (2017) went on to assert, "This should be a red flag to brands, as influencer contract value is heavily dependent on follower count, often overlooking engagement. Therefore, middling influencers cost more than micro-influencers, despite generating less engagement."

Two years later, Gartner L2 Intelligence (2019) reclassified influencers according to more detailed categories (recreated by Wilson & Arroyo, 2022 in Table 2.1), ranking success according to two objectives of reach versus audience engagement:

Notably, the minimum numbers for micro-influencers have increased, micro-influencers have now also been split into small influencers, and the term "nano" has been replaced by "advocate." Statista (2019) and other agencies and trend forecasting firms still, however, continue to use the term "nano-influencer."

**Table 2.1** Classifying and ranking influencer reach and audience engagement (Wilson & Arroyo, 2022)

| Rank | Reach | Audience engagement |
|---|---|---|
| 1 | Mega influencers: 1–7 million | Advocate influencers: 0–5K |
| 2 | Celebrity influencers: +7 million | Micro influencers: 5–25K |
| 3 | Large influencers: 250K–1 million | Large influencers: 250K–1 million |
| 4 | Small influencers: 25–100K | Celebrity influencers: +7 million |
| 5 | Medium influencers: 100–250K | Mega influencers: 1–7 million |
| 6 | Micro influencers: 5–25K | Medium influencers: 100–250K |
| 7 | Advocate influencers: 0–5K | Small influencers: 25–100K |

Schouten et al. (2020) find that consumers identify with influencers more than celebrities, with stronger feelings of similarity that lead to higher levels of trust. In turn, this wishful identification and trust mediates advertising effectiveness, making them better product endorsers. Xiao et al. (2018) describe this as a form of homophily. Bae (2019) also finds that even with consumers who are sceptical of a social media message, if they pay sufficient attention to heuristic cues and cognitive elaboration is present, then the perception of message credibility is enhanced and leads to greater purchase intention.

Furthermore, following a landmark case, according to the UK Advertising Standards Authority (ASA), anybody with more than 30,000 followers on social media is now defined as a "celebrity" and that means they are governed by advertising codes of conduct, which mean they have to declare any paid agreements and use the designated hashtags indicating this (Glenday, 2019). With an increasing ubiquity of the term "celebrity," this poses further challenges for those who appear on reality television shows and become overnight successes with a spike in followers—because what they post suddenly comes under this scrutiny, which they may be unaware of.

## A Turning Tide Against Influencer and Advertising Effectiveness?

Noguti and Waller (2020) argue that people's motivations for using media are to seek information, excitement, relaxation, emotional support, and an escape from everyday life. They make the observation that as online search and mobile apps have become more sophisticated and prevalent over the years, they are requiring less active "surfing" from individuals and this in turn increases perceptions of advertising intrusion, which potentially diminishes their overall effectiveness.

Having made these points, Voorveld et al. (2018) are critical of the term "social media" as an umbrella term used by advertising planners, as it offers little value—in the same way that broadcast media does not reflect the differences between television and radio. Their reasoning is that advertising effectiveness and engagement are bound in context over content, and the reasons for consumption differ across platforms, as each offers a unique experience. For example, Instagram is used as a pastime, for topicality and to fill empty moments. Also, Facebook and Twitter users are unappreciative of advertising.

Therefore, whilst advertisers may ensure large numbers of views, advertisements interrupt what is supposed to be a social experience, and they face a trade-off between winning attention and losing consumer acceptance of their brand (Voorveld et al., 2018). Whilst they may be critical of the term, their findings do offer reasons why brands are attempting to advertise and broadcast through leveraging the followings of influencers—as they offer more subtle and less intrusive messaging, greater context, and a snowballing of user-generated collaborative creative, which in turn leads to a multiplying effect of a creative concept.

Furthermore, "in consumer culture's current era of consent, it is the co-constructed and socially activated nature of 'consumer charisma' that has allowed YouTubers to enhance their level of authority, disrupt orthodoxies and spark interest in a new order. However, once these new orders have been established, various rules and institutions emerge to guide their influence, ultimately leading to the routinization and fading of charisma" (Cocker & Cronin, 2017, p. 467).

Following on, Cronin and Cocker (2019) argue that a zombification process occurs where influencers effectively pass for human, in an attempt to manipulate communities with artificial filtered emotions, coerced intimacy, and a manufactured notion of equality—which lead to emotional neutrality and more manageable forms of sociability and totemic worship. Whilst in many ways this is of detriment to social media tribes and goes against the raison d'être of their existence and core function, it is reflective of the impact of commercialising communication and movement towards transforming these interactions into an augmented advertising channel.

Khamis et al. (2017) were equally critical of the rise of self-branding, micro-celebrities and social media influencers: "At stake is how these practices capitalize on the apparent democratization of media production and distribution, whereby entry levels are comparatively low and potential reach, in terms of audience and influence, is spectacularly high"

(p. 205). They go on to say that "Instafame" has led to "… subjectivity to a political economy defined almost completely by consumerist logic"; and roles historically reserved for trained professionals now being occupied by quasi-experts and "the near-total extension of marketing logic and language into more areas of contemporary social life" (p. 205).

These studies demonstrate that there are differing opinions when it comes to perceived trust among micro-influencers. Most academic research focuses on the macro-influencer or celebrity industry. In contrast, there is little research that goes into detail behind the understanding of the motivations that influence consumers to follow micro-influencers, or into studying the virtual relationships consumers have with micro-influencers from a theorised and conceptual level.

# Brand Stakeholders

Windsor (1992) highlights that broad or narrow views of stakeholders' universe effect the way in which they are defined and subsequently classified. The Freeman (1984) definition takes a broad view, suggesting that "companies can indeed be vitally affected by, or they can vitally affect almost anyone" (Mitchell et al., 1997, p. 857)—whilst that expressed by Freeman and Reed (1983) is narrower, focusing instead on those whom an organisation is dependent on "for its continued survival" (p. 91).

Mitchell et al. (1997) classify stakeholders according to their power, legitimacy, and urgency, grouping them accordingly within overlapping dimensions (Fig. 2.2).

From their literature search they cite that legitimacy is rooted in either some form of contractual relationship or desirability. However, the brand communication stakeholder interplay, in turn, yields the idea that legitimacy will become problematic—as it is in fact self-governed, self-defined, and difficult to regulate. From this desirability may not be experienced by all associated parties, nor might formal contractual relationships exist. An example of this occurs when observing the prominence of the self-elected anti-branding and no-Logo movements that have been able to exert their influence.

## 2 Conceptualising Influencer, Brand, and Audience...

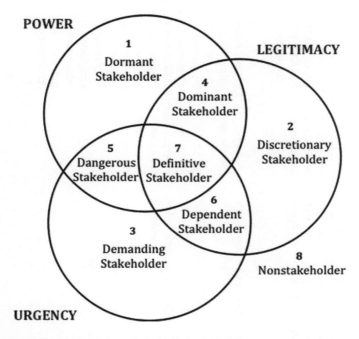

**Fig. 2.2** Stakeholder typology (Mitchell et al., 1997)

Building on their work and focusing on brands, Wilson (2011) classifies brand stakeholders according to:

Ownership/non-ownership/temporary ownership, donership (temporary ownership)
Usage/non-usage
Communication (Table 2.2)
Stake—qualified according to: bargaining power/interest/impact (Fig. 2.3).

Each of these states is seen to have a positive, negative, or neutral effect on the brand in question. The dotted line represents a notion of contractual obligations: which are actual, in a physical format; or implied and psychological. For example, when looking at the media, advertising channel partners are bound by formal written agreements, whilst journalists who act as public relations gatekeepers have no obligation to support or

**Table 2.2** Brand stakeholders (Wilson, 2011)

| Who | Main attributes | The stake | Power | Legitimacy | Urgency | Main direction of communication | Evaluation |
|---|---|---|---|---|---|---|---|
| Owner (internal) | Commercial brand accountability and interest in others' consumption | Key/ primary | High–low *(subject to role)* | High–Med *(subject to role)* | High–low *(subject to role)* | To owners, non-owners and doners | Influence, involvement and level of accountability |
| Non-owner (external) | An interest in consumption— without commercial gains | Secondary/ key | Low– high | Low–high | Low–high | To owners, non-owners | Opinion, value, influence, involvement, emotional attachment |
| User Key consumer (e.g. .celebrity, social networker) | Awareness and active brand opinion— driving consumption | Secondary/ key | Med– high | Med–high | Med–high Consistent | To users, non-users, owners and doners | Recall, recency/ frequency/ value of consumption, level of involvement, emotional attachment, pull to recommend |

| Active non-user gatekeeper (e.g. media, NGO, government, social networkers) | Awareness and active brand opinion—but no consumption | Secondary/ key | Med–high | High/low | High Temporal | To decision-making owners, users and non-users | Opinion, level of influence, pull to recommend |
|---|---|---|---|---|---|---|---|
| User Consumer | Awareness and active brand opinion—driving consumption | Secondary | Low–Med | Med | Med Consistent | To users and non–decision making owners | Recall, recency/ frequency/ value of consumption, level of involvement, emotional attachment, pull to recommend |
| Passive non-user (e.g. general public, brands, firms, intermediaries) | Awareness and passive brand opinion—but no consumption | Secondary | Low | Low | Low Fleeting | To users and non-users | Top of mind awareness, opinion, pull to recommend |

(*continued*)

**Table 2.2** (continued)

| Who | Main attributes | The stake | Power | Legitimacy | Urgency | Main direction of communication | Evaluation |
|---|---|---|---|---|---|---|---|
| Doner (external) | Drawn towards an interest in others' the consumption | Key/ secondary | Med– high | High–low | High | To owners and non-owners | Opinion, influence, involvement, emotional attachment |
| Key consumer (celebrities, social networkers) | User-initiated brand opinion, driving consumption | Key/ secondary | High– Med | High–Med | High-Med consistent | To users, non-users, owners and doners | Recall, recency/ frequency/ value of consumption, level of involvement, emotional attachment, pull to recommend |
| Media (paid for promotion) | Owner-initiated brand opinion, driving consumption | Key/ secondary | Med– high | Med–high | High Fleeting | To non-owners and decision-making Owners | Level of influence, recency/ frequency/ reach, level of involvement |

| Endorser (individuals/ firms, binding contract) | Owner-initiated brand opinion, driving consumption | Key/ secondary | Med | High | High Temporal | To non-owners, decision-making Owners | Level of influence, level of involvement, emotional attachment, compliance with agreed terms and conditions |
| Channel partner | Collaborative, driving consumption | Key/ secondary | Low– high | High | High Persistent | To owners and non-owners | Level of involvement, level of influence, reach, pull to recommend |

**Fig. 2.3** Brand stakeholder relations model (Wilson, 2011)

champion a brand. From this it can also be seen that those who share a psychological contract pose a greater potential threat to brands, due to a lack of control over their communications and ability to influence brand meanings and perceptions.

## Conceptualising Consumer Processing of Influencer-Led Advertising and Branding

Following theoretical and empirical analyses, Wilson and Arroyo (2022) present a new influencer dual process mediation model (Fig. 2.4), as an adaptation of the elaboration likelihood model and the dual mediation hypothesis model of advertising processing—building on the work of Petty and Cacioppo (1981, 1986), MacKenzie et al. (1986), Schumann et al. (2012), Karson and Fisher (2005a, b), Kamble (2014), and Schouten et al. (2020).

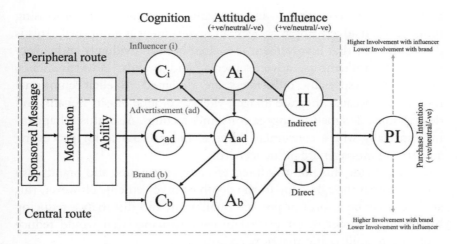

**Fig. 2.4** Influencer dual-process mediation model (Wilson & Arroyo, 2022)

They map out the conditions of cognition, resulting in elicited attitudes and influence, resulting finally in a cued intention—holding that attitudes towards influencers and advertisements follow a double loop that affects attitudes towards the brand. However, attitudes towards influencers in part operate independently via a peripheral route eliciting indirect influence.

As with conventional advertising theory, they assert that attitudes towards advertisements affect future cognition of influencers and brands.

Finally, they argue that purchase intention can be judged along a blended scale, where at the extremities:

Consumers engaged via a *peripheral route* are more highly involved with influencers than the associated brand.
Consumers engaged via the *central route* are more highly involved with the brand than the associated influencer.

In contrast to consumer behavioural dichotomies that argue for rational or emotional constructs: based upon the findings of Wilson and Arroyo (2022), they instead argue that de facto due to the involvement individually and collectively of influencers, advertisements, and brands, and especially consumers' interest and preference for processing influencer-led advertising messages, all involvement is emotional. This is due to the way that involvement is elicited both individually and collectively with influencers, advertisements, and brands. Advertisements, brands, and especially influencers are designed to elicit emotional responses—because they use images, videos, colours, music, slogans, and descriptions, designed to engage consumer feelings. Also, this is happening especially where consumers' interest and preference for processing advertising messages are influencer-led.

Having made this point, influencers, advertisements, and brands also evoke rational thought, due to the depth of involvement. However, this at times may be a form of post-rationalisation and dissonance reducing behaviour, in order to remove cognitive dissonance that would reduce motivation, ability, and therefore cognition.

In short, if consumers are not thinking and feeling to a sufficient level, then they will ignore the sponsored message—but if they are engaged, then consumers create meanings to support their reality.

## Performance Managerial Implications

A series of quantitative hard numerical values largely form the ways of assessing the effectiveness of sponsored advertising and branded content posted by influencers—which consider:

Number of social media account followers
Number of social media likes and comments on posts
Conversion, according to click-through/swipe links and promotional codes, which may or may not be linked to sales rates
Post ranking according to hashtags and geographic location

## Reshares by Followers

Each of these values is used as stand-alone metrics to establish stand out, reach, and impact—but also collaboratively, with the rationale being that critical mass is achieved through cumulative performance in a number of categories. While there is consensus on these values forming the bedrock for evaluating performance and they are used almost as a form of currency, currently, there is no one definitive benchmark, which has led to brands, agencies, and market research consultancies using these metrics to create their own ratings.

An example of this can be seen on the platform TRIBE designed for brands and content creators. They define a micro-influencer as being someone with 30,000+ followers on Facebook, Instagram, or Twitter, and charges per post are linked to the number of followers, detailed in a banding grid. TRIBE has their own rating system, but in addition they state that the quality of content and how long it took to create should also be taken into account, with regard to costing (TRIBE, 2021).

In accordance with TRIBE's recommendations, and the findings of Wilson and Arroyo (2022), the authors also argue that qualitative metrics are equally important when assessing performance. Quality, according to timeliness, context, relevance, relatability, tone, emotional connection, aesthetics, arresting uniqueness, and busy engagement from sufficient followers with immediacy, is crucial—when trying to achieve a level resonance that translates into marketing effectiveness. A key challenge with evaluating these qualitative, psychographic, more heterogeneous, and softer metrics is that while they are more insightful, they are more difficult to categorise, rank, and rate.

Furthermore, machine learning is making this task more possible. This is the process of acquiring T-shaped knowledge, also referred to as "big" and "thick" data—where breadth and depth are achieved. This approach of championing the art of science and the science of art benefits influencers as creative content creators in rewarding a wider skillset. However, over the long term this data-driven approach may take creative control away from influencers and place further power in the hands of larger firms with access to wider data points.

It is also worth mentioning that the metrics of judging influence, engagement, and effectiveness vary vastly between platforms, and a comparison between LinkedIn and TikTok offers a good example of this. LinkedIn awards for Top Voices are given to users, along with badges, who on other platforms would be considered micro-influencers, due to their number of followers. YouTube with its subscriber function raises the bar higher as to who they classify as an influencer, as many users find attracting subscribers more difficult than attracting followers on other social media platforms. This is largely because users do not need to have a profile to access YouTube in the same way as with other platforms, and less users create content, leading to them also not feeling the need to create an account. The year 2023 has also seen Meta launch a platform called Threads to rival Twitter, which will mean that metrics of effectiveness are likely to increase steeply as they grow. Furthermore, platforms such as Instagram and Twitter have changed their approach to the "blue tick" verification process, whose status among users is highly prized and interpreted beyond verification as a mark of influence and standing.

## Conclusions

Influencers who demonstrate genuine vulnerability and authenticity, possess two essential factors needed to improve the likelihood of them being more influential, trustworthy, and credible among their target stakeholder groups. Vulnerability, genuineness, and authenticity are determined by how transparent and honest an influencer is in their content and choice of brand association, through words and images. In addition, endorsing products that influencers bought, used, and believed in and stating whether they were being paid for a sponsored collaboration are some of the factors that increase perceptions of genuineness—hence their opinion would serve as a review.

Even though social media followers exhibit contradictory affective and cognitive views about influencers concerning their trustworthiness, a significant number of especially heavy usage social media users nevertheless state that they feel more comfortable purchasing a product that is recommended by an influencer.

Furthermore, while they may also express negative and perhaps paradoxical views in relation to growing consumerism in society, which influencers promote: they acknowledge that from a business perspective, it is beneficial for companies to continue collaborating with influencers—which are perhaps an indicator of some followers' aspirations to themselves become influencers, or simply an expression of where influencers, advertisements, and brands do not resonate, and therefore elicit negative feelings.

The biggest effect that influencers have on purchasing intent is indirect: where they are exposing brands to wider categories, lifestyle choices, experiences, and communities. This entices audiences to conduct further research on brands, stimulating general interest, desire, and word of mouth advocacy. Ultimately, it is judged by advertisers that this will result in consumers purchasing more of the same product, a similar product by a different brand, or different product from the same brand later on—as appetites for consumption increase through exposure, socialisation, and conditioning.

Influencer power, leading to the likelihood of direct influence, is increased when there is sufficient authenticity, context, and relevance and a personal relationship with the influencer or knowing a friend that purchased a product recommended by the influencer are present.

The influencer dual-process mediation model is an adaptation of the elaboration likelihood model and the dual mediation hypothesis model of advertising processing—where attitudes towards influencers and advertisements follow a double loop that affects attitudes towards the brand. Furthermore, in contrast to consumer behavioural dichotomies that argue for rational or emotional constructs, it instead argues that consumers' interest and preference for processing influencer-led advertising messages are all predominantly emotional, regardless of the product or service type.

Finally, qualitative metrics judging quality on a deeper level are essential components in assessing performance. Here, quality according to timeliness, context, relevance, relatability, tone, emotional connection, aesthetics, arresting uniqueness, and busy engagement from sufficient followers with immediacy is crucial—when trying to achieve a level of resonance that translates into marketing effectiveness.

# References

Amos, C., Holmes, G., & Strutton, D. (2008). Exploring the relationship between celebrity endorser effects and advertising effectiveness. *International Journal of Advertising, 27*(2), 209–234. https://doi.org/10.1080/0265048 7.2008.11073052

Association of National Advertisers. (2018, April 3). *Advertisers love influencer marketing: ANA study.* ANA Press Release: New York. https://www.ana.net/content/show/id/48437

Bae, M. (2019). Role of skepticism and message elaboration in determining consumers' response to cause-related marketing claims on Facebook brand pages. *Journal of Current Issues and Research in Advertising.* https://doi.org/1 0.1080/10641734.2019.1666071

Belk, R. W. (1988). Possessions and the extended self. *Journal of Consumer Research, 15*(2), 139–168.

Bennett, D., Diamond, W., Miller, E., & Williams, J. (2020). Understanding bad-boy celebrity endorser effectiveness: The fantasy-based relationship, hedonic consumption, and congruency model. *Journal of Current Issues and Research in Advertising, 41*(1), 1–19. https://doi.org/10.1080/1064173 4.2018.1519469

Brown, D., & Fiorella, S. (2013). *Influence marketing – How to create, manage, and measure brand influencers in social media marketing.* Que Publishing.

Brown, D., & Hayes, N. (2008). *Influencer marketing, who really influences your customers?* Elsevier Ltd. 235 pages.

Childers, C. C., Lemon, L. L., & Hoy, M. G. (2019). #Sponsored #Ad: Agency perspective on influencer marketing campaigns. *Journal of Current Issues and Research in Advertising, 40*(3), 258–274. https://doi.org/10.1080/1064173 4.2018.1521113

Chu, S.-C., Chen, H.-T., & Sung, Y. (2016). Following brands on Twitter: An extension of theory of planned behaviour. *International Journal of Advertising, 35*(3), 421–437. https://doi.org/10.1080/02650487.2015.1037708

Cocker, H. L., & Cronin, J. (2017). Charismatic authority and the YouTuber: Unpacking the new cults of personality. *Marketing Theory, 17*(4), 455–472. https://doi.org/10.1177/1470593117692022

Colliander, J., Dahlén, M., & Modig, E. (2015). Twitter for two: investigating the effects of dialogue with customers in social media. *International Journal of Advertising, 34*(2), 181–194. https://doi.org/10.1080/0265048 7.2014.996197

Cova, B., & Cova, V. (2002). Tribal marketing: The tribalisation of society and its impact on the conduct of marketing. *European Journal of Marketing, 36*(5/6), 595–620.

Cova, B., Kozinets, R. V., & Shankar, A. (2007). *"Tribes, Inc.: The new world of tribalism." Consumer tribes* (pp. 3–26). Routledge.

Cronin, J., & Cocker, H. L. (2019). Managing collective effervescence: 'Zomsumption' and postemotional fandom. *Marketing Theory, 19*(3), 281–299. https://doi.org/10.1177/1470593118787589

De Cicco, R., Iacobucci, S., & Pagliaro, S. (2020). The effect of influencer–product fit on advertising recognition and the role of an enhanced disclosure in increasing sponsorship transparency. *International Journal of Advertising*. https://doi.org/10.1080/02650487.2020.1801198

De Veirman, M., & Hudders, L. (2020). Disclosing sponsored Instagram posts: The role of material connection with the brand and message-sideness when disclosing covert advertising. *International Journal of Advertising, 39*(1), 94–130. https://doi.org/10.1080/02650487.2019.1575108

Dinesh, D. (2017). Why micro-influencers are a social media marketing imperative for 2017. *EContent, 40*(3), 14–15.

Do Nascimento, T. C., Dias Campos, R., & Suarez, M. (2020). Experimenting, partnering and bonding: A framework for the digital influencer-brand endorsement relationship. *Journal of Marketing Management*. https://doi.org/10.1080/0267257X.2020.1791933

Ebrahim, R., Ghoneim, A., Irani, Z., & Fan, Y. (2016). A brand preference and repurchase intention model: The role of consumer experience. *Journal of Marketing Management, 32*(13–14), 1230–1259. https://doi.org/10.1080/0267257X.2016.1150322

Eckhardt, G. M., Belk, R. W., & Wilson, J. A. J. (2015). The rise of inconspicuous consumption. *Journal of Marketing Management, 21*(7–8), 807–826.

Enke, N., & Borchers, N. S. (2019). Social media influencers in strategic communication: A conceptual framework for strategic social media influencer communication. *International Journal of Strategic Communication, 13*(4), 261–277. https://doi.org/10.1080/1553118X.2019.1620234

Erdogan, B. Z. (1999). Celebrity endorsement: A literature review. *Journal of Marketing Management, 15*(4), 291–314. https://doi.org/10.1362/026725799784870379

Freberg, K., Graham, K., McGaughey, K., & Freberg, L. (2011). Who are the social media influencers? A study of public perceptions of personality. *Public Relations Review, 37*(1), 90–92.

Freeman, R. E. (1984). *Strategic management: A stakeholder approach*. Pitman.

Freeman, R. E., & Reed, D. L. (1983). Stockholders and stakeholders: A new perspective on corporate governance. *California Management Review, 25*(3), 93–94.

Gandini, A. (2016). Digital work: Self-branding and the social capital in the freelance knowledge economy. *Marketing Theory, 16*(1), 123–141. https://doi.org/10.1177/1470593115607942

Gartner L2 Intelligence. (2019). *Social platforms & influencers 2019 report*. https://www.gartner.com/en/marketing/research/data-tools/influencers-2019

Gibs, J. (2017). *Measuring the efficacy of influencers*. L2 Inc, Medium. https://medium.com/@L2_Digital/measuring-the-efficacy-of-influencers-8da9deec908b

Glenday, J. (2019, July 4). ASA defines anyone with over 30,000 social media followers as a 'celebrity'. *The Drum*. https://www.thedrum.com/news/2019/07/04/asa-defines-anyone-with-over-30000-social-media-followers-celebrity

Griffin, S. (2020, January 8). Trends: So you want to be a social influencer? *Metro*. https://www.metro.news/trends-a-third-of-brits-want-to-tap-into-a-lucrative-social-media-world-but-you-need-to-put-in-the-effort-to-make-it-work/1866425/

Hayes, R. A., & Carr, C. T. (2020). Snark happens: Effects of schadenfreude on brand attitudes. *Journal of Current Issues and Research in Advertising, 41*(2), 243–256. https://doi.org/10.1080/10641734.2020.1738290

Ismail, K. (2018, December 10). Social media influencers: Mega, macro, micro or nano. *CMS Wire*. https://www.cmswire.com/digital-marketing/social-media-influencers-mega-macro-micro-or-nano/

Jin, S.-A. A., & Phua, J. (2014). Following celebrities' tweets about brands: The impact of Twitter-based electronic word-of-mouth on consumers' source credibility perception, buying intention, and social identification with celebrities. *Journal of Advertising, 43*(2), 181–195. https://doi.org/10.1080/00913367.2013.827606

Kamble, A. A. (2014). DMM model in celebrity: Brand advertisements. *SCMS Journal of Indian Management, October–December*, 89–96.

Karson, E. J., & Fisher, R. J. (2005a). Re-examining and extending the dual mediation hypothesis in an on-line advertising context. *Psychology and Marketing, 22*, 333–351.

Karson, E. J., & Fisher, R. J. (2005b). Predicting intentions to return to the web site: Extending the dual mediation hypothesis. *Journal of International Marketing, 19*(3), 2–14.

Kay, S., Mulcahy, R., & Parkinson, J. (2020). When less is more: The impact of macro and micro social media influencers' disclosure. *Journal of Marketing Management, 36*(3–4), 248–278. https://doi.org/10.1080/0267257X.2020.1718740

Khamis, S., Ang, L., & Welling, R. (2017). Self-branding, 'micro-celebrity' and the rise of social media influencers. *Celebrity Studies, 8*(2), 191–208. https://doi.org/10.1080/19392397.2016.1218292

Kozinets, R. V. (1999). E-tribalized marketing?: The strategic implications of virtual communities of consumption. *European Management Journal, 17*(3), 252–264.

Kozinets, R. V. (2006). Click to connect: Netnography and tribal advertising. *Journal of Advertising Research, 46*, 279–288.

Kozinets, R., Patterson, A., & Ashman, R. (2017). Networks of desire: How technology increases our passion to consume. *Journal of Consumer Research, 43*(5), 659–682.

Kwon, E. S., Kim, E., Sung, Y., & Yoo, C. Y. (2014). Brand followers. *International Journal of Advertising, 33*(4), 657–680. https://doi.org/10.2501/IJA-33-4-657-680

Lou, C., & Yuan, S. (2019). Influencer marketing: How message value and credibility affect consumer trust of branded content on social media. *Journal of Interactive Advertising, 19*(1), 58–73. https://doi.org/10.1080/15252019.2018.1533501

Lou, C., Tan, S.-S., & Chen, X. (2019). Investigating consumer engagement with influencer- vs. brand-promoted ads: The roles of source and disclosure. *Journal of Interactive Advertising, 19*(3), 169–186. https://doi.org/10.1080/15252019.2019.1667928

Ma, J. W., Yang, Y., & Wilson, J. A. J. (2017). A window to the ideal self: A study of UK Twitter and Chinese Sina Weibo selfie-takers and the implications for marketers. *Journal of Business Research, 74*(May), 139–142.

MacKenzie, S. B., Lutz, R. J., & Belch, G. E. (1986). The role of attitude toward the ad as a mediator of advertising effectiveness: A test of competing explanations. *Journal of Marketing Research, 23*, 130–143.

Mardon, R., Molesworth, M., & Grigore, G. (2018). YouTube Beauty Gurus and the emotional labour of tribal entrepreneurship. *Journal of Business Research, 92*(2018), 443–454. https://doi.org/10.1016/j.jbusres.2018.04.017

Markerly. (2020). *Instagram marketing: Does influencer size matter?* https://markerly.com/blog/instagram-marketing-does-influencer-size-matter/

Martínez-López, F. J., Anaya-Sánchez, R., Esteban-Millat, I., Torrez-Meruvia, H., D'Alessandro, S., & Miles, M. (2020a). Influencer marketing: Brand control, commercial orientation and post credibility. *Journal of Marketing Management.* https://doi.org/10.1080/0267257X.2020.1806906

Martínez-López, F. J., Anaya-Sánchez, R., Giordano, M. F., & Lopez-Lopez, D. (2020b). Behind influencer marketing: Key marketing decisions and their effects on followers' responses. *Journal of Marketing Management, 36*(7–8), 579–607. https://doi.org/10.1080/0267257X.2020.1738525

McCracken, G. (1989). Who is the celebrity endorser? Cultural foundations of the endorsement process. *Journal of Consumer Research, 16*(3), 310–321. https://doi.org/10.1086/209217

Mitchell, R. K., Agle, B. R., & Wood, D. J. (1997). Toward a theory of stakeholder identification and salience: Defining the principle of who and what really counts. *Academy of Management Review, 22*(4), 853–886.

Noguti, V., & Waller, D. S. (2020). Motivations to use social media: Effects on the perceived informativeness, entertainment, and intrusiveness of paid mobile advertising. *Journal of Marketing Management.* https://doi.org/1 0.1080/0267257X.2020.1799062

Petty, R. E., & Cacioppo, J. T. (1981). *Attitudes and persuasion: Classic and contemporary approaches.* Wm C. Brown.

Petty, R. E., & Cacioppo, J. T. (1986). The elaboration likelihood model of persuasion. *Advances in Experimental Social Psychology, 19*, 123–162.

Pöyry, E., Pelkonen, M., Naumanen, E., & Laaksonen, S.-M. (2019). A call for authenticity: Audience responses to social media influencer endorsements in strategic communication. *International Journal of Strategic Communication, 13*(4), 336–351. https://doi.org/10.1080/1553118X.2019.1609965

Schouten, A. P., Janssen, L., & Verspaget, M. (2020). Celebrity vs. influencer endorsements in advertising: The role of identification, credibility, and product-endorser fit. *International Journal of Advertising, 39*(2), 258–281. https://doi.org/10.1080/02650487.2019.1634898

Schumann, D. W., Kotowski, M. R., Ahn, H., & Haugtvedt, C. P. (2012). The elaboration likelihood model: A 30-year review. In S. Rodgers & E. Thorson (Eds.), *Advertising theory* (pp. 51–68). Routledge.

Shan, Y., Chen, K.-J., & Lin, J.-S. E. (2020). When social media influencers endorse brands: The effects of self-influencer congruence, parasocial identification, and perceived endorser motive. *International Journal of Advertising, 39*(5), 590–610. https://doi.org/10.1080/02650487.2019.1678322

Sirgy, J. M. (1982). Self-concept in consumer behaviour: A critical review. *Journal of Consumer Research, 9*(3), 287–300.

Statista. (2019). *Global Instagram user age & gender distribution 2019 | Statistic.* [online]. Accessed May 18, 2019, from https://www.statista.com/statistics/248769/age-distribution-of-worldwide-instagram-users/

Sung, Y., Kim, E., & Choi, S. M. (2018). #Me and brands: Understanding brand-selfie posters on social media. *International Journal of Advertising, 37*(1), 14–28. https://doi.org/10.1080/02650487.2017.1368859

TRIBE. (2021). The inside scoop on how much UK influencers ear per post. *Influencer Resources.* Accessed May 30, 2021, from https://www.tribegroup.co/blog/how-much-tribe-uk-influencers-earn-per-post

Trivedi, T., & Sama, R. (2020). The effect of influencer marketing on consumers' brand admiration and online purchase intentions: An emerging market perspective. *Journal of Internet Commerce, 19*(1), 103–124. https://doi.org/10.1080/15332861.2019.1700741

Voorveld, H. A. M., van Noort, G., Mutinga, D. G., & Bronner, F. (2018). Engagement with social media and social media advertising: The differentiating role of platform type. *Journal of Advertising, 47*(1), 38–54. https://doi.org/10.1080/00913367.2017.1405754

Wilson, J. A. J. (2011). The brand stakeholder approach – Broad and narrow-based views to managing consumer-centric brands. In A. Kapoor & C. Kulshrestha (Eds.), *Branding and sustainable competitive advantage: Building virtual presence.* IGI Global.

Wilson, J. A. J., & Arroyo, L. (2022). Conceptualising 'performance' attitudes towards social media micro-influencers. *International Journal of Business Performance Management, 23*(3), 257–284.

Windsor, D. (1992). Stakeholder management in multinational enterprises. In S. N. Brenner & S. A. Waddock (Eds.), *Proceedings of the third annual meeting of the international association for business and society* (pp. 121–128). Leuven.

Wong, K. (2014, September 10). The explosive growth of influencer marketing and what it means for you. *Forbes.* https://www.forbes.com/sites/kylewong/2014/09/10/the-explosive-growth-of-influencer-marketing-and-what-it-means-for-you/?sh=4dc0871452ac

Xiao, M., Wang, R., & Chan-Olmsted, S. (2018). Factors affecting YouTube influencer marketing credibility: A heuristic-systematic model. *Journal of Media Business Studies, 15*(3), 188–213. https://doi.org/10.1080/1652235 4.2018.1501146

Zinck, B. M. (2018, October 28). Forget celebrity influencers – Reach micro-influencers who impact your brand. *Diginomica.* https://diginomica.com/forget-celebrity-influencers-reach-micro-influencers-who-impact-your-brand

# 3

# The Effect of Social Media Influencers' Trustworthiness on Customers' Perceived Brand Value, and Purchase Intention: A Perspective of Gen Z

Li Ding

## Introduction

Generation Z refers to the people who were born between 1995 and 2010 (McKinsey & Company, 2023). The identity of Gen Z is closely associated with digital technologies, anxiety from global climate change, and financial uncertainty (Djafarova & Foots, 2022; McKinsey & Company, 2023). One of the unique characteristics of Gen Z is their "digital natives." According to a report from McKinsey & Company (2023), Gen Z young people conduct more and more daily activities online, such as working, learning, making friends, gaming, virtually traveling, and shopping. Many of these online activities are achieved through a variety of social media platforms, such as TikTok, Instagram, Snapchat, Facebook, Twitter, Pinterest, and Reddit. Therefore, Gen Z makes up a significant portion of social media users. Figures 3.1, 3.2, and 3.3 from

---

L. Ding (✉)
Faculty of Management, Institut Lyfe, Ecully, France
e-mail: lding@institutlyfe.com

© The Author(s), under exclusive license to Springer Nature Switzerland AG 2024
S. Tabari, Q. S. Ding (eds.), *Celebrity, Social Media Influencers and Brand Performance*,
https://doi.org/10.1007/978-3-031-63516-8_3

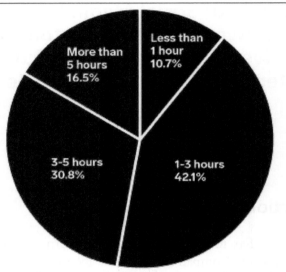

Fig. 3.1 Average time spent per day on social media

Insider Intelligence (2022) show the characteristics of US Gen Zers with social media. In the sample, nine in ten respondents spent more than one hour on social media. A number of social media platforms are popular among Gen Zers and they are open to change. The Gen Zers would like to purchase from social media. Hence, a better understanding of the relationship between Gen Zers and social media is essential to study their online consumption behaviors.

This chapter focuses on exploring the impact of Gen Z consumers' perceived trustworthiness toward Gen Z social media influencers on their brand value perceptions and further purchase intentions in the context of the restaurant sector. Social media influencers are "people who have built

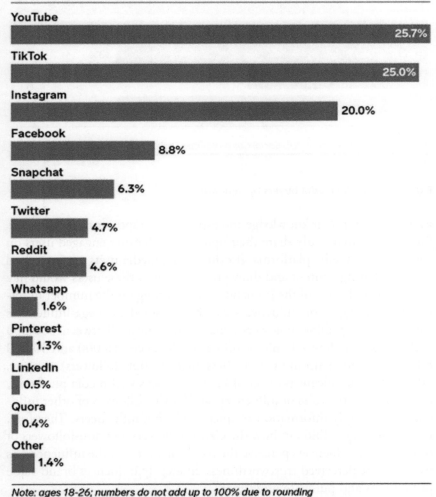

Fig. 3.2 Social media platforms

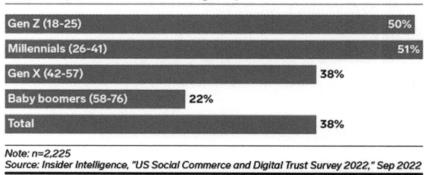

**Fig. 3.3** US social media buyers by generations

a reputation for their knowledge and expertise on a specific topic" (Geyser, 2023). They frequently share their opinions with other engaged users on certain social media platforms. If other social media users are interested in these sharing content and draw great attention, these users would like to become followers of the influencers. Depending on the number of followers, four types of influencers can be classified as mega-influencers (more than 1 million followers), macro-influencers (between 500,000 and 1 million followers), micro-influencers (between 10,000 and 50,000 followers), and nano-influencers (less than 10,000 followers) (Geyser, 2023). As a significant portion of Gen Zers use social media platforms, they may play the roles of influencers and/or the followers of other influencers, or simply information recipients of other influencers. Therefore, it is interesting to find out how the Gen Z followers and non-followers of other Gen Z influencers perceive the trustworthiness of the influencers as well as if the perceived trustworthiness differently influences brand value perceptions and purchase intentions.

Following these research questions, this chapter is structured as five sections including introduction, literature review, methodology, results, and conclusions.

## Literature Review

### Social Media Influencers

Social media influencers provide power in digital marketing at a lower cost, compared to using traditional advertising approaches (Kirkpatrick, 2016). They use their influence on social media platforms to recommend products and/or services and give descriptions to audiences in a quick manner. The delivered information may affect audiences' attitudes toward the products and/or services as well as their purchase intentions (Putri & Tiarawati, 2021; Khan et al., 2022; Bu et al., 2022). Social media influencers frequently share their experiences with downloading and reviewing by their followers who have common interests. In this way, they can obtain public opinions regarding the sharing content which influences customers' purchase intentions (Nurhandayani et al., 2019). The followers compose a large group of audiences who receive the information shared by the influencers on social media platforms. The followers present high trustworthiness toward the social media influencers they followed (Mabkhot et al., 2022). Therefore, using social media influencers as a marketing tool is effective to raise brand awareness and attract target audiences (Tuten, 2020).

Social media influencers and their audiences build the online social network and benefit from it. A social network is defined as "the collection of all the formal and informal social ties to which an actor is connected" (Che et al., 2018). Mirkovski et al. (2018) pointed out that an individual's social connectedness and other engaged activities with others reflect his/her position in a social network. The social network theory can be used to interpret the exchanged experience and other interactions among individuals in a society or community (Borgatti & Foster, 2003; Sun et al., 2022). Also, it can explain how social media influencers affect other audiences' attitudes and purchase behaviors.

The restaurant industry includes a significant number of independent restaurants which geographically diverse. In the US restaurant market, nearly 70% of restaurants are operated independently (National Restaurant Association, 2021). In recent years, with the growth of influencer marketing, more and more restaurants use food-related influencers to reduce marketing costs and attract more customers (Sun et al., 2022; Leung et al., 2022).

## Perceived Brand Value and Purchase Intention

Purchase intention refers to the genuine inclination of consumers toward commodities (Fishbein & Ajzen, 1975). This concept encompassed a combination of consumers' concerns and the likelihood of actually buying the products. Some earlier studies indicated a strong association between purchase intention and the attitude or preference consumers held for a particular brand or product (Kim & Ko, 2012; Martín-Consuegra et al., 2018). Purchase intention could also be influenced by individual perceptions and unpredictable situations (Kotler, 2003). Personal preferences and unforeseen circumstances were identified as factors that could alter purchase intention (Kotler, 2003). Purchase intention shows the inclination of consumers to purchase products/services. Essentially, the higher a customer's desire to buy a product/service, the stronger their purchase intention (Schiffman & Kanuk, 2000).

The concept of perceived value has received great attention since 1980 (Ajina, 2019). A customer's perceived brand is defined as "the consumer's overall assessment of the utility of a product based on perceptions of what is received and what is given" (Zeithaml, 1988, p. 14). It refers to the consumer's evaluation of the benefits gained versus the costs incurred. A broad scope included in this term also encompasses many factors like perceived price, benefits, quality, and cost (Mathwick et al., 2001), and further extends to the discussion of its emotional, social, epistemic, and conditional dimensions (Roh et al., 2022). Perceived value plays a critical role as the primary predictor that influences customers' preferences and behavioral intentions (Teng & Wu, 2019; Molinillo et al., 2021; Dam, 2020). Based on these insights, Hypothesis 1 is proposed as:

*H1.* Gen Z customers' perceived brand value is positively associated with their purchase intention of restaurant brands.

## Perceived Trustworthiness, Perceived Brand Value, and Purchase Intention

The perceived trustworthiness of social media influencers significantly influences consumers' purchase intentions and actual purchase behaviors (Yuan & Lou, 2020). As Cheung et al. (2020) pointed out, followers are more likely to search and obtain the information provided by social media influencers about product endorsements, when a social media influencer is seen as trustworthy. Additionally, social media influencers who consistently share informative content can build emotional connections with their followers, positively impacting their inclination to purchase the recommended products or brands (Ki et al., 2020). Brands that are associated with endorsers perceived as trustworthy tend to enjoy higher levels of brand credibility and brand attitude, resulting in increased perceived brand value and purchase intention (Fang et al., 2016; Wang & Scheinbaum, 2018). Based on these insights, Hypothesis 2 is proposed as:

*H2*. Gen Z customers' perceived trustworthiness toward Gen Z social media influencers is positively associated with their purchase intention of restaurant brands.

*H3*. Gen Z customers' perceived trustworthiness toward Gen Z social media influencers is positively associated with their perceived brand value.

*H4*. Gen Z customers' perceived brand value mediates the relationship between perceived trustworthiness toward Gen Z social media influencers and their purchase intention of restaurant brands.

## Followers and Non-Followers of Social Media Influencers

On social media platforms, parasocial relationships are formed (Tukachinsky & Stever, 2019). Parasocial relationship refers to "the long-lasting, cross-situational connection that media users have established with a media character" (Breves & Liebers, 2022, p. 775). The social media users who followed influencers, especially over a long period, may intensify and integrate with the interpersonal relationship with the influencers (Knapp et al., 2014; Breves et al., 2021). The persuasive effect of social media influencers is enhanced in the parasocial relationship. Because the followers have known the social media influencers for a long time (e.g., influencers' personal information), it may build a strong parasocial relationship. Along with the interactions on social media, followers may highly trust the influencers as their friends (Boerman & van Reijmersdal, 2020; Breves et al., 2019). With high levels of parasocial relationships, the followers were found to show less judgment toward the source credibility based on perceived brand-influencer congruence (Breves et al., 2019). Compared with non-followers, long-term followers of social media influencers showed higher levels of parasocial relationships and source credibility (Breves et al., 2021). Hence, the followers may show more favorable evaluations of the recommended products/services and high purchase intentions, if their persuasive resistance is reduced by strong parasocial relationships with the influencers (Breves et al., 2021).

The proposed research framework is presented in Fig. 3.4.

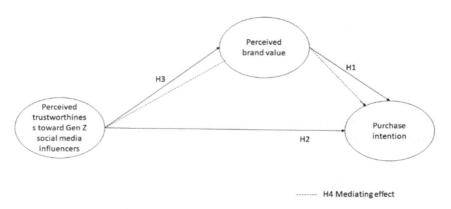

**Fig. 3.4** Proposed research framework

## Methods

This study targeted Gen Z customers who were born after 1995 but older than 18 years. The data were collected in the spring of 2023. The online surveys were distributed through the Amazon MTurk platform. The qualified participants who were in the Generation Z group were asked to provide more opinions about their perceptions regarding the social media influencers' impact on their restaurant brand purchase intention. The proposed research model indicated the minimum sample size as 68, which was estimated by G*Power 3.1.9.7 with a probability level of 0.05, a statistical power level of 0.80, and a medium effect size of 0.15 (Hair et al., 2017; Memon et al., 2020). A total of 312 usable completed questionnaires were collected.

This study conducts data collection by two groups. In the survey, Group 1 participants were asked to review the scenario that indicated they were the followers of a social media influencer. The scenario was stated as:

> Please imagine you are a follower of a famous Generation Z gastronomy influencer who has a huge number of followers on your primary-used social media account (such as Twitter, Instagram, TikTok, etc.).
>
> You knew this influencer well, for example, the influencer's public bio and recent activities. Once this influencer frequently posts comments, photos, and videos, you are always notified and would like to check those updates and/or interact with them (such as clicking Like, comment, and/or repost).
>
> If one day, you find this influencer shares his/her great dining experience in a branded restaurant on this social media account, with great photos, videos, and comments to present the variety of food dishes, sensory descriptions, and enjoyable moments of eating and interacting with restaurant staff. The menu price of this branded restaurant is reasonable compared with its products and services.
>
> The shared information by this influencer is not an official commercial advertisement. It is just a share of daily-life moments.

Group 2 participants were asked to review the scenario that indicated they were not followers of a social media influencer. The scenario was stated as:

> Please imagine you are NOT a follower of a famous Generation Z gastronomy influencer who has a huge number of followers on your primary-used social media account (such as Twitter, Instagram, TikTok, etc.). However, you knew the basic information (such as his/her name and gastronomy-related career) of this person from social media. If one day, you occasionally see reposted information from your social media network based on this influencer's sharing content on the internet.
>
> You find this influencer sharing his/her great dining experience in a branded restaurant on this social media account, with great photos, videos, and comments to present the variety of food dishes, sensory descriptions, and enjoyable moments of eating and interacting with restaurant staff. The menu price of this branded restaurant is reasonable compared with its products and services. The shared information by this influencer is not an official commercial advertisement. It is just a share of daily-life moments.

Based on the narrative scenario mentioned above, the attention check questions were given to ask if they could successfully identify themselves as the follower (Group 1) and non-follower (Group 2) of this hypothetical social media influencer in the scenario. Then the participants were asked to choose their opinions regarding their perceptions. The perceived trustworthiness toward Gen Z social media influencers was measured by three items adapted from Koay. A 7-point Likert scale was used to measure both constructs (7 = Strongly agree,..., 1= Strongly disagree). The perceived brand value was measured by two items adapted from Lien et al. (2015). Customers' purchase intention of this restaurant brand was measured by two items adapted from Lien et al. (2015) and Chiang and Jang (2007). A 5-point Likert scale was used to measure this construct (5 = Definitely,..., 1 = Definitely not). Moreover, the frequency of using social media and the number of followed social media influencers were asked. Survey participants' demographic information (i.e., age, gender, education, and income) was collected at the end of the survey. The pilot test ($n$ = 30) with Cronbach's $\alpha$ for each construct above 0.70 by SPSS 28 indicated that the internal construct consistency was acceptable.

## 3 The Effect of Social Media Influencers' Trustworthiness... 49

In order to address the potential issue of common method bias, this study employed diverse measurement scales to assess the constructs. Additionally, following the suggestion by MacKenzie and Podsakoff (2012), unrelated pictures were interspersed between the blocks of questions related to the constructs, creating psychological separation. This procedural approach was implemented to mitigate the impact of common method bias.

To validate the absence of common method bias, the study conducted Harman's single-factor test. The results indicated that the total variance explained by a single factor representing the three constructs was 47.087%. Since this percentage was below the 50% threshold, it was concluded that no significant common method bias was detected (Podsakoff et al., 2003).

The proposed paths were tested by partial least squares structural equation modeling (PLS-SEM). PLS-SEM uses "ordinary least squares (OLS) regression to minimize the error terms (i.e., the residual variance) of the endogenous constructs" and "estimates coefficients (i.e., path model relationships) that maximize the $R^2$ values of the (target) endogenous constructs" (Hair et al., 2017). PLS-SEM is suitable for small sample sizes and asymmetric distributions (Hair et al., 2017). SmartPLS 4 software was employed to analyze the data.

# Results

## Participants' Demographic Information

Table 3.1 shows the demographic information of the 312 survey participants. Of the participants, 172 (55.13%) were male and 140 (44.87%) were female; 5.19% were 20–22 years old; 51.95% were 23–25 years old; and 42.86% were 26–28 years old. Participants with a four-year college degree constituted 66.67% of the sample, while 13.78% of the participants had a master's degree. A total of 28.85% of participants had an annual household income between $50,000 and $59,999, while 15.71% of participants had an annual household income between $70,000 and

**50** L. Ding

**Table 3.1** Demographic information ($n$ = 312)

| Characteristic | Frequency | % |
|---|---|---|
| *Gender* | | |
| Male | 172 | 55.13 |
| Female | 140 | 44.87 |
| *Age* | | |
| [20–22] | 16 | 5.19 |
| [23–25] | 162 | 51.95 |
| [26–28] | 134 | 42.86 |
| *Education level* | | |
| High school graduate | 39 | 12.50 |
| Some college | 14 | 4.49 |
| 2-year college degree | 7 | 2.24 |
| 4-year college degree | 208 | 66.67 |
| Master's degree | 43 | 13.78 |
| Doctorate | 1 | 0.32 |
| *Annual household income* | | |
| Less than $10,000 | 1 | 0.32 |
| $10,000–$19,999 | 16 | 5.13 |
| $20,000–$29,999 | 11 | 3.53 |
| $30,000–$39,999 | 14 | 4.49 |
| $40,000–$49,000 | 44 | 14.10 |
| $50,000–$59,999 | 90 | 28.85 |
| $60,000–$69,999 | 46 | 14.74 |
| $70,000–$79,999 | 49 | 15.71 |
| $80,000–$89,999 | 17 | 5.45 |
| $90,000–$99,999 | 16 | 5.13 |
| $100,000–$149,999 | 7 | 2.24 |
| More than $150,000 | 1 | 0.32 |

$79,999. A total of 47.76% of participants followed 10–50 influencers on their social media accounts, whereas 38.46% followed less than 10 influencers. Figure 3.5 shows that 42.31% of participants used social media many times a day while 25.32% used social media a few times a day.

Table 3.2 presents the mean values, standard deviations, correlations, and significance levels of the model constructs.

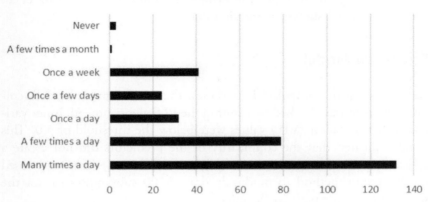

**Fig. 3.5** Frequency of using social media in daily life

**Table 3.2** Correlation table (*n* = 312)

|  | Mean | Standard deviation | 1 | 2 | 3 |
|---|---|---|---|---|---|
| 1. Perceived trustworthiness toward Gen Z social media influencers (PT) | 5.715 | 0.709 | 1 | | |
| 2. Perceived brand value (PBV) | 4.069 | 0.558 | 0.623[a] | 1 | |
| 3. Purchase intention (PI) | 4.053 | 0.500 | 0.556[a] | 0.554[a] | 1 |

[a]Significance level ≤ 0.01

## Measurement Model

Before assessing the structural model, it was essential to evaluate the measurement model's quality. The constructs under consideration, namely, perceived trustworthiness toward Gen Z social media influencers, perceived brand value, and purchase intention, were measured using reflective indicators. To ensure reliability, convergent validity, and discriminant validity, a PLS algorithm with a path weighting scheme, 300 iterations, and a stop criterion of $10^{-7}$ was employed. The results from the analysis of the measurement model showed that the average variance extracted (AVE) for all constructs exceeded 0.50, indicating acceptable convergent validity (Hair et al., 2017). Internal consistency reliability was assessed using Cronbach's α and composite reliability (CR), both of which yielded values above 0.70, meeting the criteria recommended by Hair et al. (2017). Table 3.3 shows the metric values.

## Structural Model

Before testing the proposed hypotheses, the measurement model's collinearity issue was checked by running the PLS algorithm. All inner variance inflation factor (VIF) values were below the threshold of 5.0. This result indicated that the collinearity of the predictors did not create a critical issue in the structural model (Hair et al., 2017). This study used the bootstrap method to randomly draw 5000 subsamples to test the significance of the path coefficients.

Table 3.4 and Fig. 3.6 present the testing results of the structural model path coefficients. For the direct path effects, this study found that perceived brand value positively enhanced their purchase intention ($\beta$ = 0.365, $t$ = 5.891, $p$ < 0.01). Perceived trustworthiness toward Gen Z social media influencers positively affected their purchase intention ($\beta$ = 0.341, $t$ = 5.386, $p$ < 0.01). Perceived trustworthiness toward Gen Z social media influencers positively affected their perceived brand value ($\beta$ = 0.634, $t$ = 13.718, $p$ < 0.01). H1, H2, and H3 were supported. Perceived brand value positively mediates the relationship between perceived trustworthiness toward Gen Z social media influencers and purchase intention ($\beta$ = 0.232, $t$ = 5.038, $p$ < 0.01). The $R^2$ values of perceived brand value ($R^2$ = 0.402, $p$ < 0.01) and purchase intention ($R^2$ = 0.408, $p$ < 0.01) were above 0.25, which was considered medium (Hair et al., 2017; Henseler et al., 2009).

## Multiple-Group Analysis Between Follower Group (Group 1) and Non-Follower Group (Group 2)

Further, this study also ran the multiple-group analysis (MGA) on SmartPLS to test if there was a significant difference in perceived trustworthiness's impact on perceived brand value and purchase intention

### 3 The Effect of Social Media Influencers' Trustworthiness... 53

**Table 3.3** Summary of the measurement model

| Construct and measurement items | Convergent validity | | Internal consistency reliability | | Discriminant validity |
|---|---|---|---|---|---|
| | Loadings | AVE | Composite reliability | Cronbach's alpha | HTMT ratio below 0.90 and HTMT confidence interval does not include 1 |
| Perceived trustworthiness toward Gen Z social media influencers (PT) | | 0.601 | 0.818 | 0.781 | Yes |
| PT1. This Gen Z social media influencer is dependable. | 0.801 | | | | |
| PT2. This Gen Z social media influencer is honest. | 0.749 | | | | |
| PT3. This Gen Z social media influencer is trustworthy. | 0.775 | | | | |
| Perceived brand value (PBV) | | 0.701 | 0.824 | 0.859 | Yes |
| The brand will offer good value for the price. | 0.887 | | | | |
| It is worth purchasing a product or service from this brand. | 0.785 | | | | |
| Purchase intention (PI) | | 0.644 | 0.782 | 0.868 | Yes |
| The likelihood of my purchasing the product or service from this restaurant brand is high. | 0.877 | | | | |

*(continued)*

**54**      L. Ding

**Table 3.3** (continued)

| Construct and measurement items | Convergent validity | | Internal consistency reliability | | Discriminant validity |
|---|---|---|---|---|---|
| | | | | | HTMT ratio below 0.90 and HTMT confidence interval does not include 1 |
| | Loadings | AVE | Composite reliability | Cronbach's alpha | |
| The probability that I would consider purchasing the product or service from this restaurant brand is high. | 0.720 | | | | |

**Table 3.4** PLS-SEM bootstrapping results (5000 subsamples)

| Hypothesized path | Standardized coefficient | $t$-value | $p$-value |
|---|---|---|---|
| *Direct effect* | | | |
| Perceived brand value → purchase intention (H1) | 0.365[a] | 5.891 | 0.000 |
| Perceived trustworthiness toward Gen Z social media influencers → purchase intention (H2) | 0.341[a] | 5.386 | 0.000 |
| Perceived trustworthiness toward Gen Z social media influencers → perceived brand value (H3) | 0.634[a] | 13.718 | 0.000 |
| *Indirect effect* | | | |
| Perceived trustworthiness toward Gen Z social media influencers → perceived brand value → purchase intention (H4) | 0.232[a] | 5.038 | 0.000 |
| *Total effect* | | | |
| Perceived trustworthiness toward Gen Z social media influencers → purchase intention | 0.573[a] | 10.909 | 0.000 |

[a]Significant at $p \leq 0.01$

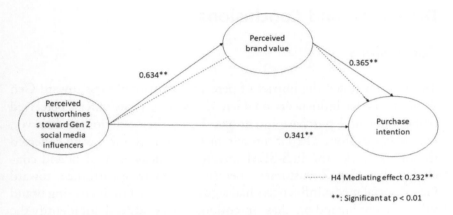

**Fig. 3.6** Basic structural model path coefficients

**Table 3.5** PLS-SEM bootstrapping MGA results (5000 subsamples)

| Hypothesized path | Difference (Group 1–Group 2) | 2-tailed p-value |
|---|---|---|
| *Direct effect* | | |
| Perceived brand value → purchase intention (H1) | −0.15 | 0.235 |
| Perceived trustworthiness toward Gen Z social media influencers → purchase intention (H2) | 0.156 | 0.216 |
| Perceived trustworthiness toward Gen Z social media influencers → perceived brand value (H3) | −0.068 | 0.407 |
| *Indirect effect* | | |
| Perceived trustworthiness toward Gen Z social media influencers → perceived brand value → purchase intention (H4) | −0.12 | 0.192 |
| *Total effect* | | |
| Perceived trustworthiness toward Gen Z social media influencers → purchase intention | 0.036 | 0.723 |

[a]Significant at $p \leq 0.01$

between the follower group (Group 1) and non-follower group (Group 2). Table 3.5 shows the MGA results and no significant impact difference was found based on the sample.

## Discussion and Conclusions

### Conclusions

This chapter tested the impact of perceived trustworthiness toward Gen Z social media influencers on Gen Z restaurant customers' perceived brand value and purchase intentions. Using the scenario-based survey, the responses from 312 US restaurant Gen Z customers were collected through MTurk. The PLS-SEM was used to analyze the data and concluded that Gen Z customers' perceived high trustworthiness toward Gen Z social media influencers had a positive impact on increasing brand value perception and purchase intentions. This study did not identify the significant effect differences between the social influencer's follower group and the non-follower group.

### Theoretical Discussions

This study makes two contributions to the influencer marketing literature. First, this study enriches the social network theory (Borgatti & Foster, 2003; Sun et al., 2022) by emphasizing Gen Z social media users and influencers. As Gen Zers are closely attached to social media platforms, their social networks are largely built online with other social media platform users. One of the interaction activities in social media networks is to connect with influencers who share their experiences and opinions. Therefore, their attitudes and judgment toward social media influencers in online social networks may influence their attitudes and evaluations toward products/services/experiences, and other daily activities, such as purchase behavior intentions. Second, this study enriches the discussions of the parasocial relationship between influencers and followers/non-followers on social media platforms. The existing literature shows the different motives of followers and non-followers to explain the brands/products/services recommended by social media influencers (Breves & Liebers, 2022). However, the current study explored the parasocial relationship in Gen Z. According to the generational theory, "certain cohorts have developed specific common characteristics based on similar sociocultural experiences" (Cabeza-Ramírez et al., 2022, p. 1436). Because Gen Zers are quite aware of the influencer marketing strategies used by companies to advertise the brands/products/services, they may feel skeptical and tricked if the recommended information is less genuine (Childers & Boatwright, 2021). Especially, many of the Gen Z users (followers/non-followers) may be also influencers on other topics on social media platforms. This perspective may help explain the insignificant impact of differences in perceived trustworthiness toward social media influencers on perceived brand value and purchase intention between the follower group and the non-follower group. Likely, the followers and non-followers treat indifferently the purposeful sharing of information by social media influencers in Gen Z.

## Practical Implications

This study provides useful implications for influencer marketing decision-makers as well as restaurant practitioners. Based on the nature of the restaurant industry, using social media influencers is an efficient way to attract potential customers' attention and awareness of the restaurants. A popular format is the foodie-type of young people exploring the local restaurants with the specialty of food in a certain region with the camera. They comment on the food and services while eating and post the recorded videos or live on social media platforms. After many food safety and quality scandals were released in the news, the effectiveness of using social media influencers to promote brands and products is weakening among young customers. The new customers who are attracted by the recommendations from social media influencers may not revisit the restaurant if the perceived value is below their expectations. It may further reduce the perceived credibility of social media influencers in the future. Therefore, the companies may strictly identify the qualifications and credibility of the social media influencers from multiple criteria, not only depending on the number of followers. When social media influencers promote brands, transparent and less-exaggerated recommendations are helpful for social media users to develop expectations with less bias. In this way, social media influencers can create long-term parasocial relationships with other users regarding the brands.

## Limitations and Future Research

This study has three main limitations that need to be addressed in future research. First, this study only emphasized the impact of perceived trustworthiness toward social influencers. To further measure the social media information source credibility, other important factors, such as social media influencers' attractiveness and their expertise may be added to the framework. Second, this study discussed the social influencers' marketing impacts from the perspective of Gen Z. A recommended future study is to compare the Gen Z sample with the samples from other generations, such as millennials. Because different generations have different patterns of using social media, for example, the number of hours spent on social media platforms and preferred social media platforms. The impacts of social media influencers on purchase intentions and behaviors may be different across generations. Identifying unique influencer marketing characteristics will help companies attract more Gen Z customers. Third, future studies may consider including key control variables (e.g., education level) and moderators (e.g., Gen Zers' sense of community) in the research framework.

# References

Ajina, A. S. (2019). The perceived value of social media marketing: An empirical study of online word-of-mouth in Saudi Arabian context. *Entrepreneurship and Sustainability Issues, 6*, 1512–1527.

Boerman, S. C., & van Reijmersdal, E. A. (2020). Disclosing influencer marketing on YouTube to children: The moderating role of para-social relationship. *Frontiers in Psychology, 10*, 3042.

Borgatti, S. P., & Foster, P. C. (2003). The network paradigm in organisational research: A review and typology. *Journal of Management, 29*(6), 991–1013.

Breves, P., & Liebers, N. (2022). # Greenfluencing. The impact of parasocial relationships with social media influencers on advertising effectiveness and followers' pro-environmental intentions. *Environmental Communication, 16*(6), 773–787.

Breves, P., Liebers, N., Abt, M., & Kunze, A. (2019). The perceived fit between Instagram influencers and the endorsed brand. *Journal of Advertising Research, 59*(4), 440–454.

Breves, P., Amrehn, J., Heidenreich, A., Liebers, N., & Schramm, H. (2021). Blind trust? The importance and interplay of parasocial relationships and advertising disclosures in explaining influencers' persuasive effects on their followers. *International Journal of Advertising, 40*(7), 1209–1229.

Bu, Y., Parkinson, J., & Thaichon, P. (2022). Influencer marketing: Homophily, customer value co-creation behaviour and purchase intention. *Journal of Retailing and Consumer Services, 66*, 102904.

Cabeza-Ramírez, L. J., Fuentes-García, F. J., Cano-Vicente, M. C., & González-Mohino, M. (2022). How generation X and millennials perceive influencers' recommendations: Perceived trustworthiness, product involvement, and perceived risk. *Journal of Theoretical and Applied Electronic Commerce Research, 17*(4), 1431–1449.

Che, Y., Li, Y., Fam, K. S., & Bai, X. (2018). Buyer-seller relationship, sales effectiveness and sales revenue: A social network perspective. *Nankai Business Review International, 9*(4), 414–436.

Cheung, M. L., Pires, G. D., Rosenberger, P. J., III, & De Oliveira, M. J. (2020). Driving COBRAs: The power of social media marketing. *Marketing Intelligence and Planning, 39*(3), 361–376.

Chiang, C. F., & Jang, S. S. (2007). The effects of perceived price and brand image on value and purchase intention: Leisure travelers' attitudes toward online hotel booking. *Journal of Hospitality & Leisure Marketing, 15*(3), 49–69.

Childers, C., & Boatwright, B. (2021). Do digital natives recognize digital influence? Generational differences and understanding of social media influencers. *Journal of Current Issues & Research in Advertising, 42*(4), 425–442.

Dam, T. C. (2020). Influence of brand trust, perceived value on brand preference and purchase intention. *The Journal of Asian Finance, Economics and Business (JAFEB), 7*(10), 939–947.

Djafarova, E., & Foots, S. (2022). Exploring ethical consumption of generation Z: Theory of planned behaviour. *Young Consumers, 23*(3), 413–431.

Fang, B., Ye, Q., Kucukusta, D., & Law, R. (2016). Analysis of the perceived value of online tourism reviews: Influence of readability and reviewer characteristics. *Tourism Management, 52*, 498–506.

Fishbein, M., & Ajzen, I. (1975). *Belief, attitude, intention and behavior: An introduction to theory and research*. Addison-Wesley Publishing.

Geyser, W. (2023). *What is an influencer? Social media influencers defined.* https://influencermarketinghub.com/what-is-an-influencer/

Hair, J. F., Jr., Hult, G. T. M., Ringle, C., & Sarstedt, M. (2017). *A primer on partial least squares structural equation modeling (PLS-SEM).* Sage Publications.

Henseler, J., Ringle, C. M., & Sinkovics, R. R. (2009). The use of partial least squares path modeling in international marketing. *Advances in International Marketing, 20,* 277–320.

Insider Intelligence. (2022). *How Gen Z consumes media in 5 charts.* https://www.insiderintelligence.com/content/how-gen-z-consumes-media-5-charts

Khan, S., Rashid, A., Rasheed, R., & Amirah, N. A. (2022). Designing a knowledge-based system (KBS) to study consumer purchase intention: The impact of digital influencers in Pakistan. *Kybernetes.*

Kim, A. J., & Ko, E. (2012). Do social media marketing activities enhance customer equity? An empirical study of luxury fashion brand. *Journal of Business Research, 65*(10).

Kirkpatrick, D. (2016, April 6). Influencer marketing Spurs 11 times the ROI over traditional tactics: Study. *Marketing Dive.* https://www.marketingdive.com/news/influencer-marketing-spurs-11-times-the-roi-over-traditional-tacticsstudy/416911/

Ki, C. W. C., Cuevas, L. M., Chong, S. M., & Lim, H. (2020). Influencer marketing: Social media influencers as human brands attaching to followers and yielding positive marketing results by fulfilling needs. *Journal of Retailing and Consumer Services, 55,* 102133.

Knapp, M. L., Vangelisti, A. L., & Caughlin, J. P. (2014). *Interpersonal communication and human relationships.* Pearson Higher Ed.

Kotler, P. (2003). *Marketing management* (11th ed.). Prentice Hall.

Leung, X. Y., Sun, J., & Asswailem, A. (2022). Attractive females versus trustworthy males: Explore gender effects in social media influencer marketing in Saudi restaurants. *International Journal of Hospitality Management, 103,* 103207.

Lien, C. H., Wen, M. J., Huang, L. C., & Wu, K. L. (2015). Online hotel booking: The effects of brand image, price, trust and value on purchase intentions. *Asia Pacific Management Review, 20*(4), 210–218.

Mabkhot, H., Isa, N. M., & Mabkhot, A. (2022). The influence of the credibility of social media influencers SMIs on the consumers' purchase intentions: Evidence from Saudi Arabia. *Sustainability, 14*(19), 12323.

MacKenzie, S. B., & Podsakoff, P. M. (2012). Common method bias in marketing: Causes, mechanisms, and procedural remedies. *Journal of Retailing, 88*(4), 542–555.

Martín-Consuegra, D., Faraoni, M., Díaz, E., & Ranfagni, S. (2018). Exploring relationships among brand credibility, purchase intention and social media for fashion brands: A conditional mediation model. *Journal of Global Fashion Marketing, 9*(3), 237–251.

Mathwick, C., Malhotra, N., & Rigdon, E. (2001). Experiential value: Conceptualization, measurement and application in the catalog and Internet shopping environment. *Journal of Retailing, 77*, 39–56.

McKinsey & Company. (2023). *What is Gen Z.* https://www.mckinsey.com/featured-insights/mckinsey-explainers/what-is-gen-z#/

Memon, M. A., Ting, H., Cheah, J. H., Thurasamy, R., Chuah, F., & Cham, T. H. (2020). Sample size for survey research: Review and recommendations. *Journal of Applied Structural Equation Modeling, 4*(2), 1–20.

Mirkovski, K., Jia, Y., Liu, L., & Chen, K. (2018). Understanding microblogging continuance intention: The direct social network perspective. *Information Technology and People, 31*(1), 215–238.

Molinillo, S., Aguilar-Illescas, R., Anaya-Sánchez, R., & Liébana-Cabanillas, F. (2021). Social commerce website design, perceived value and loyalty behavior intentions: The moderating roles of gender, age and frequency of use. *Journal of Retailing and Consumer Services, 63*, 102404.

National Restaurant Association. (2021). Restaurant Trends. National Restaurant Association. Available at: https://restaurant.org/research-and-media/research/research-reports/2021-restaurant-trends/ (Accessed on 9 July, 2024).

Nurhandayani, A., Syarief, R., & Najib, M. (2019). The impact of social media influencer and brand images to purchase intention. *Jurnal Aplikasi Manajemen, 17*, 650–661.

Podsakoff, P. M., MacKenzie, S. B., Lee, J. Y., & Podsakoff, N. P. (2003). Common method biases in behavioral research: A critical review of the literature and recommended remedies. *Journal of Applied Psychology, 88*(5), 879–903.

Putri, F. E. V. S., & Tiarawati, M. (2021). The effect of social media influencer and brand image on online purchase intention during the COVID-19 pandemic. *Ilomata International Journal of Management, 2*, 163–171.

Roh, T., Seok, J., & Kim, Y. (2022). Unveiling ways to reach organic purchase: Green perceived value, perceived knowledge, attitude, subjective norm, and trust. *Journal of Retailing and Consumer Services, 67*, 102988.

Schiffman, L. G., & Kanuk, L. L. (2000). *Consumer behavior*. Prentice Hall.

Sun, Y., Wang, R., Cao, D., & Lee, R. (2022). Who are social media influencers for luxury fashion consumption of the Chinese Gen Z? Categorisation and empirical examination. *Journal of Fashion Marketing and Management: An International Journal, 26*(4), 603–621.

Teng, Y., & Wu, K. (2019). Sustainability development in hospitality: The effect of perceived value on customers' green restaurant behavioral intention. *Sustainability, 11*, 1987.

Tukachinsky, R., & Stever, G. (2019). Theorizing development of parasocial engagement. *Communication Theory, 29*(3), 297–318.

Tuten, T. L. (2020). *Social media marketing*. Sage.

Wang, S. W., & Scheinbaum, A. C. (2018). Enhancing brand credibility via celebrity endorsement. *Journal of Advertising Research, 58*(1), 16–32.

Yuan, S., & Lou, C. (2020). How social media influencers foster relationships with followers: The roles of source credibility and fairness in parasocial relationship and product interest. *Journal of Interactive Advertising, 20*(2), 133–147.

Zeithaml, V. A. (1988). Consumer perceptions of price, quality, and value: A means-end model and synthesis of evidence. *Journal of Marketing, 52*, 2–22.

# 4

# Impact of Social Media Influencers (SMIs) on Millennials Choosing a Travel Destination

### Aafiya Mundakappadath Firose, Wei Chen, and Saloomeh Tabari

## Introduction

Influencer marketing is considered a marketing strategy adopted by the business to use opinion leaders or key individuals to positively influence the purchase decisions of the customers (McClure & Seock, 2020). It has been found that social media influencers shape followers' preferences, thus considered one of the most important marketing tools to attract millennials (AlFarraj et al., 2021; Casaló et al. *Journal of Business Research* 117:510–519, 2020). Like other industries, the tourism industry has also dramatically changed due to social media influencers (Michaelsen & Collini, 2022). This is because tourist relies more on social media to gather tourist information and are largely influenced by the opinion leaders on

---

A. M. Firose (✉) • W. Chen
Service Sector, Sheffield Hallam University, Sheffield, UK
e-mail: w.chen@shu.ac.uk

S. Tabari
Cardiff Business School, Cardiff University, Cardiff, UK
e-mail: tabaris@cardiff.ac.uk

© The Author(s), under exclusive license to Springer Nature Switzerland AG 2024
S. Tabari, Q. S. Ding (eds.), *Celebrity, Social Media Influencers and Brand Performance*,
https://doi.org/10.1007/978-3-031-63516-8_4

social media (Munar & Jacobsen, 2013). Previously influence of trust was discussed in the context of peer-to-peer marketing, electronic word of mouth, and online purchase intention; however, little attention has been paid to discussing the effect of trust on social media influencers on consumer travel decision journey (Alalwan, 2018; Cinelli et al., 2022; Enke & Borchers, 2019). Trust in the social media influencer is built due to several factors such as the credibility of the influencer (trustworthiness, expertise, and attractiveness), and the information quality that they provide (Jin et al., 2021; Hu et al., 2019). All these factors will be examined to get an insight into trust to build on social media influencers (Seçilmiş et al., 2021; Rinka & Pratt, 2018). This is because when followers see information about the brand shared by their opinion leader, it creates the desire also to have that product or service; thus, the purchase intention is generated (Hermanda et al., 2019). It is interesting to empirically examine how social media influencers encourage followers to visit a certain tourist destination (Lim et al., 2017). Several theories are used by scholars to understand purchase behaviour in existing studies such as dual process theory, self-congruence theory, and customer journey theory (Hu et al., 2019).

In recent years, SMIs have emerged as a new force in travel marketing, with their ability to reach large audiences and influence their followers' decisions (Gibson, 2022). Millennials, in particular, have been identified as a key target market for social media influencers, given their strong presence on social media platforms and their willingness to spend money on travel experiences. Despite the growing popularity of social media influencers in travel marketing, there is still a lack of understanding about the factors that contribute to their effectiveness in influencing millennials' travel decisions. This dissertation aims to explore the impact of social media influencers on millennials' choice of travel destination in the UK, with a focus on understanding the role of trust in this process. The research will seek to identify the elements that build trust in social media influencers among millennials and evaluate the factors that comprise the customer travel decision journey (Boley et al., 2022). It will also examine the impact of trust in influencers on consumer travel decision journeys, with a focus on understanding how trust influences millennials' destination choices. Additionally, the research will evaluate the credibility of social media influencers and their impact on millennials' travel decision-making.

This chapter examines how social media influencers impact millennials' decisions about where to visit in the UK. By exploring the role of trust in the effectiveness of social media influencers, this chapter provides insights into how travel marketers can develop more effective influencer marketing strategies that prioritize building trust with followers (Kinnunen, 2021). Additionally, by evaluating the credibility of social media influencers and their impact on millennials' travel decisions, finally, the chapter addresses concerns about the authenticity and transparency of influencer marketing in the travel industry, by answering the following questions:

1. How do social media influencers impact millennials' decision-making process when it comes to choosing a travel destination in the UK?
2. To what extent do millennials rely on social media influencers' recommendations for UK travel destinations over other sources of information such as travel guides or online reviews?
3. To what extent does the perceived authenticity of a travel experience in the UK influence millennials' choice of destination, and how do social media influencers play a role in shaping their perception?

## Factors That Build Trust in Social Media Influencers

Social media influencers have become a vital source of information for millennials when it comes to travel decisions (Pop et al., 2022). Influencers can create a sense of FOMO (fear of missing out) by sharing captivating and engaging content that highlights the best of a destination. This can inspire millennials to visit the UK and explore its attractions (Guerreiro et al., 2019). Social media influencers are often viewed as relatable and trustworthy. They share their personal experience and provide honest and transparent reviews of destinations which can help millennials make more informed decisions.). Weismueller et al. (2020) discussed that social media influencers have become a prominent feature of the modern marketing landscape, with many brands turning to these individuals to promote their products or services.

Firstly, source credibility is crucial with influencers who have established themselves as experts in their niche being more trusted (Cooley & Parks-Yancy, 2019). Secondly, transparency and authenticity are highly valued with audiences responding positively to influencers who are open about their experience and challenges (Tariyal et al., 2023). Thirdly, a track record of ethical behaviour and responsible content creation is important with influencers who prioritize their audience's well-being and values being more trusted (Voltolini, 2019).

Konstantinou and Jones (2022) argued that sharing both the positives and negatives of a destination as well as being open about any sponsored content or collaboration will help influencers to build transparency with their flowers. In addition, Arief et al. (2022) believe authenticity involves sharing honest opinions and experiences while transparency requires influencers to disclose any sponsored content or partnerships with travel brands. Furthermore, post-COVID-19 pandemic building trust in the travel industry among UK millennials requires influencers to prioritize authenticity and transparency (Casaló et al., 2020).

Consistency and reliability can help to establish a sense of trust and familiarity with the influencer, making it more likely that millennials will take their recommendations seriously (Alhouti & Johnson, 2022). Moreover, credibility is strengthened when influencers deliver on their promises and maintain consistency in their messaging and values over time (Weber, 2019). Such influencers can establish a loyal following and build long-term trust with their audience, ultimately influencing their travel decisions and inspiring them to explore new destinations and experiences. A study by Caraka et al. (2022) highlighted that influencers have a considerable influence on travel choices, with 40% of respondents stating they had visited a destination after seeing it on social media, and millennials trusting social media influencers' recommendations over traditional travel agencies. Online reviews and recommendations also play a role with 94% of UK millennials reading online reviews before booking holidays and 59% saying they were a key factor in their decision-making process.

Wahane (2019) stated that social media influencers who specialize in sustainable tourism are increasingly popular among millennials, with 40% seeking environmentally friendly travel options.

## Influencer and Destination

The first stage of the customer travel decision journey is the inspiration and awareness phase. This is where the customer becomes aware of potential travel destinations and begins to gather information. Social media influencers play a critical role in this stage by showcasing their travels and experiences (Dimitriou & AbouElgheit, 2019). Once a potential destination has been identified the customer begins to research and plan their trip. Social media influencers can be a valuable source of information during this stage. They can provide recommendations on where to stay, what to do, and where to eat. This is particularly true for niche influencers who specialize in a particular type of travel such as adventure travel or luxury travel (Orea-Giner & Fusté-Forné, 2023). The next stage of the customer's travel decisions is the booking and purchase stage. This is where the customer makes the final decision and books their trip. Social media influencers can have a significant impact on this stage by promoting specific destinations, hotels, or travel companies (Amagsila et al., 2022). When the trip has been booked the customer begins to experience their destination. Social media influencers continue to play a role during the stage by sharing their experiences and encouraging their followers to visit the destination; they can also provide recommendations on activities and experiences to try (Warda, 2019). According to Abad and Borbon (2021), the customer travel decision journey is a complex process that involves multiple factors, including personal preferences, budget, travel goals, and the influence of external factors like social media.

Trust is a critical factor in the success of social media influencers (Kalu, 2019). To be effective in influencing consumer behaviour, social media influencers must build a high level of trust with their followers (Ragab, 2022). This is particularly true in the travel industry where consumers are making significant financial and emotional investments in their travel experiences. Without trust, social media influencers are unlikely to have a significant impact on travel decisions. Mabkhot, Isa, and Mabkhot (2022) highlighted that trust impacts consumer travel decisions. Social media influencers can provide valuable recommendations on where to stay, what to do, and where to eat, but this recommendation is only effective if consumers trust them. The expertise of influencers (Seçilmiş et al., 2022) and their authenticity (Abreu, 2019) have a direct impact on the decision-making of their followers. Therefore, trust plays a crucial role in the influence of social media influencers on the consumer travel decision journey, particularly among millennials (Asdecker, 2022).

According to Grafström et al. (2018), "Millennials' perceptions are influenced by influencer marketing for a variety of causes, including the alignment of advertising delivered by an influencer, the level of credibility and trustworthiness of the persuasive messages, and a change in the influencer's delivery style." Furthermore, millennials are more likely than Generation X to use social media to connect with brands. Millennials are heavily involved in the digital prospect and are sometimes described as "digital natives" because they grew up in a social networking–dominated world dominated by Facebook, Twitter, Instagram, and YouTube (Moresjö & Xin, 2020). This generation has also drawn a lot of attention because it makes up a sizable portion of the consumer population with strong purchasing power and high consumption rates. Also, according to research, millennials are seen as being technologically savvy, highly educated, and mature (Ruspini, 2018). In this regard, a study by Mahmood et al. (2023) emphasized that millennials' trust in social media influencers is affected by factors such as the quality of the information provided and the transparency of sponsored content.

## Research Methods

The chapter investigates the impact of social media influencers (SMIs) on the travel destination choices of millennials in the UK, particularly in the post-COVID-19 pandemic era. The quantitative method has been employed for this study by using a survey questionnaire. The questionnaire was designed by focusing on the following areas: travel and tourism, influencer marketing, credibility, and the impact of social media influencers on travel destination choices. The questionnaire was distributed among international students studying in the UK who are also millennials. This sample was chosen as they represent a significant proportion of the travel market, and their travel behaviour has changed due to the pandemic. To ensure that the sample is representative of the target population, a random sampling technique will be employed. This random sampling technique will help ensure that the data collected is reliable and valid (Madureira, 2021).

## Sampling

Convenient-based sampling has been used to collect data. The Likert scale adopted to measure the responses of the research participants. The cross-sectional timeframe was utilized because only one-time data will be collected from the respondents (Theocharis & Papaioannou, 2020). Only 92 of the respondents were complete out of 127 and have been used for this research.

## Findings and Discussion

Out of the 92 respondents, 48 of them were male, 44 were female participants, and 11 participants preferred not to reveal their gender.

## Building Trust with Social Media Influencers

The research found that building trust with social media influencers (SMIs) is critical for successful influencer marketing. The study identified three key factors that contribute to the trustworthiness and credibility of social media influencers: transparent authenticity, and expertise. Participants emphasize that transparency in sponsored content is crucial for building trust with followers (Merenda, 2022), with 84.24% of respondents stating that they trust social media influencers who discovered sponsored content Authenticity was also identified as a significant factor in building trust, with 19.57% of participants indicating that their trust in a particular niche was found to be important, with 6.18% of participants setting up in their field.

## Impact of Social Media Influencers on Consumer Travel Decision Journey

The study highlights the importance of transparent and authentic influencer marketing strategies, which are even more critical in the current climate where consumers are more concerned about safety and trust. Influencer marketing campaigns that are transparent in their disclosure of sponsored content and promote authentic experiences are more likely to build trust with followers and, in turn, have a more significant impact on travel decision-making (Rasul et al., 2020). Moreover, the study emphasizes the need for travel brands and destination marketing organizations to collaborate with social media influencers to promote safe and responsible travel practices in the post-COVID-19 pandemic landscape. Influencers can play a crucial role in promoting responsible travel practices and encouraging followers to follow safety guidelines. Social media influencers were found to play a crucial role in influencing destination choices among millennials, with 75.19% of participants stating that they have been inspired to travel to a destination after seeing content from a social media influencer. The study also stressed that social media platforms such as Instagram and YouTube are the most commonly used platforms for travel inspiration, with 78% of participants stating that they use Instagram for travel inspiration and 51% stating that they use YouTube. Additionally, in the study on online reviews and recommendations 83% of participants stated that they are likely to research a destination before booking a trip.

The study also investigates the factors that build trust in social media influencers among millennials. The findings suggest that transparency in sponsored content, authenticity, and expertise in particular niches were key components in building trust with followers. Millennials place a high value on trust (Sesar et al., 2022), with 73% of participants stating that they are more likely to follow social media influencers who they trust. The study highlights the importance of building trust with followers and the critical roles that social media influencers play in shaping the consumer travel decision journey. Moreover, this study highlighted significant implications for destination marketing organizations, travel brands, and social media influencers, particularly in the post-COVID-19 era. The pandemic has brought unprecedented challenges to the tourism industry, with many destinations and travel brands struggling to attract visitors. Social media influencers play a critical role in promoting destinations and travel brands particularly as millennials are likely to trust recommendations from their favourites. The study emphasized the importance of transparency and authenticity in influencer marketing strategies that prioritize building trust with followers.

Overall, the study underscores the importance of social media influencers in the tourism industry and highlights the critical role that they play in shaping the consumer travel decision journey, particularly among millennials (Grafström et al., 2018). The study emphasizes the need for transparent and authentic influencer marketing strategies that prioritize building trust with followers, particularly in the post-COVID-19 era where consumers are likely to be more cautious and selective in their travel decisions.

Furthermore, this chapter provides insights into the impact of social media influencers on travel decisions highlighting the need for marketers to leverage influencer marketing effectively (Wandoko & Panggati, 2022). Additionally, it highlights the importance of the role of social media platforms and their continuance as a significant source of travel inspiration for consumers (Fig. 4.1).

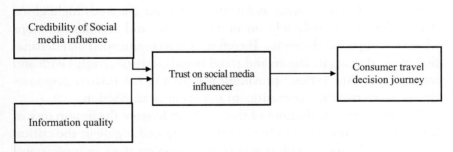

**Fig. 4.1** Conceptual framework. Source: Authors

## Recommendations and Future Study

*Emphasize transparency and authenticity*: The study found that transparency in sponsored content and authenticity were key factors in building trust with followers. Therefore, it is recommended that destination marketing organizations, travel brands and social media influencers prioritize transparency in their influencer marketing strategies, clearly disclosing sponsored content and avoiding misleading or exaggerated claims. Authenticity should also be emphasized with influences staying true to their niche and personally and brands avoiding over-scripted and generic content.

*Collaborate with micro-influencers*: While macro-influencers may have larger following the study found that micro-influencers (those with 10,000–100,000 followers) are more likely to have a stronger and more engaged relationship with their followers leading to higher levels of trust. Therefore, it is recommended that destination marketing organizations and travellers consider collaborating with micro-influencers to reach a more targeted and engaged audience.

*Utilizing Instagram and YouTube for travel inspiration*: The findings of this study emphasized the fact that Instagram and YouTube are the most commonly used platforms for travel inspiration among millennials. Therefore, it is recommended that destination marketing organizations and travel brands prioritize these platforms in their marketing strategies, creating visually appealing and informative content that inspires and informs potential travellers.

*Engage with online reviews and recommendations*: The study highlighted that millennials heavily rely on online reviews and recommendations when making travel decisions. Therefore, it is recommended that destination marketing organizations and travel brands activities engage with and respond to online reviews providing helpful and informative responses that demonstrate their commitment to customer satisfaction.

In conclusion, the findings of this study underscore the importance of trust and authenticity in influencer marketing and highlight the critical role that social media influencers play in shaping the consumer travel decision journey. By prioritizing transparency and authenticity through collaborating with micro-influencers, utilizing Instagram and

YouTube for travel inspiration, engaging with online reviews and recommendations, considering the impact of COVID-19, and conducting ongoing research and evaluation, destination managers, travel brands, and social media influencers can successfully navigate the evolving tourism industry and reach a highly engaged and trusting audience.

It would be good if future studies explore the comparison study on the impact of social media influencers on the travel decision-making process among other age groups, such as Generation X, baby boomers, and millennials. This would provide a more comprehensive understanding of the influence of social media influencers across different age groups and their impact on travel destination choices.

Future research can explore the ethical considerations surrounding social media influencer marketing, particularly in terms of disclosure and transparency in sponsored content as this would provide insight into best practices for influencer marketing that prioritize building trust with followers.

# References

Abad, P. E. S., & Borbon, N. M. D. (2021). Influence of travel vlog: Inputs for destination marketing model. *International Journal of Research, 9*(3), 47–66.

Abreu, R. (2019). *Social media micro-influencer marketing and purchasing intention of millennials: The role of perceived authenticity and trust.* Doctoral dissertation, Dublin Business School.

Alhouti, S., & Johnson, C. M. (2022). Web of lies: Drivers and consequences of social media (in) authenticity. *Journal of Promotion Management, 28*(8), 1129–1164.

Amagsila, F., Cadavis, E. M., Callueng, J. P., & Manio, J. R. (2022). The impact of influencer marketing on consumers' brand perception of travel applications. *Journal of Business and Management Studies, 4*(2), 241–255.

Arief, N. N., Gregory, A., Pangestu, A. B., Ramdlany, D. M. A., & Sanjaya, I. M. A. (2022). Employee influencer management: Evidence from state-owned enterprises in Indonesia. *Journal of Communication Management.*

Alalwan, A. A. (2018). Investigating the impact of social media advertising features on customer purchase intention. *International journal of information management, 42,* 65–77.

AlFarraj, O., Alalwan, A. A., Obeidat, Z. M., Baabdullah, A., Aldmour, R., & Al-Haddad, S. (2021). Examining the impact of influencers' credibility dimensions: attractiveness, trustworthiness and expertise on the purchase intention in the aesthetic dermatology industry. *Review of International Business and Strategy, 31*(3), 355–374.

Asdecker, B. (2022). Travel-related influencer content on Instagram: How social media fuels wanderlust and how to mitigate the effect. *Sustainability, 14*(2), 855.

Boley, B. B., Jordan, E., Woosnam, K. M., Maruyama, N., Xiao, X., & Rojas, C. (2022). Buttressing social return's influence on travel behaviour. *Current Issues in Tourism*, 1–16.

Caraka, R. E., Noh, M., Lee, Y., Toharudin, T., Tyasti, A. E., Royanow, A. F., et al. (2022). The impact of social media influencers Raffi Ahmad and Nagita Slavina on tourism visit intentions across millennials and zoomers using a hierarchical likelihood structural equation model. *Sustainability, 14*(1), 524.

Casaló, L. V., Flavián, C., & Ibáñez-Sánchez, S. (2020). Influencers on Instagram: Antecedents and consequences of opinion leadership. *Journal of Business Research, 117*, 510–519. https://doi.org/10.1016/j.jbusres.2018.07.005

Cinelli, M., Etta, G., Avalle, M., Quattrociocchi, A., Di Marco, N., Valensise, C., ... & Quattrociocchi, W. (2022). Conspiracy theories and social media platforms. *Current Opinion in Psychology, 47*, 101–407.

Cooley, D., & Parks-Yancy, R. (2019). The effect of social media on perceived information credibility and decision making. *Journal of Internet Commerce, 18*(3), 249–269.

Dimitriou, C. K., & AbouElgheit, E. (2019). Understanding generation Z's travel social decision-making. *Tourism and Hospitality Management, 25*(2), 311–334.

Enke, N., & Borchers, N. S. (2019). Management strategischer influencer-Kommunikation: Projektbericht, Leipzig, Germany.

Gibson, L. (2022). *Grabbing the bucket with both hands – A study into the presentation of self through 'Bucket List' tourism in a social-media-focused world*. Doctoral dissertation, William Angliss Institute.

Grafström, J., Jakobsson, L., & Wiede, P. (2018). *The impact of influencer marketing on consumers' attitudes*.

Guerreiro, C., Viegas, M., & Guerreiro, M. (2019). Social networks and digital influencers: Their role in customer decision journey in tourism. *Journal of Spatial and Organizational Dynamics, 7*(3), 240–260.

# 4 Impact of Social Media Influencers (SMIs) on Millennials...

Hermanda, A., Sumarwan, U., & Tinaprillia, N. (2019). The effect of social media influencer on brand image, selfconcept, and purchase intention. *Journal of Consumer Sciences, 4*(2), 76–89.

Hu, H., Zhang, D., & Wang, C. (2019). Impact of social media influencers' endorsement on application adoption: A trust transfer perspective. *Social Behavior and Personality: an international journal, 47*(11), 1–12.

Jin, S. V., Ryu, E., & Muqaddam, A. (2021). I trust what she's# endorsing on Instagram: moderating effects of parasocial interaction and social presence in fashion influencer marketing. *Journal of Fashion Marketing and Management: An International Journal, 25*(4), 665–681.

Kalu, F. (2019). *The impact of social media influencer marketing on purchase intention from an Irish male millennial's perception: A case study of Irish fashion industry.* Doctoral dissertation, Dublin, National College of Ireland.

Kinnunen, K. (2021). *The influence of social media on choosing Finnish destinations.*

Konstantinou, I., & Jones, K. (2022). Investigating Gen Z attitudes to charitable giving and donation behaviour: Social media, peers and authenticity. *Journal of Philanthropy and Marketing, 27*(3), e1764.

Lim, X. J., Radzol, A. M., Cheah, J., & Wong, M. W. (2017). The impact of social media influencers on purchase intention and the mediation effect of customer attitude. *Asian journal of business research, 7*(2), 19–36.

Mabkhot, H., Isa, N. M., & Mabkhot, A. (2022). The influence of the credibility of social media influencers SMIs on the consumers' purchase intentions: Evidence from Saudi Arabia. *Sustainability, 14*(19), 12323.

Madureira, L. B. (2021). *Stimulus from social media influencers to the Portuguese tourism and travel industry in the COVID-19 era.* Master's thesis.

Mahmood, C. K., Aboalsamh, H. M., Khalil, T., & Ali, H. (2023). *Disclosing Instagram influencers' advertising: The effect of source credibility cues on millennials' behavioral intentions.*

McClure, C., & Seock, Y. K. (2020). The role of involvement: Investigating the effect of brand's social media pages on consumer purchase intention. *Journal of retailing and consumer services, 53*, 101–975.

Merenda, S. (2022). *Strategic recommendations to Qatari emerging fashion brands: A multi method approach for the local entrepreneurs' success.*

Michaelsen, F., Collini, L., Jacob, C., Goanta, C., Kettner, S. E., Bishop, S., ... & Yesiloglu, S. (2022). The impact of influencers on advertising and consumer protection in the Single Market.

Moresjö, S., & Xin, Y. (2020). Does CSR really influence Millennials' purchase decisions?: A qualitative study on attitudes toward the fast fashion industry.

Munar, A. M., & Jacobsen, J. K. S. (2013). Trust and involvement in tourism social media and web-based travel information sources. *scandinavian Journal of Hospitality and Tourism, 13*(1), 1–19.

Orea-Giner, A., & Fusté-Forné, F. (2023). The way we live, the way we travel: Generation Z and sustainable consumption in food tourism experiences. *British Food Journal.*

Pop, R. A., Săplăcan, Z., Dabija, D. C., & Alt, M. A. (2022). The impact of social media influencers on travel decisions: The role of trust in the consumer decision journey. *Current Issues in Tourism, 25*(5), 823–843.

Ragab, A. M. (2022). How do social media influencers affect digital natives 2.0 to travel inside Egypt? Integrating the theory of planned behavior and elaboration likelihood model. *International Journal of Tourism and Hospitality Management, 5*(1), 75–105.

Rasul, T., Zaman, U., & Hoque, M. R. (2020). Examining the pulse of the tourism industry in the Asia-Pacific region: A systematic review of social media. *Tourism and Hospitality Management, 26*(1), 173–193.

Ruspini, E. (2018). Guest editorial. *Journal of Tourism Futures, 4*(1), 3–6. https://doi.org/10.1108/JTF-03-2018-069

Seçilmiş, C., Özdemir, C., & Kılıç, İ. (2022). How travel influencers affect visit intention? The roles of cognitive response, trust, COVID-19 fear and confidence in vaccine. *Current Issues in Tourism, 25*(17), 2789–2804.

Sesar, V., Martinčević, I., & Boguszewicz-Kreft, M. (2022). Relationship between advertising disclosure, influencer credibility and purchase intention. *Journal of Risk and Financial Management, 15*(7), 276.

Tariyal, A., Bisht, S., Roy, S., & Chopra, G. (2023). Assessing the impact of perceived social media usefulness on Indian millennials' online booking decision. *Journal of Marketing Analytics*, 1–17.

Theocharis, D., & Papaioannou, E. (2020). Consumers' responses on the emergence of influencer marketing in Greek market place. *International Journal of Technology Marketing, 14*(3), 283–304.

Xu (Rinka), X., & Pratt, S. (2018). Social media influencers as endorsers to promote travel destinations: an application of self-congruence theory to the Chinese Generation Y. *Journal of Travel & Tourism Marketing, 35*(7), 958–972. https://doi.org/10.1080/10548408.2018.1468851

Voltolini, E. C. (2019). *People trust in people: How Instagram has changed the way in which women from the millennial generation in Ireland are influenced by beauty brands for purchasing decision.* Doctoral dissertation, Dublin, National College of Ireland.

Wahane, A. (2019). *Impact of social media micro-influencer on the buying behavior of lifestyle product of Irish millennials.* Doctoral dissertation, Dublin, National College of Ireland.

Wandoko, W., & Panggati, I. E. (2022). The influence of digital influencer, e-WOM and information quality on customer repurchase intention toward online shop in e-marketplace during pandemic COVID-19: The mediation effect of customer trust. *Journal of Relationship Marketing, 21*(2), 148–167.

Warda, S. Y. (2019). Emirati millennials: A catalyst for innovation in the tourism industry. *Transnational Marketing Journal (TMJ), 7*(2), 131–160.

Weber, L. (2019). Restoring trust and rebuilding reputation: The critical roles of corporate purpose, earned media and the new CEO mandate. *Journal of Digital & Social Media Marketing, 6*(4), 332–340.

Weismueller, J., Harrigan, P., Wang, S., & Soutar, G. N. (2020). Influencer endorsements: How advertising disclosure and source credibility affect consumer purchase intention on social media. *Australasian marketing journal, 28*(4), 160–170.

# 5

# Advantages and Disadvantages for Brands of Using Social Media Influencers

### Eleonora Cattaneo and Yan Sun

## Introduction

Social media influencers have become very valuable to brands, especially in the fashion sector. Fashion designers court them and brand managers recognize their potential to boost brand image (Heine & Berghaus, 2014). There are several factors and dimensions involved in choosing and managing a social media influencer to endorse a brand and there are also potential downsides to relying excessively on influencers to promote fashion and luxury fashion brands (Jin et al., 2019).

This chapter will discuss:

---

E. Cattaneo (✉)
Management, Glion Institute of Higher Education, Glion, Switzerland
e-mail: eleonora.cattaneo@glion.edu

Y. Sun
Oxford Brookes Business School, Oxford Brookes University, Oxford, UK
e-mail: ysun@brookes.ac.uk

© The Author(s), under exclusive license to Springer Nature Switzerland AG 2024
S. Tabari, Q. S. Ding (eds.), *Celebrity, Social Media Influencers and Brand Performance*,
https://doi.org/10.1007/978-3-031-63516-8_5

- Social media influencer endorsement as a brand awareness creation tool for new brands
- The role of influencers in positioning and re-positioning existing brands
- The role of influencers in reviving brands
- Are all fashion brands equal? How to manage influencers in the luxury space
- When social media influencing backfires: issues in influencer strategies and management.

Endorsement of fashion brands is a strategy that undoubtedly has great importance in the fashion and luxury fashion segments (Song & Kim, 2020). The short-term results are difficult to accurately measure; however, if managed effectively, this strategy often yields long-term benefits such as increased brand loyalty and brand equity, which ultimately translate to higher sales turnover and brand value.

Influencers have evolved into retailers (Vogue, 2020), providing not only a curated offer for their followers, but the option to buy—previously reserved for brands, but extended by Instagram to include influencers. Influencers can tag the brands they're showcasing and engage with their followers, who actively look to them for inspiration, all the way through to purchase.

## Influential Marketing and Social Media/a Celebrity or an Influencer

Influencers play an important role across sectors in terms of marketing strategies and are widely used in various ways, such as to demonstrate a brand's image, to promote new product and service, or to increase public awareness (Appel et al., 2020).

In general, the term 'influencer' refers to individuals who receive payment for creating and disseminating content relating to brands (Walternrath et al., 2022). This practice is quite similar to a more traditional marketing strategy, celebrity endorsement, which has been effectively adopted in offline marketing communications and embraced by brands for decades (Bergkvist & Zhou, 2016).

Along with the dramatic rise of digital media and platforms in the past decade, the 'traditional strategy of endorsement' has transformed into

## 5 Advantages and Disadvantages for Brands of Using Social... 81

'influential marketing' and successfully adapted for the online environment (Wood & Burkhalter, 2014). Interestingly, influencers differ from traditional celebrities in a few ways. For instance, influencers enjoy a highly personal and close relationship with their followers, compared with celebrities and their audience (De Veriman et al., 2017).

Celebrities, from a traditional perspective, are individuals who become famous through professional achievement in the physical/offline environment, including in sports, acting, and writing. Conversely, influencers build their fame by sharing content via digital channels such as Twitter, Instagram, or YouTube (Audrezet et al., 2020). In other words, social media influencers are users who intensively create and passionately share relevant content in specific areas to attract a large audience online (Etter et al., 2018; Li & Du, 2017).

Compared to traditional celebrities, influencers are more approachable and remain closer to individual consumers, demonstrating significant strength in both social connectedness and network interactivity (Sun et al., 2022). Consequently, influencers are acknowledged to be more identifiable and trustworthy than celebrities, which make a huge difference to the effectiveness of advertising to consumers (Schouten et al., 2020).

The emergence of social media has completely changed communication between brands and consumers. Particularly for young generations, social media has easily surpassed traditional media and become the preferred media for consumption among young people (Southgate & Bubani, 2017).

Quite a few criteria are used to categorize social media influencers (SMIs), including the number of followers, costs per post, engagement rates, and audience characteristics (Nanji, 2017). Another way to group influencers is by the way in which they gain audiences: (1) some traditional celebrities (with non-social media origins), become SMIs after they have gained fame in the offline world, including Serena Williams and Emma Watson; (2) 'Instafamous' celebrities, who become famous only through social media by showcasing their lifestyles, including Chiara Ferragni and Sophie Quickenden (Piehler et al., 2022).

One specific type of influencer is the so-called micro-influencer, defined as those with an audience of between 1000 and 100,000 or 500,000 followers (Appel et al., 2020). Micro-influencers are very active in business collaborations because they are perceived as authentic and trustworthy through maintaining a strong, enthusiastic connection with followers (Saternus & Hinz, 2021).

In some cases, influencers have evolved into retailers (Vogue, 2020), providing not only a curated offer for their followers but the option to buy the items showcased. In 2018, Instagram extended the retail function, which had previously been reserved to brands, to individuals. Influencers can tag the brands they are showcasing and engage with their followers, who actively look to them for inspiration, all the way through to purchase. Hund and McGuigan (2019) coined the term 'shoppable life', suggesting that influencers' lifestyles have a series of elements that can be purchased and that social media platforms increasingly develop marketplace capabilities into their designs.

## An Emerging Market Perspective: India, China, Gen Z, and Brand Avoidance

Most brands are aware of unique social media platforms in mainland China, such as WeChat, Weibo, Xiaohongshu, and Douyin, which are more powerful and functional in terms of impacting consumers' purchase behaviours than their Western counterparts: Instagram and Facebook (CBBC, 2022).

For instance, WeChat is the all-in-one social media platform in China, with 900 million users daily, and the average time spent on WeChat by its users is 70 minutes per day (Statista, 2018; Sun et al., 2022). According to *JING Daily* (Pan, 2018), 100% of luxury consumption will be influenced by an online interaction by 2025. Luxury brands and retailers are getting eager to understand the digital footprints of luxury consumers, particularly young consumers. A total of 47% of millennials in China are influenced by social media in their purchase decisions and 70% of Gen Z are willing to purchase from social media platforms (Lee, 2018).

According to an anonymous source, a co-founder of a leading social media marketing agency in mainland China, the biggest difference between Chinese and UK influencers is professionalism. In China, third-party network services (multi-channel networks [MCNs]) work with multiple channels and creators to develop content, offer training, and deploy a range of resources to help influencers to become internet celebrities.

SMIs in China, including the top influencers, don't have to be 'authentic' because a strong team behind them is functioning like a powerful machine to drive them to succeed commercially in partnering with brands. This ecosystem provides an effective and efficient approach for influencers to build their fame. However, the influencer's unique style might be modified or even sacrificed for commercial reasons.

India has the largest population of Gen Y consumers, who treat the internet and SMIs as trusted sources of information and are influenced by various digital platforms during the decision making process (Kumar et al., 2018). Interestingly, consumers in India possess different attitudes towards attractive celebrity influencers and expert influencers. As suggested by Trivedi (2018), celebrity influencers have a stronger impact on the purchase of fashion products; however, when buying electronics, Indian consumers trust expert influencers (Trivedi & Sama, 2020).

In contrast to other generations, Gen Z, the future consumers, take influencers to be their own peers, who responsibly provide honest opinions and genuine information (Lou & Kim, 2019; Reinikainen et al., 2021). If influencers only act as the voice of brands for commercial purposes or represent the controlling power of brands in a negative way, brand avoidance will be triggered among Gen Z consumers and they may avoid or reject a brand (Lee et al., 2009; Reinikainen et al., 2021).

Being fully aware of influential marketing as a popular business strategy, Gen Zers expect influencers to show moral responsibility by continually searching for truth, originality, and ethics in their interactions with brands (Feng et al., 2021; Munsch, 2021). Facing global issues, including political disputes and environmental crises, brands have to take a side to clearly present their opinions to young consumers, who greatly respect diversity and believe in different truths (McKinsey, 2018).

## Social Media, Consumers, and Brands

As suggested by Campbell and Farrell (2020), three main functionalities offered by influencers are (1) audience cultivation, (2) interaction management, and (3) business endorsement. With a combination of these skillsets, influencers situate themselves as a critical component of marketing strategy, using their power to impact both consumers and brands.

Attracted by a large audience (follower) base, more and more brands have begun to partner with SMIs, and some brands even invest in selected influencers as part of their marketing strategy. Consumers (followers) clearly demonstrate a positive attitude towards influencer-produced branded content, which is seen as more organic and authentic than traditional marketing messages (Farrell et al., 2022).

Since it is less expensive than traditional celebrity endorsement, 75% of marketers include SMIs in their business plans, representing a market size of $2.3 billion in 2020 (Statista, 2020). However, the influencer-brand relationship doesn't always work out smoothly. For instance, finding the right partner is quite challenging for both influencers and brands. In other words, influencers and brands need to fit into each other's scope, considering factors such as relative connection and target consumer groups (Breves et al., 2019). The other challenge occurs in maintaining the balance of brand-sponsored posts and influencer-sponsored content. Too many brand-sponsored posts discourage consumers from continuing to interact with influencers and engage with the created content, and even lead to negative feelings towards brands (Lou et al., 2019).

User and Gratification (U&G) theory takes a user-centric approach to explain how individuals satisfy their social and psychological needs in mass communication (Katz, 1959; Ruggiero, 2000). Further applied to influencer marketing, U&G indicates four motivations (authenticity, consumerism, creative inspiration, and envy) which drive individuals to follow influencers on social media, such as Instagram (Lee et al., 2022). Focusing on young generations following influencers across media platforms, six motivations were discovered: information sharing, cool and new trends, relaxing entertainment, companionship, boredom, and information seeking (Croes & Bartels, 2021).

In contrast to traditional celebrities, SMIs offer more openness to their followers, through activities such as sharing videos, images, and details of their personal lives, and even interacting in real-time. Empowered by the latest technology, this openness makes consumers feel close to influencers and interactions take place on a personal level.

As digital bonds grow stronger, brands and influencers gradually gain a more intense relationship with their followers (potential consumers). At the same time, established trust in influencers dramatically changes

## 5  Advantages and Disadvantages for Brands of Using Social…

consumer purchase behaviour and significantly shortens the customer journey for brands (Hughes et al., 2019).

Virtual influencers, that is, computer-generated personas, are increasingly used by fashion brands to promote themselves. Lil Miquela, one of the best-known virtual influencers, had reached 2.8 million followers on Instagram in early 2023. Her Instagram headline reads '19-year-old robot' but she 'displays human emotions through her posts and interactions with her followers' (Moustakas et al., 2020). In a typical post, she will promote several brands, combining items from iconic brands such as Prada and Dior with streetwear brands and emerging start-ups.

In early 2023, a new trend emerged, with creators and influencers (particularly on TikTok) discouraging their followers from making purchases. 'De-influencing' videos had reached 208 million views on TikTok by February 2023 (Enberg, 2023). De-influencing is often directed at Gen Z buyers, who are seeking to be more responsible consumers, and is not necessarily promoting no purchase at all; rather, it offers a less commercial view of the products presented. It can be argued that the trend is a throwback to the original role that fashion bloggers had, which was reviewing products online out of genuine personal interest in the category.

## Are All Fashion Brands Equal? How to Manage Influencers in the Luxury Space

Luxury fashion brands generally came late to social media: Louis Vuitton was one of the early adopters of Facebook's store traffic ad objective in 2018 (Dugal, 2023). Luxury fashion brands were traditionally focused on physical shows and strategically located flagship stores. Before 2020, invitations to (physical) Fashion Week were reserved for celebrities, fashion journalists, and designers. The idea of a social media presence, where content cannot be fully controlled, was considered to be a threat to the carefully curated brand identity which defines luxury. Many brands also lacked the required digital capabilities to deliver owned media effectively (Kearney, 2022). Moreover, several studies suggested that the interactive and accessible nature of social media could dilute the exclusivity of a luxury brand (Blasco-Arcas et al., 2016; Tungate, 2009).

The COVID pandemic changed everything, and luxury brands quickly adapted. Not only did they develop their online presence, but they also created e-commerce options that had not been available previously. Gucci's Fall/Winter 2020 womenswear show was streamed live over 12 hours on Instagram, with a focus on the runway but also showing the backstage setup with stylists, seamstresses, and makeup artists preparing the models. Latecomers like Chanel, which had not made apparel available in its online store previously, changed approach once physical stores had to close. Luxury consumers responded enthusiastically: Hermès reported a 100% increase in online sales in the first half of 2020 and

LVMH a 64% increase in online sales for the same period. Luxury's future is clearly digital: Bain and Company projects that as many as one-third of all personal luxury purchases will take place digitally by 2025, with revenues reaching an estimated $136 billion (D'Arpizio et al., 2021). Even Bottega Veneta, which deleted its social media accounts in 2021, returned to the popular Chinese platform Sina Weibo in 2023.

Once a luxury brand is online, there is an immediate need to create engaging content, and influencers become key. Luxury brands had always collaborated with celebrities, gifting or lending items that were worn at iconic events, but these were often seen as akin to advertising. Successful luxury brand influencers create content that is not typically promotional but rather presents the brand in a subtle or aspirational way. Luxury buyers appreciate insights into the brand's heritage, into what goes on behind-the-scenes, such as the design and manufacturing processes, and lifestyle content featuring the brand in appropriate contexts: travel, events, fine dining.

Influencers need brand support to produce new and interesting content for their followers. Fendi, for example, invited influencers such as Lydia Millen (@lydiamillen) and Leonie Hanne (@leoniehanne) to its #FendiPeekabooBar pop-up in London to receive a handbag with their initials embroidered in a cursive font on the flap, a cue for impactful conversations. Dior created an opportunity for engagement around the launch of its new St Honoré bag by inviting influencer Léna Mahfouf, (@lenasituations) to prepare a St Honoré cake with renowned pastry chef Cédric Grolet in Paris. The occasion was a platform for the delivery of original and unusual content which drove engagement with the brand on multiple platforms.

## When Social Media Influencing Backfires: Issues in Influencer Strategies and Management

Influencer posts and comments must be perceived as authentic by their audiences (Belanche et al., 2021). Although, in many cases, influencers are in a paid partnership with the brand (in some countries this must be declared on the social media platform), they should avoid aggressive promotions, rather like journalists reviewing products need to be objective or risk losing credibility. Fashion influencers should also consider the context of their posts: the audience needs to see the product in an appropriate setting.

When brands collaborate with influencers, they can fail to integrate the influencer with their overall marketing strategy, which results in campaigns that are disconnected from other marketing activities. This includes follow-up engagement with influencer audiences, targeted mobile ads, and more. Blending influencer marketing with organic content and social media can lead to better engagement and connection with the target audience in the long run.

In 2021, the French clothing brand 'Bad Mood' developed partnerships with a number of different influencers with the objective of increasing sales. Results were disappointing and the brand was forced to offer major discounts to move large amounts of unsold stock. The brand mistakenly believed that influencer marketing alone could drive sales and that multiple influencers could cover all communication needs. They chose high-profile influencers with large followings, a strategy which is often not suitable for a niche brand which benefits more from cooperation with micro-influencers with a more targeted and engaged audience. One of the influencers, Nabilla (@nabillabeauty, 8.4 million followers) was paid 22,000 euros; the promo code associated to her posts generated 2300 euros (Tokami, 2021). Bad Mood's founder posted his disappointment on TikTok with a video that went viral and generated much discussion on the use of influencers.

The volume of activity is also an important consideration; an influencer who engages too little may not have sufficient impact, whereas one who posts excessively may cause information overload (Leung et al., 2022). The number and timing of posts is a subject of much debate and depends on the influencer/category/product combination.

The most heinous influencer crime is 'faking'. Influencer Johanna Olsson was accused of faking a trip to Paris. According to the followers who called her out, the images were not taken in Paris at all, they were clearly photoshopped. The Swedish blogger admitted to using backdrops, but claimed she was actually in Paris and simply used backgrounds that were better shot than the original. She could not delete the Instagram posts because they were paid partnerships with brands and justified the exercise by saying that she modified some pictures to 'inspire' her followers with better views of the locations she visited. Her followers ridiculed her response with a series of memes, photoshopping her into a number of improbable locations including the moon and positioning themselves into the photos.

The most effective influencer marketing campaigns are developed as part of an integrated strategy, with the objectives clearly defined before the influencer is selected. Obvious as this may seem, in many cases brands have been driven to mismatched partnerships because they chose an influencer based on his or her previous successes with other labels, number of followers, or presence across social media platforms, without considering fit with the brand identity and communication plan.

# Interview 1

Alessandro Fragiacomo is currently Influence Business Director at Ogilvy UK. In 2021, he was recognized by Talking Influence as one of the top 50 global players in influencer marketing.

## Can You Comment on the Evolution of Social Media Influencers in the Fashion Industry?

Fashion brands have benefitted significantly from influencer marketing campaigns in the past 10 years for several reasons. Influencers' recommendations inspire consumers to experiment with brands they might not have considered ordinarily, and influencers launch styles and trends that expose consumers to new ideas. For example, the trend of mixing luxury and fast fashion brands in the daily outfit choice was promoted by influencers showcasing a 'mix & match look'.

With the ability to stream fashion shows on social media, influencers have also gradually become a vehicle to give audiences first-view access into a world that was traditionally considered elitist and exclusive. We started with bloggers in 2006 and we are now talking about influencers becoming the face of a brand in above the line campaigns. This is what I call evolution.

## Is There a Difference Between Bloggers and Influencers?

The spectrum of influence is bigger than people realize. There is a tendency to use the term 'influencer' as a macro definition when, in reality, we can talk about at least six categories of influence: Celebrities, Creators, Media Figures, Professionals, Gatekeepers, Advocates.

The power of influencers, across the different categories, sits within the large community of followers they have access to; if they are successful, they can have an impact on millions of people. These influencers might not have always gained fame through their social media presence, they might have been media personalities, actors, athletes, or celebrities in a specific niche first, and then went on to become influencers on social media capitalizing on their personal brand.

If we specifically talk about content creators, we usually refer to people who became famous thanks to the content they create and their unique editorial style. They don't simply promote products or looks, instead they have a unique way to engage with their audiences. They tend to be more selective with any brand partnerships opportunity to stay true to their own audience and values. This allows them to become an authoritative voice in their content niche.

Bloggers are creators. They are able to influence thanks to their creativity and active fan base. They usually produce written long form content featuring their own ideas and point of view. One of the first Italian fashion bloggers, Chiara Ferragni, started her career in 2009 with a blog 'The Blonde Salad' where she introduced her personal view on fashion, the brands that she liked and a few style suggestions. Over the years, thanks to her unique approach, she developed into a content creator across multiple platforms until establishing herself as fashion entrepreneur. Her own label, Chiara Ferragni Collection, is one of a few business ventures that she manages today.

Blogging has slowly declined as new social media platforms have taken over. A fashion blogger might still have a website, or a blog, but the social media platforms would be the first point of consumption, with the blog potentially being the second one.

## Instagram or TikTok?

I would say both. TikTok relies on quick video content, which Gen Z prefers, and it's effectively an entertainment product. TikTok's ambition is to compete in the same arena of Netflix, Prime, Disney+, and similar streaming services more than the social media platforms one.

Instagram still allows for static content (i.e. photos) to exist in the industry although reels have definitely been a rising format in the past three years on the back of the TikTok success.

## Can an Influencer Campaign Help Reposition or Even Revive a Fashion Brand?

When there is a strong and innovative strategy in place, collaborating with an influencer can certainly offer renewed visibility to a fashion brand, and potentially drive awareness and conversion. It's worth noting that jumping on an influencer's popularity doesn't equal immediate success. A simple collaboration might not be enough to relaunch a brand that has run out of ideas or is no longer relevant to consumers. An influence marketing campaign is based on a values exchange between the influencers and the brand. That means, if the brand doesn't authentically look at its image first, agree on its values and commitment proposition towards customers, then it might lose the opportunity to engage with authentic content creators and create an effective partnership.

## How Do You View the Use of Influencers by Luxury Fashion Brands?

In the past decade, luxury fashion brands began to invite influencers to shows and give them front-row seats, which translated into huge visibility since, as I mentioned previously, the shows can then be streamed online to a wide audience. Luxury brands want to stay relevant and top of mind from an exclusivity status perspective. Therefore, even if many of the influencers' followers might never purchase a luxury fashion item, they would still buy into the status of the brand, its reputation and image. With the opportunity of being made aware of the brand's new collections by getting a peek into an exclusive world, consumers might be influenced with new look ideas and potentially proceed into purchase similar fast-fashion products, imitating 'the style' the luxury brand is introducing.

In the Netflix show *Bling Empire*, which focuses on the lives of ultra-rich East and Southeast Asian Americans based in Los Angeles and New York, some of the cast are actual influencers such as Dorothy Wang whose collection of Birkin bags features prominently in some episodes, and Tina Leung who partners with high-end brands such as Gucci and Tod's. The lines between influencer marketing and other forms of communication are very blurred.

## Which Particularly Successful Campaigns Come to Mind?

Emma Chamberlain and Louis Vuitton. Chamberlain is an influencer who started her career on YouTube in 2016 at the age of 15 and soon gained a prominent following thanks to her unique editing style which involves zooming, adding text to the screen and pausing to emphasize an image or scene. This approach was subsequently adopted by many content creators and is often a standard today. In March 2019, Chamberlain attended Paris Fashion Week as part of a co-branding partnership between YouTube and Louis Vuitton and in 2022 she became one of the luxury brand's ambassadors. She has maintained her otherwise thrift-chic style showcasing a diverse mix of yoga pants, crop tops, and combat boots in other posts which engage over 12 million followers on YouTube and 16 million on Instagram. The partnership with Louis Vuitton has given the luxury brand a fresh, humorous look which fits which the younger customer's expectations.

## Are There Specific Influencer Requirements in Fashion?

When we think about influencers collaborations in the fashion world the first tactic that comes to mind is 'gifting'. Gifting consists of sending a product for free to the influencers and asking them to promote it on their platforms via content creation. When influencers also receive compensation for their services we move into the territory of paid collaborations.

There are multiple influencers specializing in these types of collaborations, and it's these creators that we label as 'fashion influencers'.

Over the past four years, brands have reconsidered their strategies and decided to collaborate with creators who are not just necessarily famous in the fashion content niche, as brands started to realize that a collaboration was not just product-centred and tactical but also an opportunity to drive brand awareness and reputation as well.

A fashion collaboration is not simply limited to clothing and accessories. Fashion defines and carries status quo across various industries and walks of life. With this in mind, brands started to work with different categories of influencers: sport, lifestyle, entertainment, food etc. For example, when the Prada Café at Harrods was launched in March 2023 in London, a few influencers across different content niches were invited to visit and post about the launch, making a connection between the fashion brand and its new service offer. PrettyLittleLondon, one of the most successful lifestyle influencers in the UK, was one of these.

Overall, for luxury brands it is always important to partner with influencers who can guarantee exclusivity at least within the category and work with those who have shown previous interest in the brand rather than select purely on the basis of how famous the influencer is. Ideally, the luxury brand influencer should become a long-term brand ambassador rather than a one-off collaborator. This approach also creates an advantage for the influencer who can develop business opportunities with the brand, for example, their own capsule collection under the brand name.

Ultimately, a luxury brand needs to project authenticity, so all influencer activity needs to fit within the brand identity and look to a long-term plan rather than a short-term fix.

## Are There Any Upcoming Issues/Trends You Feel Might Change the Influencer Landscape?

- AI influencers are growing, developed by brands and creators they operate just like 'human influencers' except they allow for more control over their collaborations as the robot cannot go off-script or act in public against the brand's values. What they may lack in authenticity is compensated by a guarantee that they will be aligned with the brand.
- Metaverse fashion shows, where customers can buy pieces for their avatars, have arrived and are here to stay. Balenciaga recently staged their Spring/Summer show in the 2022 Metaverse fashion show. Virtual avatars, digital renders of real models, presented the label's collection and buyers could subsequently purchase for their own avatars. The Spring/Summer 2022 range was then made available at retailers as well.
- Brands have started looking for micro-influencers, who are loyal and passionate about the brand, over big celebrities' collaborations. They seek out existing followers of the brand and work with them to develop their online presence. A popular influencer can receive up to 50 products a day, which can oversaturate that influencer in the eye of the consumer, making it difficult to authentically connect with them and their content.
- Through a new form of advocacy, brands have started helping loyal customers to become influencers and support their journey.

## Are There Any Interesting Cases You Can Share?

There are cases of people who had a quirky presence on social media, identified by brands who then initiated collaborations with them. Francis Bourgeois became famous after posting trainspotting videos on TikTok during the pandemic—he had 2.7 million followers on the platform in early 2023. Gucci and The North Face worked with him to present their collaboration in 2022. He was filmed as a conductor checking tickets and they posted: 'It's full steam ahead for @gucci and @thenorthface as they take their second collaboration to the tracks with TikTok star and trainspotter @francis_bourgeois43.'

# 5 Advantages and Disadvantages for Brands of Using Social... 95

Khaby Lame is one of the most followed social media presences globally. The 22-year-old had started posting silent videos on TikTok, satirizing other posters' content, after losing his job at the start of the pandemic. He now has over 140 million followers on TikTok and just over 78 million more on Instagram which clearly makes him very interesting for brand associations. Lame launched a capsule collection with Boss in 2022, the Boss x Khaby collection is a mainly streetwear range which gave the Boss brand, traditionally associated with serious menswear a cool look and appeal for the younger customer.

The Adidas-Yeezy case is interesting because it shows just how quickly a collaboration can turn sour if the brand associates with a potentially controversial influencer. Kanye West is a hip-hop celebrity and a fashion influencer, and initially the Yeezy apparel and sneakers brand he created in collaboration with Adidas was an outstanding success. The products were available in limited numbers and Kanye built hype online, which resulted in a quick sell-out—sometimes in hours. Influencers were not gifted items from the collections, they had to purchase them and many stood in line or purchased on the resale market to obtain them, stoking the hype even more. Adidas and Ye (as Kanye West is now known) ended the collaboration in October 2022 after he made anti-Semitic remarks on social media, and as a result, Adidas posted a net loss of €513 million in 2022 in the wake of the 'Yeezy' line becoming unsellable.

## Advice for a Brand Starting out in the Field?

Influencer marketing is here to stay, and the power of influencers is at the core of every marketing strategy thanks to the important role that the creator economy plays for brands and customers in a constantly evolving social media landscape. It's part of an overall marketing strategy and requires professionals and experts to work on it. Creators need to be vetted carefully and brands should evaluate potential reputational risks associated with popular influencers. Being focused and working with micro-influencers who may not have many followers but have a targeted and engaged audience is a good first step.

## Interview 2

Joanna Lyle is the designer of the eponymous luxury lifestyle fashion brand. Her career began in product design; she developed numerous homeware items winning the 'Alessi Memory Containers' competition with her 'Chimu' bowl in 1990. This developed into a long collaboration with Alessi, resulting in the now iconic, egg-shaped 'Ovo' kitchen range. In 2003, Joanna launched her first collection of self-produced interior design products in collaboration with Swarovski under the name of Joanna Lyle Design. Subsequently, she began to experiment with prints using velvet, silk, and wool to develop original fabrics for interiors and a little later a range of wool and velvet scarves. Their success encouraged her to use the designs for prints and embroidery in a range of clothing and accessories. The fashion garments and accessories are manufactured by local artisans in small quantities. The brand uses carefully sourced fabrics from sustainable, often on request. The brand also developed a project using off-cuts from the garment production in collaboration with Kapdaa, a UK company that reuses fabrics, wallpapers, and off-cuts of leather to create gift items handmade by people involved in an ethical project in India. They help society to move towards sustainability and promote the concept of upcycling and traditional craftsmanship. All materials, including paper, come from ethical sources.

Joanna Lyle has a store in Milan and an online sales channel.

## Can You Please Describe Your Fashion Brand?

My key aim is to transcend the ephemeral tendencies of fashion trends and deliver timeless pieces. I am very focused on chromatic harmony in my collections, we don't use primary colours but blends mixing colours that intuitively might not seem a fit but in reality result in a perfect mix. I aim for simple shapes and original prints to create a unique look that is both casual and sophisticated.

My target customer is a woman with refined tastes, who knows and appreciates the value of something beautiful and wants this to be part of her wardrobe for years rather than a passing fad. The quality of the fabric

## 5 Advantages and Disadvantages for Brands of Using Social...

is very important, I personally select each supplier to ensure consistency and each piece is designed to last. Selecting the best Italian printers, who transfer the designs onto luxurious fabrics: silk, wool, velvet and cool cottons is also one of my primary concerns, the supply chain is constantly monitored from start to finish. All garments and accessories are entirely Made in Italy with the utmost consideration for the environment and the people involved in the production process. Each season sees fresh new additions to enrich the collection, creating clothes and accessories that will always inspire.

## When Did You Start to Use Influencers to Market Your Brand and How Did You Select Them?

We started using influencers in 2020 and selected the first one by viewing many different Instagram profiles, identifying one which would be a good fit for a niche brand and for our target customer.

We currently work with two influencers who are paid for each post, both are mature women, one is a former model. The other one selected us, she came to the store one day and liked the brand and we agreed to cooperate. It is important that the influencer reflects the brand's ethos effectively in the posts, I feel that overall both of them do. In some posts the brand is showcased with other brands, ideally there should be a good fit. In some cases the mixing and matching might not be my personal choice but it is the influencer who decides how to present the ensemble.

Some posts are very spontaneous; the influencer is inspired by a location or event and takes a picture which she then posts. In other cases, there is a professional photoshoot in a studio or on location. The influencer selects and pays the photographer and the venue, the brand pays for the individual posts.

One of our influencers has two such photoshoots a year and does twice a year go on location with the photographer.

It can happen that I don't feel a vibe when I see some posts, in that case I don't post them on the brand's Instagram. It is important to keep the owned media consistent as it communicates the brand identity to the customer. It is important to me that the influencers we partner with post in a way that showcases the brand appropriately. This means that when we are featured with other brands in the same post there is a good fit.

## How Important Is Influencer Marketing in Your Overall Approach?

Influencer marketing is very important as social media is our primary communication channel together with the website. The influencer below posted a short reel going through the product range and this resulted in 400 followers for our Instagram.

A successful campaign shows the brand at its best, not too much clutter and an authentic rather than staged feel.

Another example of a successful campaign was from the other influencer we use @easymomswissmade who often provides very spontaneous shots.

In this post the influencer @easymomswissmade has accessorized my dress with a raffia bag and hat with the dress playing the lead role as the accessories are relatively understated, a good way to showcase the brand. The beach location is great for the summer dress with the colours perfectly highlighted against the colours of the sand, water, and sky.

## Instagram, TikTok or Both?

Instagram is closer to my style. TikTok is targeted to a younger audience and very 'fast' which is not a good fit with the brand's 'slow fashion' approach. I have noticed that the Instagram algorithm has changed as it favours 'TikTok-like' content, more video-based. A year ago, a sponsored post on Instagram would result in around 300 likes, now it is more like 60… Reels are favoured on Instagram even though is some cases a picture can be more effective.

## What Would You Avoid When Using Influencers?

I would not repost something that I'm not convinced about either because the brand is matched with accessories which I don't think are a good fit or the location isn't right. I wouldn't rely too much on paid content, it comes across too much as advertising. There has to be a good balance between paid and organic. At the moment the brand partners with two mature women and I'm looking to have more diversity as clearly the influencer becomes to some extent the 'face' of the brand and we don't want our customers to feel we have a single, very focused target.

# References

Appel, G., Grewal, L., Hadi, R., & Stephen, A. T. (2020). The future of social media in marketing. *Journal of the Academy of Marketing Science, 48*(1), 79–95.

Audrezet, A., de Kerviler, G., & Moulard, J. G. (2020). Authenticity under threat: When social media influencers need to go beyond self-presentation. *Journal of Business Research, 117*, 557–569.

Belanche, D., Casaló, L. V., Flavián, M., & Ibáñez-Sánchez, S. (2021). Understanding influencer marketing: The role of congruence between influencers, products and consumers. *Journal of Business Research, 132*, 186–195.

Bergkvist, L., & Zhou, K. Q. (2016). Celebrity endorsements: A literature review and research agenda. *International Journal of Advertising, 35*(4), 642–663.

Blasco-Arcas, L., Holmqvist, J., & Vignolles, A. (2016). Brand contamination in social media: Consumers' negative influence on luxury brand perceptions—A structured abstract. In L. Petruzzellis & R. S. Winer (Eds.), *Rediscovering the essentiality of marketing: Proceedings of the 2015 Academy of*

*Marketing Science (AMS) World Marketing Congress* (pp. 265–269). Springer International Publishing.

Breves, P. L., Liebers, N., Abt, M., & Kunze, A. (2019). The perceived fit between Instagram influencers and the endorsed brand: How influencer-brand fit affects source credibility and persuasive effectiveness. *Journal of Advertising Research, 59*(4), 440–454.

Campbell, C., & Farrell, J. R. (2020). More than meets the eye: The functional components underlying influencer marketing. *Business Horizons, 63*(4), 469–479.

CBBC. (2022, August 10). What are the differences between influencer marketing in the UK and China? *FOCUS.* https://focus.cbbc.org/what-are-the-differences-between-influencer-marketing-in-the-uk-and-china/#. ZA8uCnbP3Vg

Croes, E., & Bartels, J. (2021). Young adults' motivations for following social influencers and their relationship to identification and buying behavior. *Computers in Human Behavior, 124*.

D'Arpizio, C., Levato, F., Prete, F., Gault, F., & de Montgolfier, J. (2021, January 14). The future of luxury: Bouncing back from Covid-19. *Bain & Company.* https://www.bain.com/insights/the-future-of-luxury-bouncing-back-from-covid-19/

De Veriman, M., Veroline, C., & Hudders, L. (2017). Marketing through Instagram influencers: The impact of number of followers and product divergence on brand attitude. *International Journal of Advertising, 36*(5), 798–828.

Dugal, J. (2023, April 24). *Fashion brands with a strong social media presence.* https://www.fashionabc.org/fashion-brands-with-a-strong-social-media-presence/

Enberg, J. (2023, February 22). 'De-influencing' is still… influencing. *Insider Intelligence.* https://www.insiderintelligence.com/content/de-influencing-still-influencing

Etter, M., Colleoni, C., Illia, L., Meggiorin, M., & D'Eugenio, A. (2018). Measuring organisational legitimacy in social media: Assessing citizens' judgments with sentiment analysis. *Business & Society, 57*(1), 60–97.

Farrell, J. R., Campbell, C., & Sands, S. (2022). What drives consumers to engage with influencers? Segmenting consumer response to influencers: Insights for managing social-media relationships. *Journal of Advertising Research, 62*(1), 35–48.

Feng, Y., Chen, H., & Kong, Q. (2021). An expert with whom I can identify: The role of narratives in influencer marketing. *International Journal of Advertising, 40*(7), 972–993.

Heine, K., & Berghaus, B. (2014). Luxury goes digital: How to tackle the digital luxury brand–consumer touchpoints. *Journal of Global Fashion Marketing, 5*(3), 223–234. https://www.tandfonline.com/doi/abs/10.1080/2093268 5.2014.907606

Hughes, C., Swaminathan, V., & Brookes, G. (2019). Driving brand engagement through online social influencers: An empirical investigation of sponsored blogging campaigns. *Journal of Marketing, 83*(5), 78–96.

Hund, E., & McGuigan, L. (2019). A shoppable life: Performance, selfhood, and influence in the social media storefront. *Communication Culture & Critique, 12*(1), 18–35.

Jin, S. V., Muqaddam, A., & Ryu, E. (2019). Instafamous and social media influencer marketing. *Marketing Intelligence & Planning, 37*(5), 567–579.

Katz, E. (1959). Mass communication research and the study of culture: An editorial note on a possible future for this journal. *Studies in Public Communication, 2*, 1–6.

Kearney. (2022, March 7). *How the pandemic changed the luxury industry.* https://www.kearney.com/consumer-retail/article/-/insights/how-the-pandemic-changed-the-luxury-industry

Kumar, H., Singh, M. K., & Gupta, M. P. (2018). Socio-influences of user generated content in emerging markets. *Marketing Intelligence and Planning, 36*(7), 737–749.

Lee, C. (2018, May 28). Wise up: The big mistakes luxury brands are making with China's Gen Z. *Jing Daily.* https://jingdaily.com/luxury-brands-china-gen-z

Lee, M. S. W., Motion, J., & Conroy, D. (2009). Anti-consumption and brand avoidance. *Journal of Business Research, 62*(2), 169–180.

Lee, J. A., Sudarshan, S., Sussman, K. L., Bright, L. F., & Eastin, M. S. (2022). Why are consumers following social media influencers on Instagram? Exploration of consumers' motives for following influencers and the role of materialism. *International Journal of Advertising, 41*(1), 78–100.

Leung, F. F., Gu, F. F., Li, Y., Zhang, J. Z., & Palmatier, R. W. (2022). Influencer marketing effectiveness. *Journal of Marketing, 86*(6), 93–115. https://doi.org/10.1177/00222429221102889

Li, F., & Du, T. C. (2017). Maximizing micro-blog influence in online promotion. *Expert Systems with Applications, 70*, 52–66.

Lou, C., & Kim, H. K. (2019). Fancying the new rich and famous? Explicating the roles of influencer content, credibility and parental mediation in adolescents' parasocial relationship, materialism and purchase intentions. *Frontiers in Psychology, 10*.

Lou, C., Tan, S.-S., & Chen, X. (2019). Investigating consumer engagement with influencer-vs. brand-promoted ads: The roles of source and disclosure. *Journal of Interactive Advertising, 19*(3), 169–186.

McKinsey. (2018, November 12). *'True Gen': Generation Z and its implications for companies*. https://www.mckinsey.com/featured-insights/generation-z

Moustakas, E., Lamba, N., Mahmoud, D., & Ranganathan, C. (2020, June). Blurring lines between fiction and reality: Perspectives of experts on marketing effectiveness of virtual influencers. In *2020 international conference on cyber security and protection of digital services (cyber security)* (pp. 1–6). IEEE.

Munsch, A. (2021). Millennial and generation Z digital marketing communication and advertising effectiveness: A qualitative exploration. *Journal of Global Scholars of Marketing Science, 31*(1), 10–39.

Nanji, A. (2017). *Micro-influencers vs. macro-influencers: Whose posts are more effective?* https://www.marketingprofs.com/charts/2017/32863/micro-influencers-vs-macro-influencers-which-are-more-effective-infographic

Pan, Y. (2018, November 15). China is the key for a rosy global luxury market outlook. *Jing Daily*. https://jingdaily.com/china-bain/

Piehler, R., Schade, M., Sinning, J., & Burmann, C. (2022). Traditional or 'Instafamous' celebrity? Role of origin of fame in social media influencer marketing. *Journal of Strategic Marketing, 30*(4), 408–420.

Reinikainen, H., Tan, T. M., Luona-aho, V., & Salo, J. (2021). Making and breaking relationships on social media: The impacts of brand and influencer's betrayals. *Technological Forecasting and Social Change, 171*.

Ruggiero, T. E. (2000). Uses and gratifications theory in the 21st century. *Mass Communication and Society, 3*(1), 3–37.

Saternus, Z., & Hinz, O. (2021). To #ad or not to #ad – Disclosing Instagram influencer advertising. In *PACIS 2021 proceedings* (p. 122) https://aisel.ais-net.org/pacis2021/122/

Schouten, A. P., Janssen, L., & Verspaget, M. (2020). Celebrity vs influencer endorsements in advertising: The role of identification, credibility and product-endorser fit. *International Journal of Advertising, 39*(2), 258–281.

Song, S., & Kim, H. (2020). Celebrity endorsements for luxury brands: Followers vs. non-followers on social media. *International Journal of Advertising, 39*(6), 802–823.

Southgate, D., & Bubani, G. (2017). Trust in media: The new publishing battleground. *Kantar Group and Affiliates*. https://www.kantar.com/inspiration/advertising-media/trust-in-media-the-new-publishing-battleground

Statista. (2018). *Social media in China – Statistics & facts*. https://www.statista.com/topics/1170/social-networks-in-china/

Statista. (2020). *Influencer marketing market size worldwide from 2016 to 2022*. https://www.statista.com/statistics/1092819/global-influencer-market-size/

Sun, Y., Wang, R., Cao, D., & Lee, R. (2022). Who are social media influencers for luxury fashion consumption of the Chinese Gen Z? Categorisation and empirical examination. *Journal of Fashion Marketing and Management, 26*(4).

Tokami, A. (2021). *Quel est ce drama entre Badmood Paris et les influenceurs?* https://www.yubigeek.com/drama-badmood-paris

Trivedi, J. P. (2018). Measuring the comparative efficacy of an attractive celebrity influencer vis-à-vis an expert influencer—A fashion industry perspective. *International Journal of Electronic Customer Relationship Management, 11*(3), 256–271.

Trivedi, J. P., & Sama, R. (2020). The effect of influencer marketing on consumers' brand admiration and online purchase intentions: An emerging market perspective. *Journal of Internet Commerce, 19*(1), 103–124.

Tungate, M. (2009). *Luxury world: The past, present and future of luxury brands*. Kogan Page Publishers.

Vogue. (2020). *Influencers are the retailers of the 2020s*. https://www.vogue.com/article/will-influencers-replace-retailers-2020s

Walternrath, A., Brenner, C., & Hinz, O. (2022). Some interactions are more equal than others: The effect of influencer endorsements in social media brand posts on engagement and online store performance. *Journal of Interactive Marketing, 57*(4), 541–560.

Wood, N. T., & Burkhalter, J. N. (2014). Tweet this, not that: A comparison between brand promotions in microblogging environments using celebrity and company-generated tweets. *Journal of Marketing Communications, 20*(1/2), 129–146.

# 6

# Research on the Effect of Brand Virtual Influencers on Consumers' Purchase Intention

### Guangjin Su

## Introduction

The landscape of brand endorsements has been undergoing a significant transformation in recent years. Traditional methods of celebrity endorsements are being supplemented and sometimes replaced by innovative strategies aimed at enhancing brand awareness and consumer experience (de Ruyter et al., 2018; Verhoef et al., 2009). Virtual influencers have emerged as one of the most innovative strategies in the digital age. Brands now have the option to either collaborate with an existing virtual influencer or create their own from scratch. In the former scenario, a virtual influencer can be chosen to act as the brand spokesperson or ambassador, undertake product endorsement, or even participate in the co-creation of new products. In the case of a newly created virtual influencer, the brand can invest in producing a virtual influencer that perfectly aligns with the brand values and personality.

---

G. Su (✉)
Business and Law, Northumbria University, Newcastle, UK
e-mail: elaine.su@northumbria.ac.uk

© The Author(s), under exclusive license to Springer Nature Switzerland AG 2024
S. Tabari, Q. S. Ding (eds.), *Celebrity, Social Media Influencers and Brand Performance*,
https://doi.org/10.1007/978-3-031-63516-8_6

According to Baidu, a prominent tech company, the number of virtual people projects it has undertaken for clients has doubled since 2021. These projects involve the creation and utilization of virtual influencers. The cost of such projects varies significantly, with prices ranging from as low as $2800 to a staggering $14,300 per year (Cheng, 2023). This increase in demand for virtual people projects reflects the growing interest and recognition of virtual influencers as an effective marketing tool. Brands are willing to invest in these projects to leverage virtual influencers' influence and engagement potential in reaching their target audiences.

In recent years, virtual influencers have gained significant popularity as a marketing tool utilized by companies and brands to promote their products and services (H. Kim & Park, 2023; Mrad et al., 2022; Rodrigo-Martín et al., 2021). These computer-generated or AI-driven characters play a crucial role in influencer marketing campaigns and have unique characteristics that shape consumers' perceptions and evaluations of the recommended products or services (Huang et al., 2022; H. Kim & Park, 2023; Mrad et al., 2022; Zhong, 2022). As the utilization of virtual influencers continues to rise, understanding their impact on consumer behavior has become increasingly important for marketers and researchers. This study adopts the Stimulus-Organism-Response (S-O-R) model to explore the connections between brand virtual influencers' characteristics, perceived value, and purchase intention.

## S-O-R Model

The Stimulus-Organism-Response (S-O-R) theory, originally proposed by Mehrabian and Russell (1974) in the field of environmental psychology, has been applied to marketing research by Donovan and Rossiter (1982). This framework remains relevant in current studies and has been used extensively in the field of influencer marketing (Koay et al., 2021; Kumar et al., 2018; Y. H. Lin & Jen, 2022; Loureiro et al., 2021; Patmawati & Miswanto, 2022; Yu et al., 2023; S. Zhou et al., 2021).

According to the S-O-R paradigm, environmental cues act as stimuli (S) that influence individuals' emotional and cognitive responses (O), which then trigger behavioral responses (R). In the context of brand virtual influencers, their characteristics serve as stimuli that influence consumers' perceptions and evaluations of recommended products or services. These characteristics, such as perceived attractiveness, interactivity, relevance, and popularity, can affect consumers' perceived value, and influence their purchase intention. The purpose of this study is to investigate the relationships between brand virtual influencers' characteristics, perceived value, and purchase intention and to gain insights into the underlying mechanisms and effects of virtual influencers on consumer behavior

## Brand Virtual Influencers' Characteristics as Stimuli (S)

The use of virtual influencers by companies and brands to promote products and services has gained significant momentum in recent years, leading to an increase in empirical research on the characteristics of brand virtual influencers (Huang et al., 2022; H. Kim & Park, 2023; Rodrigo-Martín et al., 2021). Previous studies have provided valuable insights into the impact of various characteristics on consumers' attitudes toward virtual influencers and their associated brands. For example, Huang et al. (2022) confirmed that factors such as the popularity, homogeneity, and relevance of virtual idols significantly affect consumers' purchase intention. Zhong (2022) revealed that interactivity, creativity, and brand storytelling in advertising content design have a positive correlation with customer brand engagement. Wu (2020) found that the trustworthiness of virtual influencers positively affects consumers' attitudes toward brands, while attractiveness and expertise have a negative impact. Tri (2022) proved that virtual influencers' credibility, attractiveness, and product-image match positively influence consumers' purchase intention. However, H. Kim and Park (2023) revealed that virtual influencers' attractiveness did not directly associate with purchase intention.

Based on these findings, this study recognizes the importance of attractiveness, interactivity, relevance, and popularity as critical characteristics of brand virtual influencers that affect consumers' purchase intention. These characteristics can be defined as follows:

1. Attractiveness: refers to the appeal and charm of brand virtual influencers and includes their physical appearance, style, and overall personality (Abbas et al., 2018; H. Kim & Park, 2023; Yu et al., 2023). This includes aesthetics, visual appeal, and the ability to captivate and engage the audience.
2. Interactivity: refers to the level of engagement and interaction between brand virtual influencers and their followers or fans and includes activities such as replying to comments, initiating conversations, and fostering a sense of community (Xu & Kim, 2022; Zhong, 2022). Interactivity fosters a stronger connection and bond between brand virtual influencers and their audience.
3. Relevance: refers to the fit between brand virtual influencers and the brands or products they promote and includes the suitability, compatibility, and congruence between the brand virtual influencer's image and values and the brand's identity (Hu, 2022; Huang et al., 2022; Shah et al., 2022; Tri, 2022). Relevance ensures that the virtual influencer resonates with the target audience and effectively conveys the brand's message.
4. Popularity: refers to the level of recognition, fame, and social prominence of the brand virtual influencers, including factors such as the number of followers, reach, and influence on social media platforms (Xu & Kim, 2022; R. Zhou & Tong, 2022). Popularity reflects the brand virtual influencer's reach and influence on their audience and can increase their credibility and perceived value.

Building on previous research, this study highlights the importance of attractiveness, interactivity, relevance, and popularity as critical characteristics for understanding consumer attitudes toward brand virtual influencers and their associated brands. By examining these dimensions, the study aims to uncover the influence of brand virtual influencers' characteristics on consumer purchase intention, with perceived value serving as a mediating variable. It is important to note that while brand virtual influencers lack expertise and rely on a team to manage their social media content, the characteristics of attractiveness, interactivity, relevance, and popularity continue to play a significant role in shaping consumer responses to brand virtual influencers and their marketing efforts.

## Perceived Value as Organism (O)

Perceived value, which has its roots in the science of consumer behavior, is crucial in explaining consumer behavior (J. H. Kim & Park, 2019; S. Zhou et al., 2022). It represents the evaluation of the benefits compared to the costs associated with buying, using, or enjoying a product or service (Zauner et al., 2015; Zeithaml, 1988). Perceived value is often divided into utilitarian value and hedonic value. Utilitarian value captures consumers' perceptions of the functional benefits and costs associated with engaging with brand virtual influencers, including factors such as cost-effectiveness, convenience, and time costs. Hedonic value, on the other hand, represents consumers' perceived emotional benefits and costs, emphasizing the enjoyment, satisfaction, and relief derived from interacting with brand virtual influencers (Babin et al., 1994; Soebandhi et al., 2019).

Perceived value is an internal psychological process of consumers when making consumption decisions and behaviors (Woodruff, 1997). Within the S-O-R framework, perceived value is often considered as the organism (O) and studied as a mediating factor between stimuli and responses (Eroglu et al., 2001; Mehrabian & Russell, 1974). Perceived value is closely related to consumer intentions, as both utilitarian and hedonic values positively influence future intentions (Chiu et al., 2014). Therefore, this study combines perceived value theory with the S-O-R model, considering perceived value as the organism (O) and purchase intention as the response (R). Perceived value has been identified as a key factor in explaining consumer behavior and is often used as a proxy for the behavior itself (Schipani, 2019; Sweeney & Soutar, 2001; S. Zhou et al., 2022). Studies based on the S-O-R model often consider perceived value as the internal response of organisms. For example, Chopdar and Balakrishnan (2020) found that perceived value as an organism is a key factor influencing consumer behavior. Based on these discussions, this study focuses on the perceived value as the organism (O).

## Purchase Intention as Response (R)

Purchase intention reflects consumers' subjective inclination to purchase products and services (Abbas et al., 2018; Herjanto et al., 2020; Khan et al., 2022; H. Kim & Park, 2023; Xu & Kim, 2022; S. Zhou et al., 2022). In the literature, the intention is often used to indicate behavior (Morwitz & Munz, 2021; S. Zhou et al., 2022). Moreover, intention is frequently treated as a response factor in studies based on the S-O-R model. Therefore, in the context of brand virtual influencers, this study focuses on purchase intention as consumers' behavioral response to their value perception, which is influenced by attractiveness, interactivity, relevance, and popularity, which act as stimuli from brand virtual influencers' characteristics.

## Conceptual Framework and Hypotheses

Based on the S-O-R model and perceived value, this study investigates the impact of brand virtual influencers on consumer behavior. The proposed framework includes the characteristics of brand virtual influencers (attractiveness, interactivity, relevance, and popularity) as external stimuli that positively affect users' perceived value as an organism (utilitarian value, hedonic value) and influence purchase intention. The research model is shown in Fig. 6.1.

## Brand Virtual Influencers' Characteristics (S) and Purchase Intention (R)

According to the S-O-R model, brand virtual influencers' characteristics are considered as stimuli (S) that can impact consumers' perceptions and attitudes (Donovan & Rossiter, 1982; Mehrabian & Russell, 1974). It is hypothesized that these characteristics will have a positive influence on consumers' purchase intention (R). When consumers have a positive perception of brand virtual influencers, it is expected that their purchase intention will be higher. This hypothesis suggests a direct relationship

# 6 Research on the Effect of Brand Virtual Influencers...

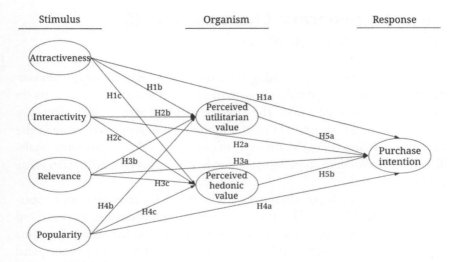

**Fig. 6.1** Research model. Source: Author

between brand virtual influencers' characteristics and consumers' purchase intention.

The influence of virtual influencers' characteristics on consumers' purchase intention has been supported by previous research. For instance, Huang et al. (2022) found that popularity, cuteness, attractiveness, relevance to the brand, and homogeneity with consumers of virtual influencers positively influence consumers' intention to buy branded clothing. Similarly, Abbas et al. (2018) found that likeability, credibility, and attractiveness have a positive effect on purchase intention. Therefore, the hypothesis proposes that virtual influencers' characteristics positively influence consumers' purchase intention.

H1a: The attractiveness of brand virtual influencers has a positive effect on consumers' purchase intention.
H2a: The interactivity of brand virtual influencers has a positive effect on consumers' purchase intention.
H3a: The relevance of brand virtual influencers has a positive effect on consumers' purchase intention.
H4a: The popularity of brand virtual influencers has a positive effect on consumers' purchase intention.

## Virtual Influencers' Characteristics (S) and Perceived Value (O)

This study focuses on examining the influence of attractiveness, interactivity, relevance, and popularity as characteristics of virtual influencers on consumers' perceived value. The characteristics of virtual influencers are considered as the stimuli (S) in the model, while perceived value is the central construct (O). The division of perceived value aligns with established frameworks from previous research, distinguishing utilitarian value and hedonic value.

The characteristics of attractiveness, interactivity, relevance, and popularity exhibited by virtual influencers can mitigate consumers' perceived risks during shopping, thus enhancing their perceived value. Previous research by Xu and Kim (2022) found that credibility, attractiveness, and interactivity have significant effects on consumers' perceived value. Yan and Mo (2020) also showed that virtual influencers demonstrating these characteristics effectively provide useful information, thereby increasing consumers' perceived value. Building on these findings, we hypothesize that attractiveness, interactivity, relevance, and popularity significantly positively affect consumers' perceived value. The attractiveness of brand virtual influencers has a positive effect on perceived utilitarian value.

H1c: The attractiveness of brand virtual influencers has a positive effect on perceived hedonic value.

H2b: The interactivity of brand virtual influencers has a positive effect on perceived utilitarian value.

H2c: The interactivity of brand virtual influencers has a positive effect on perceived hedonic value.

H3b: The relevance of brand virtual influencers has a positive effect on perceived utilitarian value.

H3c: The relevance of brand virtual influencers has a positive effect on perceived hedonic value.

H4b: The popularity of brand virtual influencers has a positive effect on perceived utilitarian value.

H4c: The popularity of brand virtual influencers has a positive effect on perceived hedonic value.

## Perceived Value (O) and Purchase Intention (R)

The higher the perceived value consumers derive, the stronger their purchase intention. Brand virtual influencers provide product information, and consumers perceive and evaluate the goods, which, in turn, affects their purchase intention (Yan & Mo, 2020). Based on previous research, this study establishes the following hypothesis to investigate the influence of perceived value on purchase intention. Numerous studies in various fields have shown that perceived value is closely related to consumers' purchase intentions and that both utilitarian and hedonic values positively influence future intentions (Babin et al., 1994; Huang et al., 2022; D. J. Kim & Hwang, 2012; Y. Li et al., 2023; Potra et al., 2018; Singh et al., 2020; Soebandhi et al., 2019). In the context of virtual influencers, previous research has found a positive effect of perceived value on users' purchase intentions (Huang et al., 2022). Therefore, the following hypothesis:

Hypothesis H5a: Perceived utilitarian value has a positive effect on purchase intention.
Hypothesis H5b: Perceived hedonic value has a positive effect on purchase intention.

## The Mediating Role of Perceived Value

In addition to examining the direct effects of the perceived value of brand virtual influencers on purchase intention, this study examines the mediating role of perceived value in the relationship between brand virtual influencers' characteristics and purchase intention. Perceived value is proposed as a mediating variable that explains how the characteristics of brand virtual influencers affect consumers' purchase intention.

Previous research has shown that perceived value mediates the impact of different stimuli on consumer behavior (Y. Li et al., 2023; Wang et al., 2020; Zhang, 2010; R. Zhou & Tong, 2022). In the context of brand virtual influencers, the characteristics of attractiveness, interactivity, relevance, and popularity can influence consumers' perception of value, which, in turn, influences their purchase intention. When consumers perceive brand virtual influencers as attractive, interactive, relevant, and popular, they are likely to derive higher utilitarian and hedonic value from their interactions and content. This higher perceived value, characterized by a positive evaluation of benefits versus costs, can have a positive impact on consumers' purchase intention.

The S-O-R model assumes that stimuli (characteristics of brand virtual influencers) influence organisms (perceived value), which then drive responses (purchase intention). To investigate the mediating role of perceived value, this study employs mediation analysis to assess the indirect effects of brand virtual influencers' characteristics on purchase intention through perceived value. Based on the proposed hypotheses, the following mediation hypotheses are formulated:

H6a: Perceived utilitarian value mediates the relationship between brand virtual influencers' attractiveness and purchase intention.

H6b: Perceived hedonic value mediates the relationship between brand virtual influencers' attractiveness and purchase intention.

H7a: Perceived utilitarian value mediates the relationship between brand virtual influencers' interactivity and purchase intention.

H7b: Perceived hedonic value mediates the relationship between brand virtual influencers' interactivity and purchase intention.

H8a: Perceived utilitarian value mediates the relationship between brand virtual influencers' relevance and purchase intention.

H8b: Perceived hedonic value mediates the relationship between brand virtual influencers' relevance and purchase intention.

H9a: Perceived utilitarian value mediates the relationship between brand virtual influencers' popularity and purchase intention.

H9b: Perceived hedonic value mediates the relationship between brand virtual influencers' popularity and purchase intention.

## Research Methodology

### Sample and Data Collection

In this study, an empirical analysis was conducted using a questionnaire. The questionnaire was distributed online to Chinese consumers. The online questionnaire consisted of two main parts designed to test the model. The first part focused on screening questions, participants' familiarity with virtual influencers and their followers, and their demographic information. Participants were asked about their awareness of and engagement with virtual influencers. In this part, participants were asked if they knew and followed the virtual influencers. The second part included measurement items for each construct of the model. The survey was conducted online in April 2023 using wjx.cn. Customers who followed the virtual influencers were selected as valid survey participants. The questionnaire was created after an extensive literature review. The first version of the questionnaire was first created in English and then translated into Chinese by two researchers who were familiar with both English and Chinese. Subsequently, the Chinese version was back-translated into English to ensure consistent accuracy. To ensure the reliability and validity of the scales, a pilot test was conducted with 70 respondents who followed virtual influencers. Based on the results of the pilot test, minor changes were made to the items before the formal survey. A formal online questionnaire was distributed via widely used social media tools such as WeChat, Tencent QQ, and Weibo. After eliminating invalid questionnaires that failed the screening questions, had too short a response time or almost invariant responses, a total of 486 valid questionnaires were obtained through random sampling methods.

### Instrument

In this study, first, all construct measures were derived from the existing literature. The questionnaire consisted of the variables, such as attractiveness, interactivity, relevance, popularity, perceived utilitarian value, perceived hedonic value, and purchase intention. Also, the respondent's demography was asked through gender, age, educational qualification, and if they followed at least one virtual influencer. The details of all constructs are presented in Table 6.2. The main questionnaire adopted a seven-point Likert scale, where 1 indicates strongly disagree, 4 indicates neither agree nor disagree, and 7 indicates strongly agree.

# Data Analysis and Results

## Descriptive Statistics

A total of 396 (81.48%) respondents followed at least one brand virtual influencer. Among the 486 respondents, 262 (53.91%) were male, and 224 (46.09%) were female. Hence, men were predominant in the sample. This corresponds to the gender makeup of the population of China. Most of the respondents were 18–25 (46.91%) years old, followed by 26–30 (44.03%) years old. The result indicated that young people embrace new technology more than old people and they are more representative than middle and old-age people in terms of virtual influencers. The educational level of respondents was as follows: 289 respondents attended diploma or bachelor's degree (59.47% of all respondents), 191 respondents obtained a master's or postgraduate degree (39.30%), with the remaining 6 respondents being PhD holders or above (1.23%). The results showed that more than half of the respondents had a diploma or bachelor's degree. The annual income of respondents varied. Overall, 40.95% of the respondents had a yearly income between 48,000 and 72,000 RMB, occupying the most significant percentage, followed by 28.40% of respondents with an annual income between 72,000 and 96,000 RMB. The third-largest group were respondents with an annual income less than 48,000 RMB, accounting for 18.72% of the total. The number of respondents with an annual income of over 96,000 RMB was 58, accounting for 11.93% of the total respondents.

Results of demographic information are displayed in Table 6.1.

## 6 Research on the Effect of Brand Virtual Influencers... 117

**Table 6.1** Demographic details of the respondents (*N* = 486)

| Items | Categories | *N* | Percent (%) | Cumulative percent (%) |
|---|---|---|---|---|
| Gender | Male | 262 | 53.91 | 53.91 |
| | Female | 224 | 46.09 | 100.00 |
| Age | 18–25 | 228 | 46.91 | 46.91 |
| | 26–30 | 214 | 44.03 | 90.94 |
| | 31–40 | 38 | 7.82 | 98.76 |
| | 41–50 | 6 | 1.24 | 100.00 |
| | Above 50 | – | – | – |
| Education | High school and below | – | – | – |
| | Diploma or bachelor's degree | 289 | 59.47 | 59.47 |
| | Master's or postgraduate degree | 191 | 39.30 | 98.77 |
| | PhD or above | 6 | 1.23 | 100.00 |
| Income | Less than 48,000 | 91 | 18.72 | 18.72 |
| | 48,000–72,000 | 199 | 40.95 | 59.67 |
| | 72,001—96,000 | 138 | 28.40 | 88.07 |
| | 96,001 and above | 58 | 11.93 | 100.00 |
| Total | | 486 | 100.0 | 100.00 |

## Measurement Model

According to Hair et al. (2014), for the establishment of internal consistency reliability, values of composite reliability (CR) must be greater than 0.7. The results shown in Table 6.2 indicate that the constructs in this study attained CR values greater than 0.802, demonstrating good internal consistency. For item reliability, an individual item must exhibit significant standardized loadings above 0.7 ($p < 0.001$) (Bagozzi & Yi, 1988). The lowest item loading was 0.705 (see Table 6.2), which was above the recommended threshold of 0.7 (Hair et al., 2011). Following Raman and Aashish (2021), to confirm convergent validity, the average variance extracted (AVE) of a construct must be over 0.5. The results showed that the AVE values of the constructs in this study were between 0.503 (interactivity) and 0.586 (attractiveness) (see Table 6.2), confirming their convergent validity. For adequate discriminant validity, the Fornell-Larcker criterion requires the square root of each construct's AVE to be greater than its correlation with each of the remaining constructs

**Table 6.2** Construct measures, factor loadings, and reliability and validity measures

| Construct | Item | Factor loadings | Reliability and validity |
|---|---|---|---|
| Attractiveness (H. Kim & Park, 2023; Masuda et al., 2022; Qiu et al., 2021) | I think the virtual influencer is quite pretty | 0.813 | CR = 0.850 AVE = 0.586 |
| | I find the virtual influencer very attractive physically | 0.782 | Cronbach's $\alpha$ = 0.850 |
| | The virtual influencer is very sexy looking | 0.770 | |
| | The virtual influencer's appearance is quite attractive | 0.808 | |
| Interactivity (Kwak & Yoh, 2021; S. C. Lin et al., 2022; Xu & Kim, 2022) | The virtual influencer is always quick to respond to comments | 0.776 | CR = 0.802 AVE = 0.503 |
| | The virtual influencer often interacts with me in the live commerce space | 0.737 | Cronbach's $\alpha$ = 0.801 |
| | The virtual influencer is always responsive and receptive to questions or opinions | 0.729 | |
| | I often check in with virtual influencers to share product information or product experiences | 0.776 | |
| Relevance (Hu, 2022; Huang et al., 2022) | It makes sense for the virtual influencer to endorse the brand/products | 0.740 | CR = 0.803 AVE = 0.506 |
| | It is appropriate that the virtual influencer endorses the brand/products | 0.734 | Cronbach's $\alpha$ = 0.803 |
| | The virtual influencer is related to the products/brand | 0.786 | |
| | Generally, the virtual influencer matches the products/brand | 0.783 | |

*(continued)*

## 6 Research on the Effect of Brand Virtual Influencers... 119

**Table 6.2** (continued)

| Construct | Item | Factor loadings | Reliability and validity |
|---|---|---|---|
| Popularity (Huang et al., 2022; R. Zhou & Tong, 2022) | I believe the virtual influencer has a lot of followers | 0.770 | CR = 0.806 AVE = 0.510 Cronbach's $\alpha$ = 0.806 |
| | I think the virtual influencer is famous | 0.773 | |
| | I think the virtual influencer is well liked | 0.771 | |
| | I think the virtual influencer is well recognized | 0.760 | |
| Perceived utilitarian value (Babin et al., 1994; Chiu et al., 2014; Soebandhi et al., 2019) | The virtual influencer I watched recommended good value for money | 0.834 | CR = 0.807 AVE = 0.583 Cronbach's $\alpha$ = 0.806 |
| | The virtual influencer can save me more time and energy when shopping | 0.767 | |
| | I can get information about stores and products easily from the virtual influencer | 0.823 | |
| Perceived hedonic value (Chiu et al., 2014; L. Li et al., 2022; Soebandhi et al., 2019; Yan & Mo, 2020) | I feel excited and happy watching the products recommended by the virtual influencer | 0.736 | CR = 0.811 AVE = 0.518 Cronbach's $\alpha$ = 0.810 |
| | I like the products recommended by the virtual influencer | 0.705 | |
| | I think I get more compliments from the virtual influencer | 0.762 | |
| | I think the products recommended by the virtual influencer can help me build a good personal image | 0.721 | |

*(continued)*

**Table 6.2** (continued)

| Construct | Item | Factor loadings | Reliability and validity |
|---|---|---|---|
| Purchase intention (Huang et al., 2022; Masuda et al., 2022; Rungruangjit, 2022; Schipani, 2019; Soebandhi et al., 2019; Tri, 2022) | Watching the virtual influencer makes me want to buy | 0.786 | CR = 0.803 AVE = 0.504 Cronbach's $\alpha$ = 0.801 |
| | If there is a need to buy, I will first buy the goods recommended by the virtual influencer | 0727 | |
| | I buy the things that the virtual influencer recommends again or more times | 0.740 | |
| | I recommend the products of the virtual influencer to my friends | 0.766 | |

*CR* composite reliability, *AVE* average variance extracted

**Table 6.3** Correlations and discriminant validity

| | ATT | INT | REL | POP | PUV | PHV | PUR |
|---|---|---|---|---|---|---|---|
| ATT | **0.766** | | | | | | |
| INT | 0.271 | **0.709** | | | | | |
| REL | 0.244 | 0.307 | **0.711** | | | | |
| POP | 0.261 | 0.199 | 0.245 | **0.714** | | | |
| PUV | 0.302 | 0.269 | 0.213 | 0.262 | **0.763** | | |
| PHV | 0.403 | 0.397 | 0.374 | 0.348 | 0.342 | **0.720** | |
| PUR | 0.278 | 0.322 | 0.287 | 0.252 | 0.313 | 0.363 | **0.710** |

Note: The square root values of the average variance extracted (AVE) are in bold
*ATT* attractiveness, *INT* interactivity, *REL* relevance, *POP* popularity, *PUV* perceived utilitarian value, *PHV* perceived hedonic value, *PUR* purchase intention

(Fornell & Larcker, 1981). As shown in Table 6.3, our results meet this requirement. Thus, the discriminant validity of each construct can be confirmed.

## Structural Model and Hypothesis Testing

The full structural model was analyzed using the maximum likelihood estimation method with AMOS 28. The overall goodness-of-fit values were satisfactory: $\chi^2/df$ =1.041, RMSEA = 0.009, CFI = 0.999, NFI = 0.980, IFI = 0.999, and TLI = 0.998. The results of hypothesis testing are shown in Table 6.4 and Fig. 6.2.

**Table 6.4** Results of path analysis

| Hypotheses paths | Unstandardized estimate | SE | z (CR) | p | Standardized estimate | Results |
|---|---|---|---|---|---|---|
| H1a: ATT→PUR | 0.074 | 0.040 | 1.839 | 0.066 | 0.084 | Not supported |
| H1b: ATT→PUV | 0.203 | 0.046 | 4.448 | 0.000 | 0.199 | Supported |
| H1c: ATT→PHV | 0.208 | 0.034 | 6.067 | 0.000 | 0.242 | Supported |
| H2a: INT→PUR | 0.147 | 0.045 | 3.298 | 0.000 | 0.149 | Supported |
| H2b: INT→PUV | 0.182 | 0.051 | 3.567 | 0.000 | 0.160 | Supported |
| H2c: INT→PHV | 0.224 | 0.039 | 5.805 | 0.000 | 0.233 | Supported |
| H3a: REL→PUR | 0.112 | 0.043 | 2.566 | 0.010 | 0.114 | Supported |
| H3b: REL→PUV | 0.086 | 0.051 | 1.696 | 0.090 | 0.076 | Not supported |
| H3c: REL→PHV | 0.188 | 0.038 | 4.909 | 0.000 | 0.197 | Supported |
| H4a: POP→PUR | 0.081 | 0.043 | 1.862 | 0.063 | 0.082 | Not supported |
| H4b: POP→PUV | 0.182 | 0.050 | 3.632 | 0.000 | 0.160 | Supported |
| H4c: POP→PHV | 0.183 | 0.038 | 4.843 | 0.000 | 0.191 | Supported |
| H5a: PUV→PUR | 0.132 | 0.038 | 3.487 | 0.000 | 0.152 | Supported |
| H5b: PHV→PUR | 0.152 | 0.050 | 3.017 | 0.003 | 0.148 | Supported |

*ATT* attractiveness, *INT* interactivity, *REL* relevance, *POP* popularity, *PUV* perceived utilitarian value, *PHV* perceived hedonic value, *PUR* purchase intention

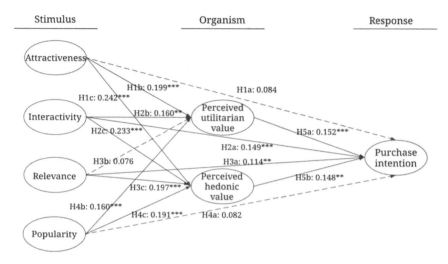

**Fig. 6.2** Research result of hypotheses testing. Note: ***Significant at $p < 0.001$; **Significant at $p < 0.01$; *Significant at $p < 0.05$

Results of hypotheses testing indicate that attractiveness was not significantly related to the customer purchase intention ($\beta = 0.084$, $p > 0.05$). But attractiveness had a significant positive impact on the perceived utilitarian value ($\beta = 0.199$, $p < 0.001$) and perceived hedonic value of virtual influencers ($\beta = 0.242$, $p < 0.001$), and thus H1a was not supported and H1b and H1c were supported. Interactivity had a positive effect on the customers' purchase intention ($\beta = 0.149$, $p < 0.001$), perceived utilitarian value ($\beta = 0.160$, $p < 0.001$), and perceived hedonic value toward virtual influencers ($\beta = 0.233$, $p < 0.001$), and thus H2a, H2b, and H2c were supported. H3a and H3c were supported in that relevance had a significant positive relationship with the customers' purchase intention ($\beta = 0.114$, $p < 0.01$) and perceived hedonic value of virtual influencers ($\beta = 0.198$, $p < 0.001$), but H3b was not supported in that relevance was not significantly related to the perceived utilitarian value ($\beta = 0.076$, $p > 0.05$).

H4a was not supported in that popularity was not significantly related to the customers' purchase intention ($\beta = 0.082$, $p > 0.05$), but H4b and H4c were supported because popularity was positively related to the perceived utilitarian value ($\beta$ = 0.160, $p$ < 0.001) and perceived hedonic value of virtual influencers ($\beta$ = 0.191, $p$ < 0.001). H5a and H5b were also supported, wherein the perceived utilitarian value ($\beta$ = 0.152, $p$ < 0.001) and perceived hedonic value ($\beta$ = 0.148, $p$ < 0.01) had significant positive relationship with customers' purchase intention toward virtual influencers.

## Mediation Test

The mediation analysis results showed that the mediating effect of perceived utilitarian value between attractiveness and purchase intention toward virtual influencers was 0.027 ($p$ < 0.05), and the 95% confidence interval [0.009, 0.057] did not include 0. Therefore, the perceived utilitarian value had a significant mediating effect between attractiveness and purchase intention toward virtual influencers. The mediating effect of perceived hedonic value between attractiveness and purchase intention toward virtual influencers was 0.028 ($p$ < 0.05), and the 95% confidence interval [0.007, 0.064] did not include 0. Therefore, the perceived hedonic value had a significant mediating effect on attractiveness and purchase intention toward virtual influencers. So, H6a and H6b were supported. H7a and H7b were also supported, wherein the perceived utilitarian value and perceived hedonic value had mediating effect on interactivity and purchase intention of virtual influencers because the result was 0.024 ($p$ < 0.05) and 0.034 ($p$ < 0.05), and the 95% confidence interval [0.005, 0.053] and [0.006, 0.064] did not include 0. The mediating effect of perceived utilitarian value between relevance and customers' purchase intention toward virtual influencers was 0.011 ($p$ > 0.05), and the 95% confidence interval [−0.004, 0.030] did include 0. But the mediating effect of perceived hedonic value between relevance and customers' purchase intention toward virtual influencers was 0.027 ($p$ < 0.05), and the 95% confidence interval [0.006, 0.056] did not include 0. Thus, H8a was not supported and H8b was supported. H9a and H9b were also supported in that perceived utilitarian value and perceived hedonic value had mediating effect on the popularity and purchase intention of virtual influencers because the result was 0.024 ($p < 0.05$) and 0.025 ($p < 0.05$), and the 95% confidence interval [0.006, 0.047] and [0.005, 0.048] did not include 0.

# Discussion and Conclusions

## Theoretical Contributions and Implications

This study contributes to the existing body of literature in several ways. First, it extends the understanding of brand virtual influencers, a relatively new and rapidly growing phenomenon in the field of digital marketing. By examining the impact of various factors such as attractiveness, interactivity, relevance, and popularity on consumers' purchase intentions, this study provides a comprehensive framework for understanding the role of brand virtual influencers in shaping consumer behavior. This research aligns with the work of Djafarova and Rushworth (2017), who explored the impact of influencers on consumer behavior, and extended it by focusing specifically on virtual influencers.

Second, this study contributes to the literature on perceived utilitarian and hedonic values. While previous studies have examined these constructs in various contexts (Chiu et al., 2014; B. Kim & Han, 2009; B. Kim & Oh, 2011; Prodanova et al., 2019; Soebandhi et al., 2019), this study is one of the first to explore their role in the context of brand virtual influencers. The findings suggest that both utilitarian and hedonic values play a significant role in shaping consumers' purchase intentions, highlighting the importance of providing both practical and enjoyable experiences for consumers.

Third, this study makes a significant contribution to the literature on consumer behavior, particularly in the context of brand virtual influencers. Specifically, it was found that interactivity and relevance directly influence purchase intentions, underscoring the importance of engagement between brand virtual influencers and their followers or fans and the fit between brand virtual influencers and the brands or products. In contrast, attractiveness and popularity did not directly influence purchase intentions. However, they significantly impacted perceived utilitarian and hedonic values. This finding suggests that while attractiveness and popularity are important factors in shaping consumers' perceptions of brand virtual influencers, they do not directly translate into purchase intentions. Instead, they contribute to the perceived utilitarian and hedonic values, which, in turn, influence purchase intentions.

## Practical Contributions and Implications

The findings of this study have several implications for marketing practitioners and researchers. Marketers should pay attention to the characteristics of virtual influencers when implementing influencer marketing strategies. Investing in virtual influencers who possess high attractiveness, interactivity, relevance, and popularity can increase consumers' purchase intention and perceived value. The study highlights the importance of utilitarian and hedonic values in driving consumers' purchase intention. Marketers should focus on creating content and experiences that provide functional benefits (utilitarian value) as well as emotional enjoyment and satisfaction (hedonic value). Understanding the mechanisms through which virtual influencers' characteristics influence consumer behavior can inform the development of effective influencer marketing campaigns. Marketers can leverage the positive impact of virtual influencers' attractiveness, interactivity, relevance, and popularity to enhance consumers' purchase intention and perceived value. Additionally, the study underscores the significance of perceived value in influencing consumers' purchase intention. Marketers should strive to create value for consumers through virtual influencers by offering utilitarian and hedonic benefits. By understanding and delivering on consumers' expectations of value, marketers can increase the effectiveness of their influencer marketing efforts. Furthermore, the findings of this study contribute to the body of knowledge on virtual influencers and their role in shaping consumer behavior. Researchers can build upon these findings to further explore the specific mechanisms and underlying psychological processes through which brand virtual influencers influence consumer attitudes and behaviors.

## Limitations and Future Research Directions

While this study provides valuable insights into the relationships between brand virtual influencers' characteristics, perceived value, and purchase intention, it is important to acknowledge its limitations. First, the study focused on a specific demographic and may not generalize to other populations. Future research could investigate the impact of brand virtual influencers on different consumer segments to provide a more comprehensive understanding. Second, the study relied on self-reported measures, which may be subject to biases and social desirability effects. Future research could employ experimental designs or objective measures to strengthen the validity of the findings. Third, the study examined the impact of brand virtual influencers' characteristics on purchase intention but did not explore the actual purchase behavior. Future research could investigate the link between brand virtual influencers and actual purchase outcomes to provide a more complete picture. Lastly, this study primarily focused on the positive aspects of brand virtual influencers. Future research could explore potential negative effects or limitations associated with brand virtual influencer marketing, such as issues of authenticity, trust, and the potential for exploitation. In conclusion, this study sheds light on the important role of brand virtual influencers in shaping consumer behavior. The findings highlight the significance of brand virtual influencers' characteristics and perceived value in driving consumers' purchase intention. By understanding these relationships, marketers can develop more effective influencer marketing strategies, ultimately enhancing consumer engagement and purchase behavior. Future research can further expand our understanding of brand virtual influencers and their impact in the dynamic landscape of digital marketing.

## References

Abbas, A., Afshan, G., Aslam, I., & Ewaz, L. (2018). The effect of celebrity endorsement on customer purchase intention: A comparative study. *Current Economics and Management Research, 4*(1), 1–10.

Babin, B. J., Darden, W. R., & Griffin, M. (1994). Work and/or fun: Measuring hedonic and utilitarian shopping value. *Journal of Consumer Research, 20*(4), 644–656.

Bagozzi, R. P., & Yi, Y. (1988). On the evaluation of structural equation models. *Journal of the Academy of Marketing Science, 16*(1), 74–94.

Cheng, E. (2023). Companies can 'hire' a virtual person for about $14k a year in China. *CNBC.* https://www.cnbc.com/2023/01/02/companies-can-hire-a-virtual-person-for-about-14k-a-year-in-china.html#:~:text=It costs about 100%2C000 yuan,by 50%25 annually through 2025

Chiu, C. M., Wang, E. T. G., Fang, Y. H., & Huang, H. Y. (2014). Understanding customers' repeat purchase intentions in B2C e-commerce: The roles of utilitarian value, hedonic value and perceived risk. *Information Systems Journal, 24*(1), 85–114. https://doi.org/10.1111/j.1365-2575.2012.00407.x

Chopdar, P. K., & Balakrishnan, J. (2020). Consumers response towards mobile commerce applications: S-O-R approach. *International Journal of Information Management, 53*(June 2019), 102106. https://doi.org/10.1016/j.ijinfomgt.2020.102106

de Ruyter, K., Isobel Keeling, D., & Ngo, L. V. (2018). When nothing is what it seems: A digital marketing research agenda. *Australasian Marketing Journal, 26*(3), 199–202. https://doi.org/10.1016/j.ausmj.2018.07.003

Djafarova, E., & Rushworth, C. (2017). Exploring the credibility of online celebrities' Instagram profiles in influencing the purchase decisions of young female users. *Computers in Human Behavior, 68*, 1–7. https://doi.org/10.1016/j.chb.2016.11.009

Donovan, R. J., & Rossiter, J. R. (1982). Store atmosphere: An environmental psychology approach. *Journal of Retailing, 58*(1), 34–57.

Eroglu, S. A., Machleit, K. A., & Davis, L. M. (2001). Atmospheric qualities of online retailing. *Journal of Business Research, 54*(2), 177–184. https://doi.org/10.1016/s0148-2963(99)00087-9

Fornell, C., & Larcker, D. F. (1981). *Structural equation models with unobservable variables and measurement error: Algebra and statistics.* Sage Publications.

Hair, J. F., Ringle, C. M., & Sarstedt, M. (2011). PLS-SEM: Indeed a silver bullet. *Journal of Marketing Theory and Practice, 19*(2), 139–152.

Hair, J. F., Gabriel, M., & Patel, V. (2014). AMOS covariance-based structural equation modeling (CB-SEM): Guidelines on its application as a marketing research tool. *Brazilian Journal of Marketing, 13*(2).

Herjanto, H., Adiwijaya, M., Wijaya, E., & Semuel, H. (2020). The effect of celebrity endorsement on Instagram fashion purchase intention: The evidence from Indonesia. *Organizations and Markets in Emerging Economies, 11*(1), 203–221. https://doi.org/10.15388/omee.2020.11.31

Hu, B. (2022). Influences of virtual spokespersons' characteristics on brand personality. In *Proceedings of the 4th international seminar on education research and social science (ISERSS 2021), 635(Iserss 2021)* (pp. 161–166). https://doi.org/10.2991/assehr.k.220107.030

Huang, Q. Q., Qu, H. J., & Li, P. (2022). The influence of virtual idol characteristics on consumers' clothing purchase intention. *Sustainability (Switzerland), 14*(14). https://doi.org/10.3390/su14148964

Khan, A., Sabir, R. I., Majid, M. B., Javaid, M. U., Anwar ul Haq, M., & Mehmood, H. (2022). Celebrity endorsements, whitening products, and consumer purchase intentions: A review of literature. *Journal of Cosmetic Dermatology, 21*(10), 4194–4204. https://doi.org/10.1111/jocd.14903

Kim, B., & Han, I. (2009). What drives the adoption of mobile data services: An approach from a value perspective. *Journal of Information Technology, 24*(1), 35–45. https://doi.org/10.1057/jit.2008.28

Kim, D. J., & Hwang, Y. (2012). A study of mobile internet user's service quality perceptions from a user's utilitarian and hedonic value tendency perspectives. *Information Systems Frontiers, 14*(2), 409–421. https://doi.org/10.1007/s10796-010-9267-8

Kim, B., & Oh, J. (2011). *The difference of determinants of acceptance and continuance of mobile data services: A value perspective.* https://doi.org/10.1016/j.eswa.2010.07.107

Kim, J. H., & Park, J. W. (2019). The effect of airport self-service characteristics on passengers' perceived value, satisfaction, and behavioral intention: Based on the SOR model. *Sustainability (Switzerland), 11*(19). https://doi.org/10.3390/su11195352

Kim, H., & Park, M. (2023). Virtual influencers' attractiveness effect on purchase intention: A moderated mediation model of the Product–Endorser fit with the brand. *Computers in Human Behavior, 143.* https://doi.org/10.1016/j.chb.2023.107703

Koay, K. Y., Teoh, C. W., & Soh, P. C.-H. (2021). Instagram influencer marketing: Perceived social media marketing activities and online impulse buying. *First Monday.* https://doi.org/10.5210/fm.v26i9.11598

Kumar, A., Adlakaha, A., & Mukherjee, K. (2018). The effect of perceived security and grievance redressal on continuance intention to use M-wallets in a developing country. *International Journal of Bank Marketing, 36*(7), 1170–1189. https://doi.org/10.1108/IJBM-04-2017-0077

Kwak, J., & Yoh, E. (2021). Effect of influencers' characteristics and consumer need satisfaction on attachment to influencer, content flow and purchase intention. *Journal of the Korean Society of Clothing and Textiles, 45*(1), 56–72.

Li, L., Kang, K., Zhao, A., & Feng, Y. (2022). The impact of social presence and facilitation factors on online consumers' impulse buying in live shopping – Celebrity endorsement as a moderating factor. *Information Technology and People*. https://doi.org/10.1108/ITP-03-2021-0203

Li, Y., Xue, J., & Deng, Z. (2023). How knowledge characteristics and platform characteristics drive users' purchase intention of online paid health knowledge? In *E-business. Digital empowerment for an intelligent future* (pp. 291–302). https://doi.org/10.1007/978-3-031-32299-0_25

Lin, Y. H., & Jen, L. C. (2022). Internet celebrity economy: Exploring the value of viewers' comment features and live streamers' marketing strategies in forecasting revenue. *NTU Management Review, 32*(1), 93–126. https://doi.org/10.6226/NTUMR.202204_32(1).0003

Lin, S. C., Tseng, H. T., Shirazi, F., Hajli, N., & Tsai, P. T. (2022). Exploring factors influencing impulse buying in live streaming shopping: A stimulus-organism-response (SOR) perspective. *Asia Pacific Journal of Marketing and Logistics*. https://doi.org/10.1108/APJML-12-2021-0903

Loureiro, S. M. C., Stylos, N., & Bellou, V. (2021). Destination atmospheric cues as key influencers of tourists' word-of-mouth communication: Tourist visitation at two Mediterranean capital cities. *Tourism Recreation Research, 46*(1), 85–108. https://doi.org/10.1080/02508281.2020.1782695

Masuda, H., Han, S. H., & Lee, J. (2022). Impacts of influencer attributes on purchase intentions in social media influencer marketing: Mediating roles of characterizations. *Technological Forecasting and Social Change, 174*(September 2021). https://doi.org/10.1016/j.techfore.2021.121246

Mehrabian, A., & Russell, J. A. (1974). *An approach to environmental psychology.* The MIT Press.

Morwitz, V. G., & Munz, K. P. (2021). *Intentions. October 2020* (pp. 26–41). https://doi.org/10.1002/arcp.1061

Mrad, M., Ramadan, Z., & Nasr, L. I. (2022). Computer-generated influencers: The rise of digital personalities. *Marketing Intelligence and Planning, 40*(5), 589–603. https://doi.org/10.1108/MIP-12-2021-0423

Patmawati, D., & Miswanto, M. (2022). The effect of social media influencers on purchase intention: The role brand awareness as a mediator. *International Journal of Entrepreneurship and Business Management, 1*(2), 170–183. https://doi.org/10.54099/ijebm.v1i2.374

Potra, S., Pugna, A., Negrea, R., & Izvercian, M. (2018). Customer perspective of value for innovative products and services. *Procedia – Social and Behavioral Sciences, 238*, 207–213. https://doi.org/10.1016/j.sbspro.2018.03.025

Prodanova, J., Ciunova-Shuleska, A., & Palamidovska-Sterjadovska, N. (2019). Enriching m-banking perceived value to achieve reuse intention. *Marketing Intelligence and Planning, 37*(6), 617–630. https://doi.org/10.1108/MIP-11-2018-0508

Qiu, L., Chen, X., & Lee, T. J. (2021). How can the celebrity endorsement effect help consumer engagement? A case of promoting tourism products through live streaming. *Sustainability (Switzerland), 13*(15). https://doi.org/10.3390/su13158655

Raman, P., & Aashish, K. (2021). To continue or not to continue: A structural analysis of antecedents of mobile payment systems in India. *The International Journal of Bank Marketing.* https://doi.org/10.1108/IJBM-04-2020-0167

Rodrigo-Martín, L., Rodrigo-Martín, I., & Muñoz-Sastre, D. (2021). Virtual influencers as an advertising tool in the promotion of brands and products. Study of the commercial activity of lil miquela. *Revista Latina de Comunicación Social, 2021*(79), 69–90. https://doi.org/10.4185/RLCS-2021-1521

Rungruangjit, W. (2022). What drives Taobao live streaming commerce? The role of parasocial relationships, congruence and source credibility in Chinese consumers' purchase intentions. *Heliyon, 8*(6), e09676. https://doi.org/10.1016/j.heliyon.2022.e09676

Schipani, P. (2019). Research on the influence of customer value on purchase intention based on service-dominant logic. *International Journal of Smart Business and Technology, 7*(1), 27–36. https://doi.org/10.21742/ijsbt.2019.7.1.03

Shah, Z., Olya, H., & Monkhouse, L. L. (2022). Developing strategies for international celebrity branding: A comparative analysis between Western and South Asian cultures. *International Marketing Review.* https://doi.org/10.1108/IMR-08-2021-0261

Singh, S., Singh, N., Kalinić, Z., & Liébana-Cabanillas, F. J. (2020). Assessing determinants influencing continued use of live streaming services: An extended perceived value theory of streaming addiction. *Expert Systems with Applications.* https://doi.org/10.1016/j.eswa.2020.114241

Soebandhi, S., Kusuma, R. A., Subagyo, H. D., Sukoco, A., Hermanto, D., & Bin Bon, A. T. (2019). Utilitarian and hedonic motivations: Its influences on search and purchase intention on Instagram. In *Proceedings of the interna-*

*tional conference on industrial engineering and operations management* (pp. 1744–1751).

Sweeney, J. C., & Soutar, G. N. (2001). Consumer perceived value: The development of a multiple item scale. *Journal of Retailing, 77*(2), 203–220.

Tri, H. M. (2022). Celebrity endorsement and purchase intention: The case of Toyota Vios in Vietnam. *Ho Chi Minh City Open University Journal of Science – Economics and Business Administration, 12*(1), 92–107. https://doi.org/10.46223/hcmcoujs.econ.en.12.1.2165.2022

Verhoef, P. C., Lemon, K. N., Parasuraman, A., Roggeveen, A., Tsiros, M., & Schlesinger, L. A. (2009). Customer experience creation: Determinants, dynamics and management strategies. *Journal of Retailing, 85*(1), 31–41. https://doi.org/10.1016/j.jretai.2008.11.001

Wang, C., Teo, T. S. H., & Liu, L. (2020). Perceived value and continuance intention in mobile government service in China. *Telematics and Informatics, 48.* https://doi.org/10.1016/j.tele.2020.101348

Woodruff, R. B. (1997). Customer value: The next source for competitive advantage. *Journal of the Academy of Marketing Science, 25*(2), 139–153.

Wu, Q. (2020). *The impact of CGI simulation virtual spokesman features on advertising effects.* Guangdong University of Foreign Studies. https://doi.org/10.27032/d.cnki.ggdwu.2020.001044

Xu, J., & Kim, H. K. (2022). A service system study on the effects of the influencers' characteristics on purchase intention. *Journal of Logistics, Informatics and Service Science, 9*(1), 136–155. https://doi.org/10.33168/LISS.2022.0110

Yan, B., & Mo, Y. (2020). The relationship of consumer perceived value, online word-of-mouth and behavioral intention in mobile E-commerce. *International Journal of Smart Business and Technology, 8*(1), 13–20. https://doi.org/10.21742/ijsbt.2020.8.1.03

Yu, J., Liang, M., & Jin, C. H. (2023). The effects of luxury brand influencer characteristics on self-brand connection: Focused on consumer perception. *Sustainability (Switzerland), 15*(8). https://doi.org/10.3390/su15086937

Zauner, A., Koller, M., & Hatak, I. (2015). Customer perceived value—Conceptualization and avenues for future research. *Cogent Psychology, 2*(1), 1–17. https://doi.org/10.1080/23311908.2015.1061782

Zeithaml, V. A. (1988). Consumer perceptions of price, quality, and value: A means-end model and synthesis of evidence. *Journal of Marketing, 52*(3), 2–22. https://doi.org/10.1177/002224298805200302

Zhang, E. M. (2010). Understanding the acceptance of mobile SMS advertising among young Chinese consumers. *Psychology & Marketing, 30*(6), 461–469. https://doi.org/10.1002/mar

Zhong, L. (2022). Analyses of the relationship between virtual influencers' endorsements and customer brand engagement in social media. In *Proceedings of the 2022 international conference on creative industry and knowledge economy (CIKE 2022), 651(Cike)* (pp. 37–41). https://doi.org/10.2991/aebmr.k.220404.007

Zhou, R., & Tong, L. (2022). A study on the influencing factors of consumers' purchase intention during livestreaming e-commerce: The mediating effect of emotion. *Frontiers in Psychology, 13*(May), 1–15. https://doi.org/10.3389/fpsyg.2022.903023

Zhou, S., Blazquez, M., McCormick, H., & Barnes, L. (2021). How social media influencers' narrative strategies benefit cultivating influencer marketing: Tackling issues of cultural barriers, commercialised content, and sponsorship disclosure. *Journal of Business Research, 134*(November 2019), 122–142. https://doi.org/10.1016/j.jbusres.2021.05.011

Zhou, S., Li, T., Yang, S., & Chen, Y. (2022). What drives consumers' purchase intention of online paid knowledge? A stimulus-organism-response perspective. *Electronic Commerce Research and Applications, 52*. https://doi.org/10.1016/j.elerap.2022.101126

# 7

# Play or Attack? Navigating Identity in the Virtual World, a Conceptual Perspective on Virtual Influencers and Influencer Marketing

### Esther Ruitong Cui

## Virtual Reality: From Abstract Concept to Tangible Realities

The notion of the virtual has evolved significantly since its initial conception as a speculative and exciting frontier of future possibilities (Heim, 1993). This evolution has led to virtual reality (VR) becoming deeply entrenched in the fabric of our physical reality. Indeed, the metaphysical dimension of VR, previously considered purely theoretical, has transitioned into more tangible forms, as evidenced by immersive virtual realities, intricate simulations, interactions, artificiality and networking communications that pervade many fields (Heim, 1993; da Silva Oliveira & Chimenti, 2021; Leung et al., 2022). Such technological breakthroughs mark a significant shift in the ways we interact, giving birth to an ever-evolving landscape that is equally captivating and complex (Luttrell & Wallace, 2021; Leung et al., 2022).

---

E. R. Cui (✉)
Department of Materials, University of Manchester, Manchester, UK
e-mail: ruitong.cui@postgrad.manchester.ac.uk

© The Author(s), under exclusive license to Springer Nature Switzerland AG 2024
S. Tabari, Q. S. Ding (eds.), *Celebrity, Social Media Influencers and Brand Performance*,
https://doi.org/10.1007/978-3-031-63516-8_7

Among these tangible manifestations, the virtual realm, comprising virtual reality (VR), augmented reality (AR) and the metaverse, diverges from being a mere digital replica of the physical world (Roo & Hachet, 2017; Hollensen et al., 2022; Rospigliosi, 2022). Instead, it embodies its own unique set of principles, dynamics and simulated environments that profoundly impact social media users' identities, interactions and experiences (Osório et al., 2006; Fowler, 2015). These environments are often designed to invoke creativity and portray elements of fantasy or dystopia (Nusselder, 2009; Nikolova, 2021), inevitably shaping how users perceive themselves and others in these spaces.

The increasing interweaving of our physical lives with digital personas portrayed on social media calls for a sophisticated conceptualisation of reality, one that acknowledges the impacts of these blended spaces on our identities (Munar, 2010; Kasza, 2017). Such an understanding is pivotal not only for comprehending the intricate processes of identity formation within these virtual realms but also for successfully navigating the evolving landscape of our increasingly digitalised world. However, this discernment extends beyond cognitive endeavours or mere individual experiences and interpretations; it informs people's perceptions, shaping and reshaping their identities and, ultimately, impacting their sense of self and interaction with others in these spaces (Creeber, 2009; Gupta, 2023). Thus, the impact of what is real and what is unreal is not confined to a screen or a device; rather, it pervades the real world, affecting human perceptions of the self, the ways people interact with others and, ultimately, people's overall experiences of reality.

## The Fine Line: Interplay Between the Real and the Unreal

Hawkins (1977) pioneered the conceptualisation of *perceived reality*, explaining that the perception of reality is not limited to a simplistic dichotomy of real and unreal. Rather, reality exists on a spectrum from complete reality to complete unreality (Shapiro & Chock, 2003). Dey et al. (2020) suggest that perceived reality unveils a dynamic continuum of experiences interacting reciprocally. On one end of the spectrum lies our physical reality, which is delineated by concrete and perceptible experiences. On the other extreme, we encounter the digital environment, a space that, despite its intangible physical nature, can evoke emotional responses reminiscent of those triggered by physically real experiences. Occupying the space in between these extremes are a plethora of experiences that blend elements of the real and unreal (Shapiro & Chock, 2003). Instances of this are found in phenomena such as VR experiences and digital social interactions (Shapiro & McDonald, 1995).

Furthermore, our interactions with these digital spaces tend to reflect, to varying extents, our real-world experiences. This phenomenon, referred to as the *mirror*, engendering a new form of reality that lies between the real and unreal (Turkle, 1999; Thomas, 2007). The complexity involved in making reality judgements in the digital environment, as was originally observed when television became prevalent (Hawkins, 1977), involves creating fictional entities mirroring aspects of human existence, such as physical and emotional characteristics and behaviours (Hoffner & Cantor, 1991). These characters, while inherently unreal, emulate aspects of human existence, compelling us to draw parallels between the real and the unreal (Stallabrass, 1993; Gibson, 2007).

The challenges of crafting authentic representations within these digital spaces mirror the multifaceted nature of human experiences, which encompasses the multifaceted interplay of personal, social, and technological influences (Gautam et al., 2018). Despite the inherently fictional nature of these characters, individuals instinctively seek elements of reality within these spaces (Green et al., 2004). Indeed, the representation of these characters is based not merely on their ability to mimic physical or behavioural aspects of humanity but, rather, on their capacity to resonate with our shared experiences, emotions, and intricacies. Even as we recognise these constructs as fictional fabrications, their capacity to mirror and, in some instances, distort reality emphasises their profound influence on self-perception and the comprehension of societal norms (Ibrahim, 2018).

Social media's inclination to present idealised 'truth' or spread misinformation exemplifies how these mirrored realities shape individual and societal understanding on a large scale (Miller, 1997; Newton, 2013).

This reflection of reality subsequently forms the basis of individual and collective identities as social judgements about these realities, which were initially exclusive to the physical human lives, permeate our interactions with the unreal (Shapiro & Lang, 1991). The ways in which social media has impacted society, culture and politics underlie the importance of the fluid, complex interplay between the real and the unreal in the digitally intertwined world. As we navigate the virtual world of influence, understanding the intrinsic relationship between reality and unreality is important given the constant blurring of lines between the real and unreal and the pervasive impact of this interplay on all aspects of our lives (Wakefield et al., 2003; Van Evra, 2004). Therefore, the integrity of the reality reflected in these virtual environments can amplify their influence and magnify their potential to offer valuable insights into the dynamics of identity formation (Childers & Boatwright, 2021; Leung et al., 2022).

## Diversifying the Sphere of Virtual Influence

Against this backdrop, we see a tangible manifestation of this digital revolution in the rise of social media and virtual influencers. The advent of social media has provided consumers with new avenues via which to explore and present their identities, with influencer marketing being a significant factor in this phenomenon (Childers & Boatwright, 2021). In particular, the influencer-marketing landscape is diversifying, seamlessly integrating a wide spectrum of technologies ranging from AR filters to VR experiences to shape contemporary marketing practices (Childers & Boatwright, 2021; Hung, 2021; Lou et al., 2023). Virtual influencers, who have emerged as prominent figures, took the form of computer-generated avatars and possessed authentic, human-like identities (Stein et al., 2022). These entities are powered with artificial intelligence (AI) and visually rendered as immersive, real-time constructed human beings in a digital world (Sands et al., 2022). The virtual influencer landscape allows consumers to connect in more authentic and dynamic ways and provides brands many opportunities to experiment with novel marketing approaches (Lou et al., 2023). According to the State of Influencer Marketing Benchmark Report (2023), the influencer-marketing industry is projected to be worth 21.1 billion US dollars by 2023. Moreover, it has been suggested that 63% of brands intend to incorporate AI into their influencer campaigns, with two-thirds of them planning to use AI to identify influencers (Geyser, 2023).

The emergence of virtual influencers—humanoid fictional characters with appealing personalities—has broadened brand's sphere of influence, captivating audiences in unprecedented ways (Merchant, 2006; Robinson, 2020). Nonetheless, the ascendance of virtual influencers has elicited pressing questions regarding the evolution of marketing techniques, ethics, motivation and communication (Leung et al., 2022). Scholars have largely expressed optimism regarding technological advancements, suggesting that virtual influencers have the potential to facilitate authentic connections, foster positive communities and drive meaningful social changes (Hyder, 2016). Virtual influencers, as exemplified by Lil Miquela, represent a fusion of technology and creativity, residing entirely within the virtual world (Blanton & Carbajal, 2022). They mimic activities akin to their human counterparts—they generate social media content, endorse brands, advocate for social issues and causes and interact with their audiences (Leung et al., 2022). The creation of such entities is meticulous, incorporating human-like traits, preferences and narratives to present a coherent and credible virtual identity. Furthermore, these advancements offer opportunities to enhance virtual influencers' self-representation and engagement with their audience, thereby complementing the role traditionally held by established figures of influence, such as celebrities and social media influencers (Schaffer, 2020; Hung, 2021). Such identities, as encapsulated by digital entities, in this case, virtual influencers, are a notable manifestation of the digital revolution (Arsenyan & Mirowska, 2021).

An intriguing line of thought emerges when we transpose the complexity of identity onto a digital stage, where we are prompted to consider the performance of identity change when the setting becomes virtual (Cover, 2015). Virtual coexistence environments, while providing a recreational space in which individuals can explore and experiment with their identities, can be transformed into conflict zones, in which personal identities become vulnerable to attacks (Dwivedi et al., 2022). In this new context, virtual influencers incite profound inquiries about the essence of identity in virtual settings. Furthermore, this broad situation also urges us to ponder upon the role of virtual influencers in steering the identity formation of social media users. Along with opening new avenues for real and unreal identity construction and engagement, the following questions arise: are individuals refining their online personas more selectively, accentuating certain virtual aspects while minimising or completely omitting others? What are the consequences of these strategic identity presentations facilitated by virtual influencers? Do virtual influencers have a positive impact, serving as a catalyst for the self, or do they pose a threat to individual identity?

## A Glance at Identity Studies and Its Digital Formation

The field of identity studies, rooted in the social sciences, extends the concept of identity beyond individual confines and examines how our social environment, cultural background and broader societal shifts, including the impacts of globalisation and the rise of new technologies, influence our sense of self (Erikson, 1993; Edwards & Usher, 2007; Buckingham, 2008). The study of identity, however, at its heart, involves an individual's introspective quest, one that revolves around the questions 'who am I?' and 'who are you?' (Bamberg, 2011). Such inquiries often encompass both the explicit or implicit questioning of one's identity, which is influenced by a variety of individual and collective factors, as well as directed or introspective inquiries that further enrich our understanding of the concept (Schwartz et al., 2011).

Building on the foundational understanding of identity, Erikson's (1968, 1993) work provides a significant contribution to the discourse on identity formation and psychosocial development, asserting that identity development is an ongoing, complex process, one that is continuously influenced by multiple personal and social factors. Erikson underscored the critical role of social relationships in shaping an individual's personality and development throughout every stage of human life. Consequently, he viewed identity not as static but, rather, as transforming in response to the changing dynamics of our personal lives and the societies in which we live.

Expanding on this, Brown (2015) later explained that the distinction between personal and social identities is not a drastic one; rather, these identities are inherently intertwined. This perspective reinforces Erikson's emphasis on the mutual influence, during identity development, and interplay between these two facets of identity, reinforcing the concept of identity as a multifaceted construct. On the personal level, self-definition and introspection are instrumental to understanding personal goals, values, beliefs and spiritual inclinations (Marcia, 1966; MacDonald, 2011). They often facilitate a process of self-discovery and self-evaluation, providing a pathway via which individuals can delve more deeply into their psyches and form unique identities.

On the social level, interactions with our environment are believed to have a significant impact on the formation of an individual's identity (Swan, 2005). Through the process of dialogue and shared experiences, individuals are presented with diverse perspectives that have the potential to either confirm or challenge their pre-existing beliefs regarding themselves and their surroundings. The phenomenon of socialisation, which manifests in diverse settings, including familial units, peer groups, communal networks and the wider societal framework, significantly contributes to the formation of an individual's identity (Ting-Toomey, 2005).

Identities are also formed, in part, by social categories, such as race, ethnicity, gender, sexuality and class, which can affect one's sense of belonging and self-perception (Tajfel & Turner, 2004). These identification categories, according to Main et al. (1985), are crucial for individuals attempting to navigate the social world and establish connections with others who have similar experiences or characteristics. The dynamics of these categories, their composition and the ways they are shaped, sustained and transformed over time underscore the fluidity and complexity of identity.

In the era preceding the advent of digitalisation, identity formation was somewhat constrained by the tangible aspects of the present and the necessity to draw upon a comparatively restricted range of past experiences. However, the landscape of identity development has undergone a profound transformation, one in which the boundaries that once confined identity formation to physical realities and experiences have been stretched and reshaped by the vast digital realm. In this new context, individuals are no longer solely reliant on their immediate surroundings or past encounters to shape their sense of self.

This shift necessitates a deeper examination of identity in the virtual realm, moving beyond simply observing individual online presentations or the crafting of virtual influencers' personas. Instead, it calls for investigating how the concept of identity transcends the individual by interacting with the reshaped social and cultural contexts brought about by digital platforms and virtual environments. In this context, the virtual domain mirrors and influences identity formation, expression and understanding.

## Digital Identity Formation and Active Construction

Much like the physical one, the virtual world is one space in which individual and social identities interact and evolve. In this new context, the ability to manipulate one's identity could potentially surpass traditional frameworks of identity formation (Erikson, 1968; Nagy & Koles, 2014). In this line of inquiry, the dual nature of the virtual world can exist as a realm that is entirely separated from reality or as a space that exists somewhere in between the real and unreal. Individuals can curate and project various facets of their identities, allowing for a multiplicity of self-expression (Saren et al., 2013).

From television to the internet and social networks, the intricate process of identity formation unfolds in the changing landscape of electronic media (McLuhan, 1964). These digital environments have drastically transformed how we perceive ourselves and others, driving the development of human identities in new and unforeseen directions. Resonating with McLuhan's (1964) concept of 'the Global Village', the digital environment is an interactive ecology in which all components—individuals, information and interfaces—are interdependent and mutually influential. In this digital environment, our identities are not singularly constructed; rather, they are the result of constant negotiation and interaction with various elements within this ecosystem.

Eyerman and Jamison (1995) further argue that individuals are concurrently creators and consumers, influencers and influenced, who actively participate in the dynamic process of identity formation and reformation. This intertwining of physical and digital realities catalyses a dual process of identity formation, from passive reflection to active constructions of the self (Willett, 2008). On one hand, individuals gain self-awareness within these digital networks, discovering and creating their identities through interactions with various digital content and communities (Turkle, 1999). On the other hand, they become increasingly cognisant of others, absorbing new perspectives, challenging pre-existing beliefs and continually redefining their self-concepts in light of these experiences (Shin, 2018).

## Identity Being Fragmented

As previously stated, the convergence of physical and digital realities has transformed the concept of identity such that it fluctuates along a spectrum of the real and the unreal (Shapiro & Chock, 2003). Online personas serve as mirror reflections, amplifications or divergent versions of our actual selves, with the precise form being contingent on the medias we engage with, the audiences we interact with and the contexts in which these digital exchanges occur (Cover, 2015). Such intertwining of self- and other-awareness fosters the emergence of computer-like identities, a type of fragmented identity, as most prominently exemplified by virtual influencers (Gregory, 2022; Breakwell, 2023). These identities blur the lines between the physical and the virtual, extending our cognitive processes into the digital realm.

We continually negotiate our sense of self within these domains, making decisions that correspond with their perceived identities and modifying their behaviour in response to feedback (Rogers, 2011; Kimmons & Veletsianos, 2014; Adams & Hannaford, 1999; Windley, 2005). This interaction with the virtual environment forms a feedback loop that leads to the formation of an evolving digital identity. In this context, virtual spaces facilitate social interaction by allowing us to connect, share experiences and develop relationships (Yee, 2006). By comparing our self-perceptions with those of others, these social interactions allow us to affirm or contest their identities (Williams, 2007; Williams et al., 2009). Hu et al. (2020) found that alterations in human behaviour originating in the virtual domain tended to transfer to subsequent physical interactions, in which individuals may align themselves with the values and characteristics projected by these digital personas, thereby altering their own self-concept.

Moreover, the belief in the progressive qualities and potential of new technologies is firmly rooted in individual and societal attitudes (Borgmann, 1984; Bookchin, 2015). The digital era offers individuals expanded opportunities for self-presentation and the exploration and formulation of their identities. This is emphasised by virtual environments, digital personas and interactive platforms, all of which underscore the intricacies of identity formation and representation.

## Performative Identity of Virtual Influencer

Virtual influencers exemplify fragmentation and represent an intersection between human creativity and advanced technology. By their nature, project identities that are meticulously crafted, encapsulating an intricate balance of relatability and idealism, bring to life characters that are simultaneously familiar and extraordinary (Arsenyan & Mirowska, 2021). Through their immersive online presences, they create connections with social media users in a way that mirrors real-life social interactions (Dwivedi et al., 2022).

This persona creation unfolds on a virtual stage, echoing Goffman's dramaturgical perspective on identity, highlighting the intricacies of self-presentation and impression management in social situations (Goffman, 1959). Virtual influencers emerge as the new actors in this theatre, with their characteristics and performances signifying a new convergence of influencer marketing. In his seminal work *The Presentation of Self in Everyday Life* (1959), Goffman developed the concept of *dramaturgy*, drawing an analogy between social interaction and theatrical performances. He envisaged individuals as actors who present varying facets of themselves in different social contexts, adopting roles and personas as dictated by the situation. In the same vein, virtual influencers manipulate their understanding of audience expectations and platform dynamics to influence their presentation and followers' perceptions (Yee, 2006). This strategic interaction becomes apparent when we consider Goffman's frontstage-backstage dichotomy.

According to Goffman (1959), the frontstage refers to the public-facing aspect of a performance, in which individuals create and present relatable and engaging personas to connect with their audience. The backstage area provides a hidden environment for individuals to unwind and prepare in, without being observed by the general public. The performers meticulously strategize regarding their content, test various personas, and improve their acts in the backstage area prior to showcasing them for their viewers (Yee, 2006). This division highlights the impression-management tactics utilised by virtual influencers, who create appealing and relatable personas to effectively interact with their followers in a positive manner.

However, the performative nature of the virtual-influencer identity is also highlighted by the portrayal of virtual influencers as hyper-idealised entities that are meticulously crafted for marketing purposes (Kiely et al., 2015). The relevance of *hyper-personal communication*, as proposed by Walther (1996; Walther et al., 2015), is significant in this context. Walther's (1996) concept of *hyper-personal communication* emphasises the potential benefits and drawbacks of online interactions in enabling selective self-presentation. It suggests that online interpersonal interactions may result in idealised relationships and distorted self-perception.

In a positive light, virtual influencers serve as models by influencing how their followers perceive and present themselves online (Conti et al., 2022). Intentionally altering their self-presentation, social media users can tailor their identities to the platform or audience (Chua & Chang, 2016; DeVito et al., 2018). On the other hand, a distorted self-presentation can be viewed as an attack on identity, as it highlights the potential harm that can result from the performative nature of virtual influencers and the identities they present (Walther et al., 2011; Walther, 2022). The idealised portrayal of virtual influencers may generate unrealistic expectations and perpetuate a culture of comparison and self-doubt among their audiences (Miyake, 2023; Mouritzen et al., 2023). In addition, constant exposure to idealised digital personas may result in feelings of inadequacy or discontent with one's own identity (Gardner & Davis, 2013; Audrezet & Koles, 2023). Consequently, the influence of virtual influencers adds another layer to the intricate relationships between online identities, self-presentation and the construction of the self. It emphasises the potential harm caused by the performative aspects of virtual influencer culture.

## Virtual Influencer: Play or Attack?

As the examination of virtual identity progresses, it becomes apparent that two opposing elements, 'play' and 'attack', have considerable influence in terms of shaping the landscape. The concept of 'play' involves the investigation of one's identity and the expression of oneself in the digital domain. Conversely, 'attack' refers to the possible obstacles and drawbacks that individuals may face in this context. The objective of this section is to analyse the potential benefits and downsides linked of virtual influencers for human identity.

## The Playful Influence of Identity

As highlighted in influencer-marketing research, the strategic significance of virtual influencers lies in the engagement of firms and brands with these online influencers so as to leverage their unique resources and engage their followers on social media, ultimately enhancing firm performance (Leung et al., 2022; Sands et al., 2022). This trend marks a noteworthy transformation in the realm of influencer marketing, with extensive ramifications for digital society. These virtual entities have the ability to inspire creativity, foster social interactions and influence decision-making processes (Hergueux & Jacquemet, 2015; Leung et al., 2022).

For example, virtual identities are constructed by certain preferences and aversions, which subsequently impact consistent behaviours and reactions in various situations. Sokolova and Kefi (2020) conducted research that revealed an increase in para-social interaction, which is a psychological bond between a media personality and a member of the audience, following exposure to online influencers. The study indicates that virtual influencers possess the ability to exert an influence on consumer behaviour, as well as having an impact on the formation of identity and decision-making processes. Thus, the alignment of virtual influencers has been observed to augment their credibility and foster a perception of authenticity that effectively resonates with their audience.

Moreover, Hudders et al. (2021) emphasise the significance of virtual influencers as intermediaries for communication in digital contexts. Virtual influencers act as intermediaries, enabling interactions and engagement among users in the digital domain. Through their curated personas and content, virtual influencers serve as a means of connecting individuals with the digital realm by means of their carefully crafted personas and content, thereby fostering a sense of community and connectedness.

Consider the case of Lil Miquela, who exerts considerable influence within her communities (Sands et al., 2022). She uses social media platforms to cultivate a sense of genuineness and connection with her followers by virtue of her commitment to social causes and collaborations with established influencers and corporations (Miao et al., 2022). She frequently employs her platform to advocate for causes such as racial equality and LGBTQ+ rights (Guthrie, 2022), fostering an authentic and connected relationship with her followers. According to Choudhry et al. (2022), her influence spans the domains of fashion and music, augmenting her appeal. Her ability to shape online personas, thereby aligning them with the expectations of her digital communities, has also been recognised (Dwivedi et al., 2023).

Moreover, these virtual influencers serve a greater purpose beyond facilitating online interaction and engagement; they act as agents that stimulate significant conversations within the digital realm. They stimulate discussions pertaining to diversity, representation and self-expression, thus prompting users to reconsider and redefine conventional standards of identity (Marwick, 2013). According to Robinson (2020), virtual influencers can influence individual identity beyond physical boundaries, promoting self-exploration and interconnectedness.

## The Attack Influence on Identity

Simultaneously, the utilisation of social media enables individuals to create and exhibit a preferred persona to others, potentially deviating from their authentic selves (Goffman, 1959). However, the interactive nature of virtual and social settings has prompted apprehension regarding the violation of one's identity (Wang et al., 2009). The convergence of the virtual and physical realms in immersive online environments may result in the unauthorised exploitation or manipulation of personal data, thereby jeopardising individuals' privacy and identities.

The issue of identity theft is a prevalent concern that arises from the utilisation of avatars, particularly personalised avatars, in the context of social media and social media influencers' influence on identity development (Falchuk et al., 2018). The act of generating digital personas and divulging personal information in virtual domains can render individuals susceptible to identity theft, whereby nefarious agents may manipulate their online identities for deceptive objectives, resulting in substantial anguish (Katyal, 2003; Parkinson et al., 2018). This proposition posits that the assimilation and ramifications of virtual influencers may not be as unambiguous as those of their human equivalents (Suler, 2016). The absence of tangible existence and the notion of virtual influencers as computer-generated entities may have an impact on the degree of trust and genuineness that influencers' followers associate with them (Choudhry et al., 2022), thereby impacting their efficacy and influence.

In addition, the idealised characteristics of virtual influencers have the potential to establish impractical benchmarks for their followers, which could result in unfavourable consequences regarding self-representation (de Brito Silva et al., 2022). This phenomenon has the potential to foster adverse self-evaluations and induce a sense of obligation to conform to unrealistic standards. This phenomenon possesses the capacity to cultivate unfavourable self-assessments and elicit a feeling of duty to comply with impractical benchmarks (Peltola, 2019; Nisandzic, 2020). The perception of virtual influencers is distinct from that of human influencers. According to Leung et al. (2022), human influencers are frequently regarded as more trustworthy and credible than virtual influencers. This implies that the adoption and impact of virtual influencers may not be a straightforward process.

The depiction of idealised digital avatars, which stand in contrast to individuals' real-life experiences, can lead to a sense of inadequacy and distorted self-perceptions. According to Turkle (1999), when individuals engage with various virtual influencers and personas online, they may undergo a fragmentation of their self-concept as they adapt and conform to the various identities that correspond to the expectations and values espoused by these influencers. The phenomenon of identity fragmentation may result in the detachment of an individual's genuine self from the virtual personas they present, leading to a distorted self-image and a feeling of insincerity (Kim et al., 2023; Yang et al., 2023).

More specifically, the potential effects of virtual influencers on individuals' self-esteem, body image and overall well-being are noteworthy due to the distorted portrayal of reality they present (Mackson et al., 2019; Mirowska & Arsenyan, 2023). Perpetual exposure to meticulously crafted and idealised digital identities may generate impractical beauty benchmarks and cultivate a climate of contrast, meaning that individuals may find themselves constantly comparing to others. This results in unfavourable body perceptions and reduced self-confidence among adherents (Mirowska & Arsenyan, 2023). Moreover, the perceived disparity between the idealised virtual realm and the actual experiences of individuals may lead to a feeling of discontent and disillusionment, which could impact their general welfare and psychological state (Niehuis et al., 2011; Miyake, 2023).

An investigation into 'play' and 'attack' within the context of virtual identity reveals a multitude of intricate and dynamic facets that both enhance and pose difficulties for the digital environment. The emergence of virtual influencers has significantly transformed the digital landscape, providing avenues for innovation, communal engagement and self-discovery. These individuals, who have significant influence, also play a crucial role in initiating important discussions regarding the topics of representation and diversity. Notwithstanding this, it is imperative to acknowledge the risk factors linked to these technological advancements, which include identity theft, privacy infringement, the establishment of impractical benchmarks and potential unfavourable impacts on self-regard. The aforementioned paradigm resembles the current academic discussion surrounding influencer marketing, which centres on the tactics utilised by digital influencers to carefully shape their public image and construct compelling and relatable personalities.

## A Conceptual Reflection and a Look Forwards

Attempting to understand the meaning of identity and the impact of virtual influencers on human identity necessitates acknowledging the theoretical nature of this pursuit. This exploration is conceptual, not empirical. The objective of this discourse is to explore the realm of concepts and theories, scrutinising fundamental ideas and elucidating the intangible aspects of digital existence.

In this light, the emergence of virtual influencers prompts inquiries into the fundamental nature of identity. Notwithstanding their fictional and artificial nature, they prompt a revaluation of the concept of existence and identity in a realm where the boundaries between reality and virtuality are blurred, as are those between human and artificial. The digital constructs that mirror and resonate with human attributes thus challenge and redefine the notions of identity and self. These constructs inhabit a dimension that lacks the tangible human experiences needed to shape identity.

A comprehensive exploration of virtual influencers entails engaging with the notion of what is real and what is unreal within the context of the contemporary digital landscape. Virtual influencers construct storylines and identities that evoke a sense of genuineness, thereby promoting authentic connections with their audiences. However, the attribution of authenticity to these virtual entities remains a subject of inquiry. Alternatively, could their identities be construed as a mere result of algorithmic computations, cultural conventions, and market inclinations?

The act of interacting with virtual influencers, when viewed through a postmodern lens, brings to the forefront the concept of identity fragmentation. As individuals engage with digital personas and potentially alter their personal virtual identities based on these interactions, the idea of a true and unified self appears to be disintegrating, yielding to a fluid, multifaceted construction of identity. The process of transitioning into multiple identities can result in both a sense of freedom and disorientation as individuals navigate through the complex terrain of their various identities.

Concurrently, the advent of virtual influencers gives rise to ethical predicaments that necessitate thoughtful consideration. The digital realm is characterised by persistent power dynamics, and its advancements are accompanied by concerns regarding privacy, unrealistic expectations and potential negative effects on identity (Gardner & Davis, 2013). This inquiry elicits reflection on whether the formation of these digital entities is a one-way process or these constructions, in turn, are influencing the individuals who engage with them.

The aforementioned conceptual exploration highlights the necessity of maintaining a critical and attentive approach towards our interactions within the digital realm. The emergence of virtual influencers can be perceived as a multifaceted phenomenon that has the potential to enhance our means of self-expression, while also posing a plausible risk to our self-conceptualisation and overall welfare. Thus, it is imperative to uphold a consciousness of our individual sense of identity as we address the complex dynamics between the tangible and intangible realms, as well as between human and digital agents of influence. The process of negotiating and navigating identities is poised to play a pivotal role in shaping our comprehension of the self in the era of digital technology.

## Concluding Thoughts

The emergence and dissemination of virtual influencers signify a significant development in the progression of digital personas and communication, indicating a crucial transition in the way people perceive themselves and others in the virtual domain. Upon exploring the intricacies of identity manipulation and conflicts within the domain of virtual influencers, it is evident that this sphere presents a plethora of advantageous prospects, as well as complex obstacles.

This chapter highlights the concept of play, which underscores the potential of virtual influencers to stimulate innovation, foster communal engagement and influence the self-concepts and cognitive processes of their audience. In the digital realm, they serve as influential intermediaries, fostering connections between users and stimulating significant conversations on topics such as diversity, representation and self-expression. Nevertheless, the ramifications of these digital avatars are not uniform and are characterised by a sense of duality, with the complementary aspect being exemplified by the attack.

The emergence of virtual influencers has given rise to various pressing concerns, including the possibility of identity theft, privacy violation and the promotion of unrealistic standards of beauty and success. These concerns have the potential to negatively impact individuals' self-esteem and overall well-being. Moreover, the digitally produced entities, which are characterised by their impeccable portrayals and altered storylines, have the potential to intensify feelings of insufficiency and dissatisfaction, ultimately resulting in a distorted perception of the self among their adherents.

This chapter introduced a novel aspect to the process of constructing online identities and presenting oneself, despite a complex and dichotomous influence that warrants careful scrutiny and management. As an academic community, it is imperative to consistently analyse these patterns, comprehending their ramifications and proactively moulding the conversation surrounding them to guarantee that the digital realm progresses in a way that is beneficial, comprehensive and morally justifiable.

The domain of virtual influencers is in a state of perpetual change, and the present investigation provides a momentary glimpse of this ever-evolving terrain. The intention of this analysis is to enhance the comprehension of the intricate association between virtual influencers and the development of identity, thereby stimulating additional discourse and exploration in this field. The development of digital identities in the metaverse and beyond necessitates sustained inquiry, discourse and self-reflection to promote constructive, comprehensive and principled participation in the digital realm.

# References

Adams, R. J., & Hannaford, B. (1999). Stable haptic interaction with virtual environments. *IEEE Transactions on Robotics and Automation, 15*(3), 465–474.

Arsenyan, J., & Mirowska, A. (2021). Almost human? A comparative case study on the social media presence of virtual influencers. *International Journal of Human-Computer Studies, 155*, 102694.

Audrezet, A., & Koles, B. (2023). Virtual influencer as a brand avatar in interactive marketing. In *The Palgrave handbook of Interactive Marketing* (pp. 353–376). Springer International Publishing.

Bamberg, M. (2011). Who am I? Narration and its contribution to self and identity. *Theory & Psychology, 21*(1), 3–24.

Blanton, R., & Carbajal, D. (2022). Not a girl, not yet a woman: A critical case study on social media, deception, and Lil Miquela. In *Research anthology on usage, identity, and impact of social media on society and culture* (pp. 894–909). IGI Global.

Bookchin, M. (2015). *The next revolution: Popular assemblies and the promise of direct democracy*. Verso Books.

Borgmann, A. (1984). *Technology and the character of contemporary life: A philosophical inquiry*. University of Chicago Press.

Breakwell, G. M. (2023). *Identity: Unique and Shared*. SAGE Publications.

Brown, A. D. (2015). Identities and identity work in organizations. *International Journal of Management Reviews, 17*(1), 20–40.

Buckingham, D. (2008). *Introducing identity*. MacArthur Foundation Digital Media and Learning Initiative.

Childers, C., & Boatwright, B. (2021). Do digital natives recognize digital influence? Generational differences and understanding of social media influencers. *Journal of Current Issues and Research in Advertising, 42*(4), 425–442.

Choudhry, A., Han, J., Xu, X., & Huang, Y. (2022). "I felt a little crazy following a doll" investigating real influence of virtual influencers on their followers. *Proceedings of the ACM on Human-Computer Interaction, 6*(GROUP), 1–28.

Chua, T. H. H., & Chang, L. (2016). Follow me and like my beautiful selfies: Singapore teenage girls' engagement in self-presentation and peer comparison on social media. *Computers in Human Behavior, 55*, 190–197.

Conti, M., Gathani, J., & Tricomi, P. P. (2022). Virtual influencers in online social media. *IEEE Communications Magazine, 60*(8), 86–91.

Cover, R. (2015). *Digital identities: Creating and communicating the online self.* Academic Press.

Creeber, G. (2009). Digital theory: Theorizing new media. In *Digital cultures. Understanding new media* (pp. 11–22).

da Silva Oliveira, A. B., & Chimenti, P. (2021). "Humanized robots": A proposition of categories to understand virtual influencers. *Australasian Journal of Information Systems, 25*.

de Brito Silva, M. J., de Oliveira Ramos Delfino, L., Alves Cerqueira, K., & de Oliveira Campos, P. (2022). Avatar marketing: A study on the engagement and authenticity of virtual influencers on Instagram. *Social Network Analysis and Mining, 12*(1), 130.

DeVito, M. A., Walker, A. M., & Birnholtz, J. (2018). 'Too gay for Facebook' presenting LGBTQ+ identity throughout the personal social media ecosystem. *Proceedings of the ACM on Human-Computer Interaction, 2*(CSCW), 1–23.

Dey, B. L., Yen, D., & Samuel, L. (2020). Digital consumer culture and digital acculturation. *International Journal of Information Management, 51*, 102057.

Dwivedi, Y. K., Hughes, L., Baabdullah, A. M., Ribeiro-Navarrete, S., Giannakis, M., Al-Debei, M. M., Dennehy, D., Metri, B., Buhalis, D., Cheung, C. M., & Conboy, K. (2022). Metaverse beyond the hype: Multidisciplinary perspectives on emerging challenges, opportunities, and agenda for research, practice and policy. *International Journal of Information Management, 66*, 102542.

Dwivedi, Y. K., Hughes, L., Wang, Y., Alalwan, A. A., Ahn, S. J., Balakrishnan, J., Barta, S., Belk, R., Buhalis, D., Dutot, V., & Felix, R. (2023). Metaverse marketing: How the metaverse will shape the future of consumer research and practice. *Psychology & Marketing, 40*(4), 750–776.

Edwards, R., & Usher, R. (2007). *Globalisation & pedagogy: Space, place and identity*. Routledge.

Erikson, E. H. (1968). *Identity youth and crisis* (Vol. 7). WW Norton & Company.

Erikson, E. H., 1993. *Childhood and society*. WW Norton & Company.

Eyerman, R., & Jamison, A. (1995). Social movements and cultural transformation: Popular music in the 1960s. *Media, Culture and Society, 17*(3), 449–468.

Falchuk, B., Loeb, S., & Neff, R. (2018). The social metaverse: Battle for privacy. *IEEE Technology and Society Magazine, 37*(2), 52–61.

Fowler, C. (2015). Virtual reality and learning: Where is the pedagogy? *British Journal of Educational Technology, 46*(2), 412–422.

Gardner, H., & Davis, K. (2013). *The app generation: How today's youth navigate identity, intimacy, and imagination in a digital world*. Yale University Press.

Gautam, A., Williams, D., Terry, K., Robinson, K., & Newbill, P. (2018). Mirror worlds: Examining the affordances of a next generation immersive learning environment. *TechTrends, 62*, 119–125.

Geyser, W. (2023). *The state of influencer marketing 2023: Benchmark report, influencer marketing hub*. Accessed June 9, 2023, from https://influencermarketinghub.com/influencer-marketing-benchmark-report/

Gibson, J. (2007). *Fiction and the weave of life*. OUP.

Goffman, E. (1959). *The presentation of self in everyday life: Selections*.

Green, M. C., Brock, T. C., & Kaufman, G. F. (2004). Understanding media enjoyment: The role of transportation into narrative worlds. *Communication Theory, 14*(4), 311–327.

Gregory, A. (2022). Artificial intelligence, big data and all change. In *Research handbook on strategic communication* (pp. 209–220). Edward Elgar Publishing.

Guthrie, S. R. D. (2022). The OFCC Project: A Collaborative-Action Ethnography. Master's thesis, San Diego State University.

Gupta, P. (2023). Understanding consumer behavior in virtual ecosystems: Adoption of immersive technologies in metaverse among consumers. In *Handbook of research on consumer behavioral analytics in metaverse and the adoption of a virtual world* (pp. 130–152). IGI Global.

Hawkins, R. P. (1977). The dimensional structure of children's perceptions of television reality. *Communication Research, 4*(3), 299–320.

Heim, M. (1993). *The metaphysics of virtual reality*. Oxford University Press on Demand.

Hergueux, J., & Jacquemet, N. (2015). Social preferences in the online laboratory: A randomized experiment. *Experimental Economics, 18*, 251–283.

Hoffner, C., & Cantor, J. (1991). Perceiving and responding to mass media characters. *Responding to the Screen: Reception and Reaction Processes, 1*, 63–101.

Hollensen, S., Kotler, P., & Opresnik, M. O. (2022). Metaverse—The new marketing universe. *Journal of Business Strategy*.

Hu, L., Min, Q., Han, S., & Liu, Z. (2020). Understanding followers' stickiness to digital influencers: The effect of psychological responses. *International Journal of Information Management, 54*, 102169.

Hudders, L., De Jans, S., & De Veirman, M. (2021). The commercialization of social media stars: A literature review and conceptual framework on the strategic use of social media influencers. *International Journal of Advertising,* *40*(3), 327–375.

Hung, K. (2021). Celebrity, influencer, and brand endorsement: Processes and effects. In *Oxford research encyclopedia of communication.*

Hyder, S. (2016). *The zen of social media marketing: An easier way to build credibility, generate buzz, and increase revenue.* BenBella Books, Inc.

Ibrahim, Y. (2018). *Production of the 'self' in the digital age.* Springer.

Kasza, J. (2017). Post modern identity: "In between" real and virtual. *World Scientific News, 78,* 41–57.

Katyal, S. K. (2003). The new surveillance. *Case Western Reserve Law Review, 54,* 297.

Kiely, E., Ging, D., Kitching, K., & Leane, M. (2015). *The sexualisation and commercialisation of children in Ireland: An exploratory study.*

Kim, D., Kim, E., & Shoenberger, H. (2023). The next hype in social media advertising: Examining virtual influencers' brand endorsement effectiveness. *Frontiers in Psychology, 14,* 485.

Kimmons, R., & Veletsianos, G. (2014). The fragmented educator 2.0: Social networking sites, acceptable identity fragments, and the identity constellation. *Computers & Education, 72,* 292–301.

Leung, F. F., Gu, F. F., & Palmatier, R. W. (2022). Online influencer marketing. *Journal of the Academy of Marketing Science,* 1–26.

Lou, C., Taylor, C. R., & Zhou, X. (2023). Influencer marketing on social media: How different social media platforms afford influencer–follower relation and drive advertising effectiveness. *Journal of Current Issues and Research in Advertising, 44*(1), 60–87.

Luttrell, R., & Wallace, A. A. (2021). *Social media and society: An introduction to the mass media landscape.* Rowman & Littlefield.

MacDonald, D. A. (2011). Spiritual identity: Individual perspectives. In *Handbook of identity theory and research* (pp. 531–544). Springer New York.

Mackson, S. B., Brochu, P. M., & Schneider, B. A. (2019). Instagram: Friend or foe? The application's association with psychological well-being. *New Media & Society, 21*(10), 2160–2182.

Main, M., Kaplan, N., & Cassidy, J. (1985). Security in infancy, childhood, and adulthood: A move to the level of representation. In *Monographs of the society for research in child development* (pp. 66–104).

Marcia, J. E. (1966). Development and validation of ego-identity status. *Journal of Personality and Social Psychology, 3*(5), 551.

Marwick, A. E. (2013). *Status update: Celebrity, publicity, and branding in the social media age*. Yale University Press.

McLuhan, M. (1964). Media hot and cold. In *Understanding media: The extensions of man* (pp. 22–32).

Merchant, G. (2006). Identity, social networks and online communication. *E-Learning and Digital Media, 3*(2), 235–244.

Miao, F., Kozlenkova, I. V., Wang, H., Xie, T., & Palmatier, R. W. (2022). An emerging theory of avatar marketing. *Journal of Marketing, 86*(1), 67–90.

Miller, D. (1997). *Material culture and mass consumerism*. John Wiley & Sons.

Mirowska, A., & Arsenyan, J. (2023). Sweet escape: The role of empathy in social media engagement with human versus virtual influencers. *International Journal of Human-Computer Studies, 174*, 103008.

Miyake, E. (2023). I am a virtual girl from Tokyo: Virtual influencers, digital-orientalism and the (Im) materiality of race and gender. *Journal of Consumer Culture, 23*(1), 209–228.

Mouritzen, S. L. T., Penttinen, V., & Pedersen, S. (2023). Virtual influencer marketing: The good, the bad and the unreal. *European Journal of Marketing*. https://doi.org/10.1108/EJM-12-2022-0915

Munar, A. M. (2010). Digital exhibitionism: The age of exposure. *Culture Unbound, 2*(3), 401–422.

Nagy, P., & Koles, B. (2014). The digital transformation of human identity: Towards a conceptual model of virtual identity in virtual worlds. *Convergence, 20*(3), 276–292.

Newton, J. (2013). *The burden of visual truth: The role of photojournalism in mediating reality*. Routledge.

Niehuis, S., Lee, K. H., Reifman, A., Swenson, A., & Hunsaker, S. (2011). Idealization and disillusionment in intimate relationships: A review of theory, method, and research. *Journal of Family Theory & Review, 3*(4), 273–302.

Nikolova, A. (2021). *Transforming reality: An artistic exploration of interactive virtual environments*. Doctoral dissertation, University of Lethbridge.

Nisandzic, M. (2020). *Are you even real? Virtual influencers on Instagram and the role of authenticity in the virtual influencer consumer relationship*. Doctoral dissertation, Master's thesis, Leopold-Franzens-University Innsbruck.

Nusselder, A. (2009). *Interface fantasy: A Lacanian cyborg ontology*. MIT Press.

Osório, F. S., Musse, S. R., Vieira, R., Heinen, M. R., & Paiva, D. C. (2006). Increasing reality in virtual reality applications through physical and behavioural simulation. In *Proceedings of the virtual concept conference* (Vol. 1, pp. 1–45).

Parkinson, B., Millard, D. E., O'Hara, K., & Giordano, R. (2018). The digitally extended self: A lexicological analysis of personal data. *Journal of Information Science, 44*(4), 552–565.

Peltola, L. (2019). *Making sense of the relationship between social media influencers on Instagram and the consumers who follow them.* Thesis paper.

Robinson, B. (2020). Towards an ontology and ethics of virtual influencers. *Australasian Journal of Information Systems, 24.*

Rogers, L. (2011). Developing simulations in multi-user virtual environments to enhance healthcare education. *British Journal of Educational Technology, 42*(4), 608–615.

Roo, J. S., & Hachet, M. (2017). One reality: Augmenting how the physical world is experienced by combining multiple mixed reality modalities. In *Proceedings of the 30th annual ACM symposium on user interface software and technology* (pp. 787–795).

Rospigliosi, P. A. (2022). Metaverse or simulacra? Roblox, Minecraft, Meta and the turn to virtual reality for education, socialisation and work. *Interactive Learning Environments, 30*(1), 1–3.

Sands, S., Ferraro, C., Demsar, V., & Chandler, G. (2022). False idols: Unpacking the opportunities and challenges of falsity in the context of virtual influencers. *Business Horizons, 65*(6), 777–778.

Saren, M., Harwood, T., Ward, J., & Venkatesh, A. (2013). Marketing beyond the frontier? Researching the new marketing landscape of virtual worlds. *Journal of Marketing Management, 29*(13–14), 1435–1442.

Schaffer, N. (2020). *The age of influence: The power of influencers to elevate your brand.* HarperCollins Leadership.

Schwartz, S. J., Luyckx, K., & Vignoles, V. L. (Eds.). (2011). *Handbook of identity theory and research.* Springer Science & Business Media.

Shapiro, M. A., & Chock, T. M. (2003). Psychological processes in perceiving reality. *Media Psychology, 5*(2), 163–198.

Shapiro, M. A., & Lang, A. (1991). Making television reality: Unconscious processes in the construction of social reality. *Communication Research, 18*(5), 685–705.

Shapiro, M. A., & McDonald, D. G. (1995). Implications of virtual reality for judgments about reality. *Communication in the Age of Virtual Reality, 323.*

Shin, D. (2018). Empathy and embodied experience in virtual environment: To what extent can virtual reality stimulate empathy and embodied experience? *Computers in Human Behavior, 78,* 64–73.

Sokolova, K., & Kefi, H. (2020). Instagram and YouTube bloggers promote it, why should I buy? How credibility and parasocial interaction influence purchase intentions. *Journal of Retailing and Consumer Services, 53*, 101742.

Stallabrass, J. (1993). Just gaming: Allegory and economy in computer games. *New Left Review*, 83–83.

Stein, J. P., Linda Breves, P., & Anders, N. (2022). *Parasocial interactions with real and virtual influencers: The role of perceived similarity and human-likeness* (p. 14614448221102900). *New Media & Society*.

Suler, J. R. (2016). *Psychology of the digital age: Humans become electric.* Cambridge University Press.

Swan, K. (2005). A constructivist model for thinking about learning online. *Elements of Quality Online Education: Engaging Communities, 6*, 13–31.

Tajfel, H., & Turner, J. C. (2004). The social identity theory of intergroup behavior. In *Political psychology* (pp. 276–293). Psychology Press.

Thomas, A. (2007). *Youth online: Identity and literacy in the digital age* (Vol. 19). Peter Lang.

Ting-Toomey, S. (2005). Identity negotiation theory: Crossing cultural boundaries. In *Theorizing about intercultural communication* (pp. 211–233).

Turkle, S. (1999). Cyberspace and identity. *Contemporary Sociology, 28*(6), 643–648.

Van Evra, J. (2004). *Television and child development.* Routledge.

Wakefield, M., Flay, B., Nichter, M., & Giovino, G. (2003). Role of the media in influencing trajectories of youth smoking. *Addiction, 98*, 79–103.

Walther, J. B. (1996). Computer-mediated communication: Impersonal, interpersonal, and hyperpersonal interaction. *Communication Research, 23*(1), 3–43.

Walther, J. B. (2022). Social media and online hate. *Current Opinion in Psychology, 45*, 101298. https://doi.org/10.1016/j.copsyc.2021.12.010

Walther, J. B., Liang, Y. J., DeAndrea, D. C., Tong, S. T., Carr, C. T., Spottswood, E. L., & Amichai-Hamburger, Y. (2011). The effect of feedback on identity shift in computer-mediated communication. *Media Psychology, 14*(1), 1–26.

Walther, J. B., Van Der Heide, B., Ramirez, A., Jr., Burgoon, J. K., & Peña, J. (2015). Interpersonal and hyperpersonal dimensions of computer-mediated communication. In *The handbook of the psychology of communication technology* (pp. 1–22).

Wang, Z., Walther, J. B., & Hancock, J. T. (2009). Social identification and interpersonal communication in computer-mediated communication: What you do versus who you are in virtual groups. *Human Communication Research, 35*(1), 59–85.

Willett, R. (2008). *Consumer citizens online: Structure, agency, and gender in online participation*. MacArthur Foundation Digital Media and Learning Initiative.

Williams, M. (2007). Avatar watching: Participant observation in graphical online environments. *Qualitative Research, 7*(1), 5–24.

Williams, D., Consalvo, M., Caplan, S., & Yee, N. (2009). Looking for gender: Gender roles and behaviours among online gamers. *Journal of Communication, 59*(4), 700–725.

Windley, P. J. (2005). *Digital identity: Unmasking identity management architecture (IMA)*. O'Reilly Media, Inc.

Yang, J., Chuenterawong, P., Lee, H., Tian, Y., & Chock, T. M. (2023). Human versus virtual influencer: The effect of humanness and interactivity on persuasive CSR messaging. *Journal of Interactive Advertising*, 1–18.

Yee, N. (2006). The psychology of massively multi-user online role-playing games: Motivations, emotional investment, relationships and problematic usage. In *Avatars at work and play: Collaboration and interaction in shared virtual environments* (pp. 187–207).

# 8

# Virtual World, Fear of Missing Out and Its Impact on Impulsive Buying

Saloomeh Tabari and Qing Shan Ding

## Introduction

Social media influencers (SMIs) are people "who gained popularity through their social platform and their presence and content, like YouTubers, and Instafamous" (Aw & Chuah, 2021, p. 146). SMIs' expertise is to create unique and authentic content about brands and products through tutorials and product reviews with their followers (Lee & Watkins, 2016). Statista (2022a) reported that as of 2022, 4.65 billion people worldwide actively use social media, which is expected to increase. It is estimated that in 2027 this number will increase to 5.85 billion users (Statista, 2022b). The popularity of social media personalities provided opportunities for social media

---

S. Tabari (✉)
Cardiff Business School, Cardiff University, Cardiff, UK
e-mail: tabaris@cardiff.ac.uk

Q. S. Ding
Huddersfield Business School, University of Huddersfield, Huddersfield, UK
e-mail: Q.s.ding@hud.ac.uk

© The Author(s), under exclusive license to Springer Nature Switzerland AG 2024
S. Tabari, Q. S. Ding (eds.), *Celebrity, Social Media Influencers and Brand Performance*,
https://doi.org/10.1007/978-3-031-63516-8_8

influencers (SMI) who help brands to change their consumer attitudes (Freberg et al., 2011). Oberlo (2021) revealed that about 73 percent of marketers believe that social media platforms may be used to effectively support the execution of their marketing efforts.

The research stated that in the USA and UK, nearly half of the consumers are avoiding ad-based media, and their consumption decision is mostly based on them subscribing to different services where they can avoid ads (Campaign, 2023). The increasing popularity of live streaming has provided its use as a tool to enhance sales by several retails and service firms (Mao et al., 2022). The rise of social media and the increase in popularity of social platforms such as TikTok, Instagram, WeChat and Douyin opened a new door for marketers and brands and celebrities. During the COVID-19 pandemic, most brands moved to the virtual world, with some faster than they were expecting, which changed the world of marketing and connecting with customers, especially with younger generations. As a result of the rise in social networking platforms' popularity, the importance of communication, building connection and trust with customers is increasing (Piranda et al., 2022; Silvia & Anwar, 2021), providing direct shopping opportunities through the platforms. Wang (2021) states that brands can expand through social media either directly via their own page or indirectly via communities which provide an opportunity for customers to join the community and communicate with one another. In recent years, the rise of social media influencers (SMIs) has played a significant role in changing consumer behaviour and their buying behaviour journey. Dinh and Lee (2021) argued that influencer imitation has a significant impact on social comparison, captured in the fear of missing out (FOMO) effect, which affects the purchase intention of the endorsed product. Furthermore, followers of SMIs have shown impulsive purchases of fashion and cosmetic products (Prihana Gunawan & Permadi Iskandar, 2020). The trust gained by SMIs has a significant role in enhancing the urge-to-buy (UTB) impulsively on social networking sites (Shamim & Islam, 2022).

The effects of influencers as brand communicator tools have been discussed in the literature (Carlson et al., 2020; Wang et al., 2021; Valsesia et al., 2020; Ryu & Jin, 2019), as they boost customer engagement (Al-Emadi & Ben Yahia, 2020; Hughes et al., 2019; Lee & Theokary,

2020; Tafesse & Wood, 2021) and adaptation and purchase intention (Corrêa et al., 2020; Weismueller et al., 2020; Zhang et al., 2021). Furthermore, a few studies focused on the particularity of social media influencers in impacting consumer impulse buying behaviour (Shamim & Islam, 2022; Hu et al., 2019; Lou & Yuan, 2019; Wangshu & Guanhua, 2020; Zafar et al., 2020, 2021; Liang et al., 2021) and only a handful of research explored the factors that lead to impulsive buying on SMIs topic (Xiang et al., 2016; Chung et al., 2017; Chen et al., 2016, 2019; Mavlanova et al., 2012; Yadav et al., 2013). To the best knowledge of the authors, there has been very limited research (e.g. Dinh & Lee, 2021) exploring the impact of social media influencers and the virtual world on urge-to-buy (UTB) because of fear of missing out (FOMO).

This chapter aims to explore the impact of the virtual world and SMIs on UTB and impulse buying because of FOMO among followers and peer groups. To achieve this aim, the chapter questions are outlined as follows:

(a) What is the role of SMIs in the virtual world towards the impulse buying behaviour of their followers?
(b) What are the reasons for UTB and impulse buying?
(c) Are the virtual world and SMIs the reason for FOMO and UTB?

The chapter first discusses SMIs and their impact on changes in consumer behaviour and shopping behaviour, followed by social influence theory, and then looks at FOMO, impulse buying and UTB literature and the effect of SMIs on consumption patterns. Finally, the chapter provides a conceptual framework and propositions for future study.

## Social Media Influencers, Social Influence Theory and Social Identity

Influencers are a new type of celebrity that has an impact on customer opinion. brands by implementing this tactic have an opportunity to influence their customers' purchasing decisions (Claude, 2018). Influencers have a positive effect on customers' trust towards brands (Lou

& Yuan, 2019; Reinikainen et al., 2020) through their own platforms. Schouten et al. (2021) found that customers feel closer similarity to influencers compared to celebrities. As a result, they have more trust in influencers and their commitment to brands.

With the increase of influencer marketing and the positive impact of the influencer on their followers' decision-making behaviour, brands at first were predominantly interested in mega-influencers, with followers counting in the millions. In recent times, they are more interested to collaborate with micro-influencers, with less than 10,000 followers, who represent niche and specific interest areas like gym clothing, lifestyle and vegan products (Pittman & Abell, 2021). Brands and firms changed their strategies towards interactive marketing by adopting sponsoring influencers to promote their products and services on Instagram, TikTok, YouTube, Twitch and other platforms (Ge & Gretzel, 2018).

Influencers are the source of trendsetters in today's virtual world who utilise specific skills to build relationships with their followers. This provides them with the ability to influence their followers' behaviour by voicing their opinions with a strong sense of credibility and trust attached to them. As a result of their experiences and skills, their followers see them as opinion leaders (Reale, 2019).

Influencers build psychological bonds with their followers by communicating and sharing their personal information about their interests, beliefs, fashion, cosmetics, lifestyles, travel, cooking and photography (Audrezet et al., 2018; Lou et al, 2020; Jin et al., 2019; Ladhari et al., 2020). They create a very powerful online identity with their followers by communicating their narratives in an authentic way through sharing videos, photos and daily activities, which attract followers to engage with them (Khamis et al., 2017; Childers et al., 2019; Audrezet et al., 2018; Belanche et al., 2020; Ki et al., 2020; Ladhari et al., 2020) and legitimate their online identities (Lou et al., 2020; Sokolova & Kefi, 2020). Social influence theory has been introduced by Kelman (1961, 1974, 2006) and distinguishes three processes: compliance, identification and internationalisation. Researchers like Kapitan and Silvera (2016), Sokolova and Kefi (2020), and Tafesse and Wood (2021) used this theory to understand the relationship between influencers and their followers.

Compliance happens when individuals gain approval or avoid disapproval from the influencer which affects their behaviour (Kelman, 1974, 2006). Identification happens when the followers create and build a self-defining relationship with the influencer and slowly becomes part of the followers' self-image and self-concept (Kelman, 1974, 2006). In the internationalisation process, the followers adopt the encouragement because they believe the content is useful in resolving a problem and their personal orientation and value system, like adopting the new behaviour due to the influencers' recommendation (Kelman, 1974, 2006; McCormick, 2016). Followers accept the changes based on influencers' recommendations because they fit with their value system (Kapitan & Silvera, 2016; Sokolova & Kefi, 2020). Therefore, followers accept encouragement from SMIs because they see them as popular, credible, relatable and trustworthy (De Veirman et al., 2017; Kapitan & Silvera, 2016; Ki et al., 2020; Kim & Kim, 2020; Ladhari et al., 2020; Schouten et al., 2020; Sokolova & Kefi, 2020). Trejo-Pech and Thach's (2021) study indicated that individuals interpret the influencer's recommendations as highly authentic and unique.

## Fear of Missing Out, Impulse Buying and Urge-to-Buy

FOMO has been defined by different scholars as a term used to express being left out of something occurring on social media (Gil et al., 2015). Similarly, Zhang et al. (2020, p. 1631) defined it as "a feeling of fear of potential negative consequences from inaction on a perceived opportunity".

Anderson and de Palma (2011) believed that the increase in information from brands may lead to the fear of missing out on a potentially better offer or product. The results of the study on the impact of influencers on cosmetic shopping by Rahmawati and Sijabat (2022) showed that they have a positive effect on consumer purchase intentions and imitation of the fear of missing out on the trend. The concept of FOMO has reflected an emerging consumer phenomenon (Good & Hyman, 2021;

Hodkinson, 2016; Celik et al., 2019; Kang et al., 2019) and is still a new concept in the marketing literature. Dinh and Lee (2021) stated that there is no quantitative research to examine the influencer's effect through FOMO. The increase in dependency on technology among Generation Y and Z compared to the previous generations and heavier usage of social media platforms, like TikTok, Twitch, Snapchat and Douyin, among Gen Zs, the gaming generation, had a direct impact on self-isolation behaviour among these groups. They are more engaged with digital influencers and accept their recommendations due to the identification process of social influence theory and closeness, trust and accepting them as opinion leaders. Peer pressure and being accepted by them increased their fear of missing out and therefore they try hard to be like them.

Research by Jin and Ryu (2020) stated that the buying intention of female customers increased when social media influencers, whom they perceive as friends, endorsed the products. This may be linked to the social identity, feeling of belonging to certain groups and having significance emotion and value, because of being a member of the group (Tajfel, 1972) and trying to look and act like them. Previous research indeed indicated the impact of SMIs on purchase intention and online buying of their followers (Wangshu & Guanhua, 2020; Weismueller et al., 2020).

Impulsive buying behaviour can be considered an irrational decision (Luna-Arocas et al., 2000). Amos et al. (2014) and Islam et al. (2019) discussed that unplanned buying generally is a result of an urgent desire and strong feeling which lead to UTB and occur after exposure to a specific external stimulus (Applebaum, 1951; Rook, 1987b). Luo (2005) and Hwang and Zhang (2018) suggested that social factors such as the presence of others and online para-social interaction play a crucial role in the impulse buying of customers/followers. The two key factors for impulse buying of followers are either because so many people were buying and having it or because they could not resist the temptation of not having it (Chen et al., 2021; Verhagen & Van Dolen, 2011). Furthermore, trusting the influencer can be considered the main factor in impulse buying (Chen et al., 2021). A strong desire of having a product because it is a trend and others have it leads to an unplanned purchase. Chung et al. (2017) described UTB as a purchase intention without prior planning. Some studies suggested that UTB is a proxy variable for impulse buying behaviour (Chen et al., 2016; Xiang et al., 2016). The UTB and impulse buying behaviour are directly related to the FOMO of followers, who do not want to miss out on the trends. This is in line with Dinh and Lee (2021) who stated that SMI imitations have a significant impact on social comparison and FOMO and have a direct effect on the purchase decision of the endorsed product and service. Research by the TikTok group (2021) showed that almost 70 per cent of their users believe that TikTok communities have the power to create change in culture and consumption patterns.

## Conclusion and Propositions for the Future Study

Whether we like it or not, social media is here to stay with an improvement in virtual activities and an increase in digital influencers such as social media influencers, virtual influencers and Metaverse. As Hudders et al. (2021) stated, the research on social influencers is thriving and is expected to expand further. Social media influencers gained a lot more attention and became the main marketing strategy of brands, especially after the 2019 pandemic. From well-established to small brands all looking to sponsor social media influencers, macro or micro, to promote their products and services. They are using SMIs to create a trend among followers, specifically the young and techno-savvy generation. They use the FOMO phenomenon to change consumer buying behaviour and increase their customer engagement through SMIs. Based on the review of extant literature in previous sections, the following propositions have been developed for future study in this area:

*Proposition 1*: SMI recommendations have a direct effect on a new trend among their followers.
*Proposition 2*: SMI activities have a direct impact on the fear of missing out (FOMO) on the new trend among followers from the same group.
*Proposition 3*: UTB is a result of FOMO from trends created by SMIs.

*Proposition 4*: Impulse buying is a result of FOMO in followers to create the feeling of belonging to a group or community and creating self-identity closer to the SMIs.

We capture these developments in a conceptual framework presented in Fig. 8.1.

Researchers suggested that brands should use the plausible effect of FOMO to persuade consumers to buy and increase their engagement (e.g. Rahmawati & Sijabat, 2022; Hodkinson, 2016; Özden, 2022). Most of the exciting research provided suggestions to brands on how to increase their engagement and sales, but questions arise about the ethical perspective of using the FOMO phenomenon on consumers and the result of the UTB and impulse buying on unnecessary shopping and one-time use products, either of poor quality or change of the trend, and a consequent impact on sustainability and environmental waste issues.

Today, virtual influencers or avatars are emerging worldwide and getting the attention of young customers, especially Alpha or Twitch Generation, and many luxury brands like Gucci, Dior and LV have already adopted this as their marketing strategy. Therefore, the future of

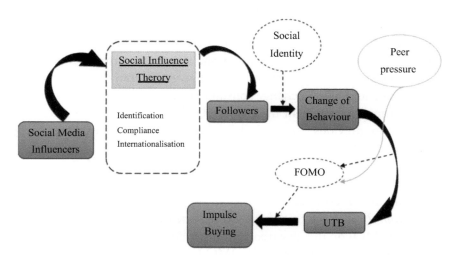

**Fig. 8.1** Conceptual framework, SMIs' influence on UTB because of FOMO and peer pressure of followers. Source: Authors

marketing seems to be very different from the traditional way of advertising and what currently brands are implementing. The new marketing strategy appears to be more affordable and provides more engagement among brands and consumers. On the other hand, the micro social media influencers, those with less than millions of followers, are still the main source of trust for customers like Gen Y and Z. Therefore, they are here to stay for a while as a main marketing strategy of brands. We suggest that while brands use this method of marketing to engage with their customers and enhance their sales, they need to remain cautious of the well-being of customers and related ethical issues and try to promote sustainable purchasing behaviour.

# References

Al-Emadi, F. A., & Ben Yahia, I. (2020). Ordinary celebrities related criteria to harvest fame and influence on social media. *Journal of Research in Interactive Marketing, 14*(2), 195–213.

Amos, C., Holmes, G. R., & Keneson, W. C. (2014). A meta-analysis of consumer impulse buying. *Journal of Retailing and Consumer Services, 21*(2), 86–97.

Anderson, S. P., & de Palma, A. (2011). Departement D'Economie. *Cahier n, 2010*, 23.

Applebaum, W. (1951). Studying customer behavior in retail stores. *Journal of Marketing, 16*(2), 172–178. https://doi.org/10.1177/002224295101600204

Audrezet, A., De Kerviler, G., & Moulard, J. G. (2018). Authenticity under threat: When social media influencers need to go beyond self-presentation. *Journal of Business Research*.

Aw, E. C.-X., & Chuah, S. H.-W. (2021). Stop the unattainable ideal for an ordinary me! Fostering parasocial relationships with social media influencers: The role of self-discrepancy. *Journal of Business Research, 132*, 146–157.

Belanche, D., Flavián, M., & Ibáñez-Sánchez, S, 2020. Followers' reactions to influencers' Instagram posts. Spanish Journal of Marketing – ESIC 1–17. https://doi.org/10.1108/SJME-11-2019-0100

Carlson, B. D., Donavan, D. T., Deitz, G. D., Bauer, B. C., & Lala, V. (2020). A customer-focused approach to improve celebrity endorser effectiveness. *Journal of Business Research, 109*, 221–235.

Celik, I. K., Eru, O., & Cop, R. (2019). The effectsof consumers' FoMo tendencies on impulsebuying and the effects of impulse buying on post-purchase regret: An investigation on retail stores. *BRAIN—Broad Research in Artificial Intelligence and Neuroscience, 10*(3), 124–138. https://lumenpublishing.com/journals/index.php/brain/article/view/2189

Campaign (2023). https://www.campaignlive.co.uk/article/modern-love-story/1812713? utm_medium=EMAIL&utm_campaign=promotion&utm_source=20230321&utm_content=230321JY01&spMailingID=28007223&spUserID=ODk1NTMwNzg2MDY4S0&spJobID=2421209531&spReportId=Accessed December 2023.

Chen, J. V., Su, B.-C., & Widjaja, A. E. (2016). Facebook C2C social commerce: A study of online impulse buying. *Decision Support Systems, 83*, 57–69.

Chen, Y., Lu, Y., Wang, B., & Pan, Z. (2019). How do product recommendations affect impulse buying? An empirical study on WeChat social commerce. *Information & Management, 56*(2), 236–248. https://doi.org/10.1016/j.im.2018.09.002

Chen, M., Xie, Z., Zhang, J., & Li, Y. (2021). Internet celebrities' impact on luxury fashion impulse buying. *Journal of Theoretical and Applied Electronic Commerce Research, 16*, 2470–2489.

Childers, C. C., Lemon, L. L., & Hoy, M. G. (2019). # sponsored# ad: Agency perspective on influencer marketing campaigns. *Journal of Current Issues and Research in Advertising, 40*(3), 258–274. https://doi.org/10.1080/10641734.2018.1521113

Chung, N., Song, H. G., & Lee, H. (2017). Consumers' impulsive buying behavior of restaurant products in social commerce. *International Journal of Contemporary Hospitality Management, 29*(2), 709–731. https://doi.org/10.1108/IJCHM-10-2015-0608

Claude, L. M. (2018). *Influencers impact on the decision-making among Generation Y & Z Swedish females when purchasing fast fashion.* http://www.diva-portal.org/smash/get/diva2:1214227/FULLTEXT01.pdf

Corrêa, S. C. H., Soares, J. L., Christino, J. M. M., Gosling, M. d. S., & Gonçalves, C. A. (2020). The influence of YouTubers on followers' use intention. *Journal of Research in Interactive Marketing, 14*(2), 173–194.

De Veirman, M., Cauberghe, V., & Hudders, L. (2017). Marketing through Instagram influencers: The impact of number of followers and product divergence on brand attitude. *International Journal of Advertising, 36*(5), 798–828.

Dinh, T. C. T., & Lee, Y. (2021). "I want to be as trendy as influencers"–How "fear of missing out" leads to buying intention for products endorsed by social media influencers. *Journal of Research in Interactive Marketing, 16*(3), 346–364.

Freberg, K., Graham, K., McGaughey, K., & Freberg, L. A. (2011). Who are the social media influencers? A study of public perceptions of personality. *Public relations review, 37*(1), 90–92.

Ge, J., & Gretzel, U. (2018). Emoji rhetoric: A social media influencer perspective. *Journal of Marketing Management, 34*(15/16), 1272–1295.

Gil, F., Chamarro, A., & Oberst, U. (2015). Addiction to online social networks: A question of "fear of missing out"? *Journal of Behavioral Addictions, 4*(Suppl. S1), 51–52.

Good, M. C., & Hyman, M. R. (2021). Direct and indirect effects of fear-of-missing-out appeals on purchase likelihood. *Journal of Consumer Behaviour, 20*(3), 564–576.

Gunawan, N. P., & Iskandar, I. B. P. (2020). Analyzing the impact of fashion influencer on online impulsive buying behavior. *KnE Social Sciences*, 350–363.

Hodkinson, C. (2016). "Fear of missing out" (FOMO) marketing appeals: A conceptual model. *Journal of Marketing Communications, 25*(1), 1–24. https://doi.org/10.1080/13527266.2016.1234504 (PDF) Direct and indirect effects of fear-of-missing-out appeals on purchase likelihood. Available from: https://www.researchgate.net/publication/345397739_Direct_and_indirect_effects_of_fear-of-missing-out_appeals_on_purchase_likelihood#fullTextFileContent [accessed Jul 08 2024].

Hu, X., Chen, X., & Davison, R. M. (2019). Social support, source credibility, social influence, and impulsive purchase behavior in social commerce. *International Journal of Electronic Commerce, 23*(3), 297–327.

Hudders, L., De Jans, S., & De Veirman, M. (2021). The commercialization of social media stars: A literature review and conceptual framework on the strategic use of social media influencers. *International Journal of Advertising, 40*(3), 327–375. https://doi.org/10.1080/02650487.2020.1836925

Hughes, C., Swaminathan, V., & Brooks, G. (2019). Driving brand engagement through online social influencers: An empirical investigation of sponsored blogging campaigns. *Journal of Marketing, 83*(5), 78–96.

Hwang, K., & Zhang, Q. (2018). Influence of parasocial relationship between digital celebrities and their followers on followers' purchase and electronic word-of-mouth intentions, and persuasion knowledge. *Computers in Human Behavior, 87*, 155–173.

Islam, T., Islam, R., Pitafi, A. H., Xiaobei, L., Rehmani, M., Irfan, M., & Mubarak, M. S. (2019). The impact of corporate social responsibility on customer loyalty: The mediating role of corporate reputation, customer satisfaction, and trust. *Sustainable Production and Consumption, 25,* 123–135. https://doi.org/10.1016/j.spc.2020.07.019

Jin, S. V., & Ryu, E. (2020). "I'll buy what she's #wearing": The roles of envy toward and parasocial interaction with influencers in Instagram celebrity-based brand endorsement and social commerce. *Journal of Retailing and Consumer Services, 55,* 102121.

Jin, S. V., Muqaddam, A., & Ryu, E. (2019). Instafamous and social media influencer marketing. *Marketing Intelligence & Planning, 37*(5), 567–579. https://doi.org/10.1108/MIP-09-2018-0375

Kang, I., Cui, H., & Son, J. (2019). Conformityconsumption behavior and FOMO. *Sustainability, 11*(17), 4734–4752. https://doi.org/10.3390/su11174734

Kapitan, S., & Silvera, D. H. (2016). From digital media influencers to celebrity endorsers: Attributions drive endorser effectiveness. *Marketing Letters, 27*(3), 553–567.

Kelman, H. C. (1961). Processes of opinion change. *Public Opinion Quarterly, 25,* 57–78. https://doi.org/10.1086/266996

Kelman, H. C. (1974). Further thoughts on the processes of compliance, identification, and internalization. In J. T. Tedeschi (Ed.), *Social power and political influence* (pp. 126–171). Aldine.

Kelman, H. C. (2006). Interests, relationships, identities: Three central issues for individuals and groups in negotiating their social environment. *Annual Review of Psychology, 57,* 1–26. https://doi.org/10.1146/annurev.psych.57.102904.190156

Ki, C., Cuevas, L. M., Chong, S. M., & Lim, H. (2020). Influencer marketing: Social media influencers as human brands attaching to followers and yielding positive marketing results by fulfilling needs. *Journal of Retailing and Consumer Services, 55,* 1–11.

Kim, D. Y., & Kim, H. Y. (2020). Influencer advertising on social media: The multiple inference model on influencer-product congruence and sponsorship disclosure. *Journal of Business Research.* https://doi.org/10.1016/j.jbusres.2020.02.020

Khamis, S., L. Ang, and R. Welling. 2017. Self-branding, 'micro-celebrity' and the rise of social media influencers. *Celebrity Studies, 8*(2), 191–208

Ladhari, R., Massa, E., & Skandrani, H. (2020). YouTube vloggers' popularity and influence: The roles of homophily, emotional attachment, and expertise. *Journal of Retailing and Consumer Services, 54,* 102027. https://doi.org/10.1016/j.jretconser.2019.102027

Lee, M. T., & Theokary, C. (2020). The superstar social media influencer: Exploiting linguistic style and emotional contagion over content? *Journal of Business Research, 132*, 860–871.

Lee, J. E., & Watkins, B. (2016). YouTube vloggers' influence on consumer luxury brand perceptions and intentions. *Journal of Business Research, 69*(12), 5753–5760.

Liang, X., Hu, X., Islam, T., & Mubarik, M. S. (2021). *A systematic review of emerging human.*

Lou, C., & Yuan, S. (2019). Influencer marketing: How message value and credibility affect consumer trust of branded content on social media. *Journal of Interactive Advertising, 19*(1), 58–73.

Lou, C., Tan, S. S., & Chen, X. (2019). Investigating consumer engagement with influencer-vs. brand-promoted ads: The roles of source and disclosure. *Journal of Interactive Advertising, 19*(3), 1–18. https://doi.org/10.108 0/15252019.2019.1667928

Lou, C., Ma, W., & Feng, Y. (2020). A sponsorship disclosure is not enough? How advertising literacy intervention affects consumer reactions to sponsored influencer posts. *Journal of Promotion Management, 27*(2), 278–305

Luna-Arocas, R., Tang, T. L. P., & Quintanilla Pardo, I. (2000). Money attitudes and achievement motivation: Predicting money as a motivator and intrinsic motivation. *25th annual colloquium of international association for research in economic psychology, July, Baden, Vienna.*

Luo, X. (2005). How does shopping with others influence impulsive purchasing? *Journal of Consumer Psychology, 15*, 288–294.

Mao, Z., Du, Z., Yuan, R., & Miao, Q. (2022). Short-term or long-term cooperation between retailer and MCN? New launched products sales strategies in live streaming e-commerce. *Journal of Retailing and Consumer Services, 67*, 102996. https://doi.org/10.1016/j.jretconser.2022.102996

Mavlanova, T., Benbunan-Fich, R., & Koufaris, M. (2012). Signaling theory and information asymmetry in online commerce. *Information & Management, 49*(5), 240–247.

McCormick, K. (2016). Celebrity endorsements: Influence of a product-endorser match on Millennials attitudes and purchase intentions. *Journal of Retailing and Consumer Services, 32*, 39–45. https://doi.org/10.1016/j. jretconser.2016.05.012

Özden, A. (2022). "Not ignoring the FOMO (fear of missing out) effect" as a new way to persuade consumer to buy. In R. Yilmaz & B. Koc (Eds.), *Narrative theory in the post-truth era* (pp. 117–131).

OBERLO (2021). How many people have smartphones in 2021? Retrieved 2024, from https://www.oberlo.com/statistics/how-many-peoplehave-smartphones

Piranda, D. R., Sinaga, D. Z., & Putri, E. E. (2022). Online marketing strategy in facebook marketplace as a digital marketing tool. *Journal of Humanities, Social Sciences and Business (JHSSB), 1*(3), 1–8. https://doi.org/10.55047/jhssb.v1i2.123

Pittman, M., & Abell, A. (2021). More trust in fewer followers: Diverging effects of popularity metrics and green orientation social media influencers. *Journal of Interactive Marketing, 56,* 70–82.

Rahmawati, I., & Sijabat, R. (2022). Analysis of influencer's imitation behavior phenomenon, fear of missing out about the impact on purchase intention on local cosmetic products endorsed by social media influencers. *Budapest International Research and Critics Institute-Journal (BIRCI-Journal), 5*(2).

Reale, M. (2019). Digital market, bloggers, and trendsetters: The new world of advertising law. *Laws, 8*(3), 21.

Reinikainen, H., Munnukka, J., Maity, D., & Luoma-aho, V. (2020). 'You really are a great big sister'—Parasocial relationships, credibility, and the moderating role of audience comments in influencer marketing. *Journal of Marketing Management, 36*(3–4), 279–298.

Rook, D. W. (1987b). The buying impulse. *The Journal of Consumer Research, 14*(2), 189–199.

Ryu, E., & Jin, S. V. (2019). Instagram fashionistas, luxury visual image strategies and vanity. *The Journal of Product and Brand Management, 29*(3), 355–368.

Schouten, A. P., Janssen, L., & Verspaget, M. (2020). Celebrity vs. influencer endorsements in advertising: The role of identification, credibility, and product-endorser fit. *International Journal of Advertising, 39*(2), 258–281.

Schouten, A. P., Janssen, L., & Verspaget, M. (2021). Celebrity vs. Influencer endorsements in advertising: the role of identification, credibility, and Product-Endorser fit. In Leveraged marketing communications (pp. 208-231). Routledge

Shamim, K., & Islam, T. (2022). Digital influencer marketing: How message credibility and media credibility affect trust and impulsive buying. *Journal of Global Scholars of Marketing Science, 32*(4), 601–626. https://doi.org/10.1080/21639159.2022.2052342

Silvia, G., & Anwar, K. U. S. (2021). Pengaruh E-Commerce Terhadap Perilaku Konsumen Tokopedia Pada Masyarakat Kota Jambi. *Transekonomika: Akuntansi, Bisnis Dan Keuangan, 1*(3), 240–251.

Sokolova, K., & Kefi, H. (2020). Instagram and YouTube bloggers promote it, why should I buy? How credibility and parasocial interaction influence purchase intentions. *Journal of Retailing and Consumer Services, 53*, 1–9. https://doi.org/10.1016/j.jretconser.2019.01.011

Statista. (2022a). *Global digital population as of April 2022 (in billions).* https://www.statista.com/statistics/617136/digital-population-worldwide/?utm_source=statista_system&utm_medium=email&utm_campaign=statistic_update_mail&utm_term=statistik_abo

Statista. (2022b). *Number of social network users worldwide from 2018 to 2027 (in billions).* Accessed April 1, 2023, from https://www.statista.com/statistics/278414/number-of-worldwide-social-network-users/

Tafesse, W., & Wood, B. P. (2021). Followers' engagement with Instagram influencers: The role of influencers' content and engagement strategy. *Journal of Retailing and Consumer Services, 58*, 1–9.

Tajfel, H. (1972). Experiments in a vacuum. In J. Isreal & H. Tajfel (Eds.), *The context of social psychology*. Academic Press.

The power of social media marketing, Oberlo. (2021). Accessed December 2022, from https://www.oberlo.com/blog/social-media-marketing-statistics

TikTok. (2021). *New studies quantify TikTok's growing impact on culture and music.* Accessed April 17, 2023, from https://newsroom.tiktok.com/en-us/new-studies-quantify-tiktoks-growing-impact-on-culture-and-music

Trejo-Pech, C. O., & Thach, S. (2021). A review of articles in the Journal of Global Scholars of Marketing Science (JGSMS) special issue on Marketing Management in International Contexts. *Journal of Global Scholars of Marketing Science, 31*(1), 1–9.

Valsesia, F., Proserpio, D., & Nunes, J. C. (2020). The positive effect of not following others on social media. *Journal of Marketing Research (JMR), 57*(6), 1152–1168.

Verhagen, T., & Van Dolen, W. (2011). The influence of online store beliefs on consumer online impulse buying: A model and empirical application. *Information Management, 48*, 320–327.

Wang, T., Thai, T. D.-H., Ly, P. T. M., & Chi, T. P. (2021). Turning social endorsement into brand passion. *Journal of Business Research, 126*, 429–439.

Wangshu, G., & Guanhua, W. (2020). *How influencers marketing motivates consumers' buying behaviour: A focus group investigation of the impulse buying behaviour via Chinese millennials' lens.*

Weismueller, J., Harrigan, P., Wang, S., & Soutar, G. N. (2020). Influencer endorsements: How advertising disclosure and source credibility affect consumer purchase intention on social media. *Australasian Marketing Journal, 28*(4), 160–170.

Xiang, L., Zheng, X., Lee, M. K., & Zhao, D. (2016). Exploring consumers' impulse buying behavior on social commerce platform: The role of parasocial interaction. *International Journal of Information Management, 36*(3), 333–347.

Yadav, M. S., de Valck, K., Hennig-Thurau, T., Hoffman, D. L., & Spann, M. (2013). Social commerce: A contingency framework for assessing marketing potential. *Journal of Interactive Marketing, 27*(4), 311–323. https://doi.org/10.1016/j.intmar.2013.09.001

Zafar, A. U., Qiu, J., & Shahzad, M. (2020). Do digital celebrities' relationships and social climate matter? Impulse buying in f-commerce. *Internet Research, 30*(6), 1731–1762.

Zafar, A. U., Qiu, J., Li, Y., Wang, J., & Shahzad, M. (2021). The impact of social media celebrities' posts and contextual interactions on impulse buying in social commerce. *Computers in Human Behavior, 115*, 106178.

Zhang, Z., Jimenez, F. R., & Cicala, J. E. (2020). Fear of missing out scale: A self-concept perspective. *Psychology & Marketing, 37*(11), 1619–1634.

Zhang, W., Chintagunta, P. K., & Kalwani, M. U. (2021). Social media, influencers, and adoption of an eco-friendly product: Field experiment evidence from rural China. *Journal of Marketing, 85*(3), 10–27.

# 9

# Virtual Influencers: The Future of Marketing and Branding?

Chen Yang and Yan Sun

## Introduction

Virtual influencers, as computer-generated human avatars, have gained increasing attention from both academia and industry in recent years. As defined by Tan and Liew (2020), virtual influencers refer to 'embodied virtual agents' presenting vivid human personalities and carrying storylines to create natural user-agent interactions.

Virtual influencers often appear as members of 'Generation Z' and receive a hearty welcome from young audiences (Moustakas et al., 2020). High-end brands, including Porsche and Louis Vuitton, are collaborating

---

C. Yang (✉)
Marketing and Management, Greenwich Business School, University of Greenwich, London, UK
e-mail: c.yang@greenwich.ac.uk

Y. Sun
Oxford Brookes Business School, Oxford Brookes University, Oxford, UK
e-mail: ysun@brookes.ac.uk

© The Author(s), under exclusive license to Springer Nature Switzerland AG 2024
S. Tabari, Q. S. Ding (eds.), *Celebrity, Social Media Influencers and Brand Performance*,
https://doi.org/10.1007/978-3-031-63516-8_9

with virtual influencers to reach younger generations. Virtual influencers also provide a potential solution for brands to reduce risks of working with human influencers due to their unpredictable behaviour (Sands et al., 2022).

Representations of virtual influencers are deeply rooted in their cultural contexts. Leading virtual influencers Lil Miquela (USA), Liu Yexi (China) and Imma (Japan) combine cultural elements from their countries into their social media narrative strategies.

We will start this chapter with a discussion of definitions from various perspectives, before focusing on the ways that virtual influencers engage with target audiences. We will then compare virtual influencers in various markets under different cultural contexts. Finally, we will explore the impacts virtual influencers make on brand image and brand identity.

# (Human) Influencers

Social media influencers are individuals who have established a significant presence on social media platforms and can influence the opinions, behaviour and purchasing decisions of their followers (Cooley & Parks-Yancy, 2019).

The term 'influencer' is derived from the word 'influence', which means the ability to affect or sway someone's opinions or actions. Opinion leaders have existed for a long time in traditional mass media such as TV, films and newspapers. In a study conducted during the 1940 presidential election in the USA, Lazarsfeld et al. (1948) pointed out that mass media normally do not have a direct impact on consumers' behaviour patterns. Instead, the opinion leaders who interpret the information that is received from a distant body of knowledge will act as a 'passive segment' to affect people's minds and actions. Social media influencers have emerged as a new form of opinion leader, and their popularity stems from their social prestige, expertise and ability to connect with their followers on a personal level (Kim & Kim, 2021; Nouri, 2018). They often have a large following on social media platforms, such as Instagram, YouTube, TikTok and X, and their content can reach millions of people worldwide.

Authenticity is an essential element of an influencer's relationship with their followers. The definition of authenticity varies across different academic fields. Within the field of social psychology, this concept can be defined as the degree to which an individual's self-presentation reflects their true self and is perceived as genuine by others. In the context of social media influencers, authenticity refers to the extent to which their content and endorsements align with their personal beliefs, values and interests and are perceived as sincere by their followers (Audrezet et al., 2020).

Authenticity is crucial for successful self-branding, and features of self-branding on social media aim to create a sense of engagement that appears authentic while still prioritising benefits to the market (Banet-Weiser, 2011). According to Hearn (2008), self-branding is the process of constructing a meta-narrative and meta-image of oneself through the use of cultural meanings and images drawn from mainstream cultural industries, with the purpose of obtaining social capital and financial benefit. This idea enables individuals to become a brand through the activities of their followers and fans. To achieve success, creators need to make their identity construction a consumable product that is accepted by their audience, forming a connection between themselves and consumers. Marwick (2013) called this carefully monitored and highly commercialised self-branding the 'edited self'. According to DeCordova (2001), the Hollywood star system is based on the notion that the private lives of stars are more fascinating to the public than their fictional characters. This means that the typical celebrity persona is often created through deliberate performance (Marwick & Boyd, 2011). They suggest that celebrities use their public image to give the impression of behind-the-scenes access to their lives while acknowledging that this persona is often artificial. In the social media era, influencers also tend to commodify their personal life through creating a 'staged authenticity'.

However, authenticity is not always straightforward in the world of social media influencers. Influencers may face pressure to present a curated and idealised version of themselves or to promote products and brands that may not align with their personal values or interests (Scolere et al., 2018). Balancing the demands of authenticity with the expectations of brands and followers can be a challenging task for influencers, and the potential for conflicts of interest can be high.

On the one hand, a successful collaboration can create a positive association between a brand, influencers and their followers, and this can be invaluable in building brand loyalty and increasing sales (Clark & Melancon, 2013). On the other hand, if the product does not align with the selected influencers' values or those of their followers, it will cause negative impacts on product reputation, the trust between influencers and their followers, and the purchase intention and product attitude of the consumers (Kim & Kim, 2021).

## Virtual Influencers

In recent years, a new phenomenon has emerged in the world of social media marketing: virtual influencers. Unlike traditional social media influencers, who are real people, virtual influencers are computer-generated characters that exist only in the digital realm. These virtual entities have generated significant buzz in the marketing world, as they offer a new way for brands to engage with their audiences and target specific demographics.

A virtual influencer can be defined as a computer-generated character that is designed to have their unique presence, personas and storyline (Arsenyan & Mirowska, 2021; Sands et al., 2022). Similar to human influencers, virtual influencers frequently interact with users in a shared digital environment (Gammoh et al., 2018; Audrezet & Koles, 2023). Sometimes, real human beings choose to select a computer-generated avatar to present themselves in an online environment such as a game or chat room. However, the majority of well-known virtual influencers on social media (such as the four cases discussed later) are completely invented characters created by a production team. One advantage is that the company can ensure content consistency and avoid unexpected interruptions such as sickness or conflicts between human influencers and companies. When influencers are considered as commodified entities in business activities, the ability to produce consistent and risk-free value is highly prioritised by participants in the market.

## 9 Virtual Influencers: The Future of Marketing and Branding?

The development of virtual influencers has been driven by advancements in technology, particularly in the areas of artificial intelligence (AI) and computer graphics. The ability to create realistic-looking characters that can interact with humans in a natural and engaging way has opened up new opportunities for brands to engage with their audiences and promote their products and services.

However, one of the major challenges facing the producers of virtual influencers is building their authenticity. Unlike traditional influencers, who are real people with their own personalities and life experiences, virtual influencers are entirely fabricated. This can make it difficult for audience to connect with them on a personal level and can lead to questions about their authenticity (Molin & Nordgren, 2019).

To address this challenge, the producers of virtual influencers have developed a range of strategies, such as giving them distinct personalities, interests, and backstories and allowing them to interact with their audiences in a human-like way. A study done by Andersson and Sobek (2020) found that virtual influencers' authenticity is determined by four factors: purpose, personality, continuity and transparency. Purpose refers to a simple and clear idea of why the virtual influencer is created. Secondly, the virtual influencer's personality needs to be perceived as genuine and relatable by their consumers. Continuity emphasises that the sense of authenticity has to be consistent during the time of interacting with consumers. Lastly, transparency refers to the producers' values and opinions, which must remain somewhat similar to the virtual influencers they create, and brand collaboration information, which should be easily accessible to the public. This postmodern idea of recreating a 'staged authenticity' puts more emphasis on the feelings of the consumers and less on actual realism (Wong et al., 2023).

Despite their potential benefits, virtual influencers also raise a number of potential issues. Many of these discussions focus on the issues arising from the lack of authenticity of these fabricated characters. For example, there are ethical concerns regarding the use of computer-generated personas to promote products and services (Mrad et al., 2022). Additionally, issues surrounding intellectual property (IP) ownership and the legitimacy of virtual influencers participating in social rights movements

## Now? Social (Media) Commerce

Launched in 2004, Facebook (now called Meta) was originally built to connect Harvard students on campus. Following dramatic growth over two decades, in 2022, Facebook/Meta had roughly 2.96 billion monthly active users worldwide (Statista, 2023). Social media (SM) has completely changed the way we communicate and connect with each other. Furthermore, SM has transformed the way business operates by integrating new technologies and channels of commerce.

One step beyond e-commerce, social commerce (SC) refers to (1) a virtual shopping environment which empowers consumers to interact with platforms using social tools (Stephen & Toubia, 2010); (2) a computer-mediated environment to support interactions among community members, where brand values are co-created by consumers through the process of communication (Wang & Yu, 2017).

Two types of SC contexts were observed in the past decade: (1) incorporating commercial features into social network service (SNS) and (2) integrating social networking features into traditional e-commerce sites (Huang & Benyoucef, 2013; Zhang et al., 2014).

SC offers an innovative and interactive format for consumers to collaborate with each other during the online shopping process (Lim, 2020). Consumer-generated content is considered to be a new version of word of mouth (WOM) and a credible source to help consumers make purchase decisions (Lin et al., 2019; Lin & Wang, 2022). SC sites include social network-driven sales platforms, peer recommendation websites, group buying websites, peer-to-peer sales platforms, user-curated shopping websites, social shopping websites and participatory commerce websites (Tajvidi et al., 2020).

During the Covid-19 pandemic, SM and SC have had an even stronger impact on our daily lives during periods when most people had to stay at home to avoid face-to-face interaction due to lockdowns announced by authorities. With little interaction in the physical world, people have

## 9 Virtual Influencers: The Future of Marketing and Branding?

relied on SM and SC to continue their daily lives. The whole world has been dependent on the Internet and digital environments to move forwards during the pandemic. In Malaysia, small and micro-enterprises achieved huge success during the pandemic by operating across social media commerce platforms, such as Facebook, Twitter, YouTube, Instagram and Pinterest (Hassan & Shahzad, 2022). Another new emerging market in Asia-Pacific, Indonesia became the fastest-growing e-commerce market, where social media plays a significant role of pushing online sales in the fashion sector (Gifford, 2019).

SC and SM have become key drivers in the past decade and led to a lot of changes across sectors, including the allocation of time and resources (Dwivedi et al., 2015). Traditional marketing tactics, such as promotions and offers taking place in a physical setting, can't capture customers' attention anymore. Social media platforms have become a fundamental hub for daily interaction among individuals and businesses (French, 2017).

Consumers are keen to share all types of experiences and opinions on social media every day. On the other hand, individuals often blindly accept content and information shared on social media without verification (Shareef et al., 2019, 2020). With audiences misled by false information and fake news, confusion, disturbance and unrest can emerge overnight in business sectors and political environments. Undoubtedly, trust is a burning issue for any parties involved with social media and social commerce. As a complex human behaviour, trust is influenced by multidimensional parameters and formatted between socially associated members (Shin, 2010; Haclyakupoglu & Zhang, 2015). It is a challenging process to develop trust on social media, which is an extremely dynamic environment, and unexpected behaviours in virtual settings can lead to consequences in the physical world.

# Case Studies with an International Perspective

## Lil Miquela

Lil Miquela is a virtual influencer created by Brud, a Los Angeles–based startup, in 2016. Miquela is portrayed as a 19-year-old Brazilian-American girl known for her striking appearance, which includes blue hair, oversized sunglasses and a polished and fashionable style. Miquela's polished, stylised image and celebrity lifestyle appeal to many young people who aspire to a similar lifestyle. In 2018, Lil Miquela was listed as one of the 25 most influential people on the Internet by Time (2018). This popularity is reflected in the engagement rate for her content, which appears to be three times higher than the average human influencer's (The Influencer Marketing Factory, 2022).

Lil Miquela's ability to engage with consumers has quickly attracted interest from brands. In 2020, Samsung invited Lil Miquela with other human celebrities, including Millie Bobbie Brown, Ninja and Steve Aoki, to participate in their campaign #TeamGalaxy. Because of the collaboration with Miquela, Samsung has successfully enhanced the innovative and futuristic features of the brand identity (Blanton & Carbajal, 2022; Sands et al., 2022). It is worth noting that the campaign was not restricted to social media platforms but achieved a much wider impact across mass media.

According to Stéphanie Genz (2015), Lil Miquela's authenticity is used as a way to make her seem more real and valuable in the postfeminist attention economy. Lil Miquela addresses real-world issues, responds to social media trolls and takes pictures with real people to create a sense of authenticity (Mei, 2021). An example of this is a promotional video released by Calvin Klein in 2019, in which human supermodel Bella Hadid kisses Lil Miquela. This mix of real and artificial characteristics both confuses and intrigues audiences. Lil Miquela's perceived authenticity is similar to that of a typical influencer, as she shares personal details with her audience. However, she is not a real person, and her authenticity is simply a representation of an archetype. Some fans are

## 9 Virtual Influencers: The Future of Marketing and Branding? 183

surprised by how much they relate to her, while others are confused by how a robot can display emotions and interact with humans.

Sands et al. (2022) also pointed out that, compared with human influencers, narratives created through brand partnerships can be more accepted by consumers. Lil Miquela has appeared using Samsung on Instagram and other social media platforms since the partnership was announced. This avoids potential anger from consumers which is often prompted by inconsistent product usage by human influencers online and offline (in their everyday lives). Furthermore, because Lil Miquela was created for the purpose of commercialisation, audiences are not surprised to find out about brand partnerships, and therefore, these business activities will not harm the sense of 'authenticity' created by virtual influencers (Sands et al., 2022).

To make the character more 'real', Brud created a group of virtual characters on Instagram and developed many storylines between them. Miquela invited her boyfriend—another virtual influencer, Nick Killan— to appear in her music video 'Speak Up', and she also appears frequently in her friend Bermuda's posts. Just like Miquela, these virtual influencers act as models, artists and musicians in Los Angeles. They have 'cool' jobs and a fantasy lifestyle. The stories between them are like a TV drama on Instagram that never stops. This strong storytelling ability also encourages their followers to keep engaging with their social media posts (Bringé, 2022).

However, some critics argue that the creation of virtual influencers like Miquela is a form of cultural appropriation. As a non-human entity, the 'Brazilian-American' Miquela does not have a lived experience or cultural background, nor did any of her creators have this particular background. Therefore, it is questionable for Miquela to claim that she represents any particular culture; rather, she reflects the desires and values of her creators and audience. While her activism on social justice issues (such as 'Black Lives Matter') has garnered praise, her creation and popularity raise important questions about 'commercialised fake justice' and the blurring of reality and fiction in the age of social media (Clein, 2019). As virtual influencers become increasingly popular, it will be important for creators and brands alike to critically examine the cultural implications of their existence and the messages they promote.

Also, the emergence of virtual influencers has brought up another important concern—how to protect the intellectual property (IP) associated with the content generated by different entities. Miquela is a prime example of this, as she endorses Prada products and even has her music on Spotify. With the significant financial investment involved in these endeavours, legal contracts must address important questions such as the ownership of the virtual influencer's output (Christina, 2019). It remains unclear whether the brand whose product the virtual influencer is promoting or the artist who conceived and developed the virtual influencer should have ownership. Additionally, the origin of the IP (internally created or external) may affect the legal agreements' terms. Therefore, it is crucial to consider intellectual property issues when deciding whether to hire an external artist or work with an in-house team. As the virtual influencer industry continues to grow, it is essential to establish clear legal guidelines to protect the IP rights of all involved parties.

## Liu Yexi

Liu Yexi is a virtual influencer created by the Chinese tech company CreateOne. She was launched in 2019 and quickly became a sensation in the Chinese social media landscape. Liu Yexi's Douyin account gained over 1.3 million followers within 24 hours after her first video was posted, and this rapid growth of popularity quickly attracted attention from brands. This case study explores the rise of Liu Yexi as a virtual influencer and the factors that contributed to her success. CreateOne is a Chinese technology company that specialises in the development of virtual characters and their social media account operations. The company created Liu Yexi to cater to the growing demand for digital content in China. Liu Yexi was designed to be a beautiful, stylish and intelligent young woman who has an identical make-up style.

CreateOne's marketing strategy for Liu Yexi was to leverage the power of social media to create a buzz around her. Similarly to Brud, CreateOne created a visually stunning Douyin account for her and designed several series of short dramas around her. To make the virtual character more 'localised', the content was rooted deeply in Chinese culture, with elements including Kung Fu, Chinese traditional opera and calligraphy. However, Liu Yexi's Douyin posts are carefully curated to appeal to her target audience, which consists mainly of young, urban Chinese consumers (Dang, 2023). Therefore, the production team set Liu's story in a modern Chinese city, but Liu wears traditional Chinese clothes and hairstyles. The videos posted on Douyin also focus on social issues in modern Chinese society, such as mental health and self-care, which creates a sense of aspiration among her followers. This localisation strategy led to Liu's popularity with well-educated urban consumers.

In recent years, the revival of Chinese traditional culture has become a new trend among younger generations in China. Traditional culture and recreation practices have not only appeared in film and media but also spread to clothing, cosmetics and music industries. Many local brands have embraced the trend and adopted it into their brand identities. However, those local brands have struggled to gain trust from high-income consumers in urban cities (Chan et al., 2009). Liu's production team created a virtual world which combined a strong futuristic feel with traditional Chinese cultural elements, which gives local brands a great opportunity to approach higher-income consumers whilst also maintaining a consistent brand narrative.

Another key element of Liu Yexi's marketing strategy is her engagement with her followers. Liu Yexi interacts with her followers by responding to their comments and messages. She also hosts live-streaming events where she talks about her life, shares beauty tips and showcases her favourite products. This interaction creates a sense of intimacy and loyalty amongst her followers, who see her as a friend rather than as a Computer-generated avatar.

Several factors have contributed to Liu Yexi's success as a virtual influencer. One of the most significant factors is the growing popularity of virtual influencers in China. According to the research report published by iiMedia (2023), the core market scale of China's virtual influencers industry has reached to approximately 16.8 billion USD in 2022 and is expected to reach to 66.9 billion USD in 2025. Technology companies like CreateOne have focused on producing virtual influencers to partner with brands, and many Chinese brands are also investing in creating their own virtual idols.

However, the popularity of Liu Yexi seems to be falling quickly, compared with the time she was launched. Some people argue that this is due to the long production period for her content (Feng, 2022). Each video takes the production team roughly one month to make. Also, some articles (eg., Xinkedu, 2022) criticise the stories created on Liu's account for being too simple, due to the restriction of technical tools and production periods. With a low posting frequency and the fading novelty of this concept, it is hard to keep people's attention, especially on Douyin, where attention is measured in seconds.

## Imma

Imma is a well-known virtual influencer in Japan, a digital model created by the company Aww Inc. Imma has gained a significant following for her realistic appearance and fashion-forward content. Imma was first introduced to the public in 2019, and since then, she has gained over 100,000 followers on Instagram. Her content focuses on fashion and beauty, and she is often seen wearing high-end brands such as Chanel and Prada. Imma's creators have made an effort to make her character relatable and authentic, and she often engages with her followers by responding to comments and sharing behind-the-scenes glimpses of her life.

One of the reasons for Imma's success is her realistic appearance. Unlike some virtual influencers who have a clearly digital appearance, Imma's creators have endeavoured to make her look as lifelike as possible. She has a realistic face, complete with freckles and blemishes, and her poses and movements are designed to mimic those of a real human model. This level of realism has helped to make her more relatable to her followers and has contributed to her success. One of Imma's most successful marketing cases was her collaboration with Japanese fashion brand A Bathing Ape (BAPE) in 2019. The collaboration included a limited-edition clothing line featuring Imma and BAPE's signature ape logo. The line was promoted through a series of social media posts featuring Imma wearing the clothing, as well as through in-store displays and a pop-up shop in Tokyo.

## 9 Virtual Influencers: The Future of Marketing and Branding? 187

The collaboration was a huge success, with the limited-edition clothing selling out within minutes of its release. The pop-up shop in Tokyo also drew significant crowds, with fans lining up for hours to purchase the clothing and take photos with Imma. The collaboration generated significant buzz on social media, with fans sharing photos and videos of the clothing and the pop-up shop. One reason for the success of this marketing collaboration was the strong brand alignment between Imma and BAPE. Both brands have a young, fashion-forward audience, and the collaboration allowed Imma to tap into BAPE's established fan base. Additionally, the limited-edition aspect of the clothing line created a sense of exclusivity and urgency among fans, which helped to drive sales and generate buzz.

Although Imma received a warm welcome from younger generations in Japan, like many influencers and virtual influencers, she is also facing criticism for promoting an unrealistic and unattainable beauty ideal that reflects the 'Asian beauty standard'. Imma is seen as reinforcing the 'Asian beauty standard' because her appearance is based on conventional beauty standards that are prevalent in many East Asian countries. The 'Asian beauty standard' is heavily influenced by societal expectations and values that prioritise features such as pale skin, large eyes and a small nose and mouth. These ideals have been perpetuated through various cultural mediums, including media, advertising and even traditional folklore.

Imma is often praised for her expressive eyes, flawless skin, luscious lips and perfect hair, which represent the ideal of eternal youthfulness and perfection that surpasses filters and modifications. However, Imma's popularity also raises concerns about the role of digital technologies in shaping our perceptions of beauty and the representation of women in popular media. The paradoxical embodiment of Imma as both an idealised beauty and a product of digital artifice is reflective of the tensions within postfeminist digital culture. On the one hand, women are expected to conform to heteronormative beauty standards and maintain an appealing appearance that is often associated with youthfulness. On the other hand, there is growing criticism of the over-sexualisation and objectification of women online, which has led to regulatory debates and discussions about the impact of digital media on women's self-esteem and mental health (Djafarova & Rushworth, 2017).

Moreover, the use of virtual models like Imma in Western popular media reinforces racial and gender differences by materialising them through the consumption of virtuality. In much content posted on social media, Imma appears in locations with typical Japanese architecture and wears a kimono, creating a sense of 'myth' from a Western perspective. Miyake (2023) has argued that, considering the company's international background, the company may be utilising these semiotics to satisfy the 'techno-Orientalist' gaze of its global consumers.

In conclusion, while Imma has achieved significant success as a virtual influencer, it is important to consider the cultural implications of her representation. Virtual influencers may perpetuate narrow stereotypes and contribute to a culture of superficiality and consumerism. As the trend of virtual influencers continues to grow, it is important for brands and creators to be mindful of these concerns and work to promote a diverse and inclusive representation of culture.

## The Future? Marketing and Branding in Digital Environment

Following therise of SC, social media influencers further enhance the impact of SM on our society, particularly boosting the two-way communication between individuals and businesses. The power of influencers is evident in various markets and countries. In 2011, the top live streamer in China, Viya, successfully sold $30 million worth of products to her millions of followers within a few hours, which was a headline story across various media for weeks (Wu et al., 2022).

However, human influencers may be involved in inappropriate communication and scandals, leading to PR crises and inflicting serious damage on brands and their customers. Virtual influencers offer another option for business today. A few global brands, including Prada, Samsung, Unilever and KFC, have already partnered with virtual influencers in marketing campaigns (da Silva Oliveira & Chimenti, 2021). What is next? In the short term, definitely AI. In the long term, the metaverse,

# 9 Virtual Influencers: The Future of Marketing and Branding?

perhaps. As AI technology continues to evolve, it is likely that virtual influencers will become more sophisticated and realistic.

One potential area where AI could have a significant impact on the development of virtual influencers is in their ability to learn and adapt to user interactions. Currently, most virtual influencers are either manually managed by human producers or pre-programmed with a set of responses to specific prompts and questions. However, as AI technology advances, virtual influencers could become more responsive to user input, learning from previous interactions and adapting their responses to better meet the needs of individual users.

Another area where AI could influence the development of virtual influencers is in their ability to create content. Currently, most virtual influencers are created by human designers, who use 3D modelling software to create their appearance and animations. However, with the development of AI image generation tools such as Midjourney, it may become possible to generate virtual influencers automatically, using machine learning algorithms to create unique images and videos within a very short period of time.

It is widely agreed that it is still early days for the metaverse. According to McKinsey (2022), the metaverse provides an immersive environment which exists in real time; the virtual and physical worlds become parallel. If the metaverse is taken as an evolution of the Internet today, from a marketing perspective, the metaverse represents an opportunity to successfully engage customers in a new environment without capacity limits and geographic boundaries.

Surprisingly, leading brands are already embracing the metaverse by redeveloping the rules of marketing. Facebook rebranded as Meta in 2021 and announced plans to bring the metaverse to real life. A month later, Microsoft announced a proposal to acquire a gaming giant (Activision) to build blocks for the metaverse. Leading virtual influencers and their production companies are also ready to join the game. Brud, the company that created Miquela, was acquired by a blockchain company called DapperLabs, which led to a transition to a decentralised autonomous organisation (DAO) named Brud DAO. This change means that Miquela will now be owned and driven by her community, with the use of crypto-based methods to showcase her story across various Web

3.0 platforms. This new approach will give fans a more significant role in shaping Miquela's narrative, allowing them to become co-creators and participate in ownership and voting using tokens, rather than simply voting on social media posts. This new development represents an exciting experiment in the future of decentralised media, where communities collectively own and create intellectual property. Miquela has already launched a project called 'Villa M', which focuses on buying digital furniture in the metaverse, as part of a community-building initiative (Cowen, 2022).

Future consumers? Gen Z. Gen Z refers to individuals born between 1996 and 2012, who are the first generation of true digital natives (McKinsey, 2018). Unlike previous generations, Gen Z has no experience of what life was like before the Internet appeared.

Nearly one-third of Gen Z spend six hours or longer on their smartphones across the Asia-Pacific area, and this age group greatly rely on social media to connect in both virtual and physical worlds (McKinsey, 2020). Willing to accept different truths, comfortable with virtual identities, having grown up with social media and being familiar with online gaming, perhaps Gen Z will transition more smoothly into the metaverse than older generations.

# References

Andersson, V., & Sobek, T. (2020). *Virtual avatars, virtual influencers & authenticity*. MSc thesis, University of Gothenburg. https://gupea.ub.gu.se/handle/2077/64928

Arsenyan, J., & Mirowska, A. (2021). Almost human? A comparative case study on the social media presence of virtual influencers. *International Journal of Human-Computer Studies, 155*, 102694.

Audrezet, A., & Koles, B. (2023). Virtual influencer as a brand avatar in interactive marketing. In C. L. Wang (Ed.), *The Palgrave handbook of interactive marketing*. Palgrave Macmillan.

Audrezet, A., De Kerviler, G., & Moulard, J. G. (2020). Authenticity under threat: When social media influencers need to go beyond self-presentation. *Journal of Business Research, 117*, 557–569.

Banet-Weiser, S. (2011). Convergence on the street: Rethinking the authentic/commercial binary. *Cultural Studies, 25*(4–5), 641–658.

Blanton, R., & Carbajal, D. (2022). Not a girl, not yet a woman: A critical case study on social media, deception, and Lil Miquela. In Information Resources Management Association (Ed.), *Research anthology on usage, identity, and impact of social media on society and culture* (pp. 894–909). IGI Global.

Bringé, A. (2022, October 18). The rise of virtual influencer and what it means for brands. *Forbes.* https://www.forbes.com/sites/forbescommunicationscouncil/2022/10/18/the-rise-of-virtual-influencers-and-what-it-means-for-brands/?sh=36d581446b56

Chan, T. S., Cui, G., & Zhou, N. (2009). Competition between foreign and domestic brands: A study of consumer purchases in China. *Journal of Global Marketing, 22*(3), 181–197.

Christina. (2019). *Lil Miquela—The new "It-Girl" that received $6m funding.* https://1e9.community/t/lil-miquela-the-new-it-girl-that-received-6m-funding/280

Clark, M., & Melancon, J. (2013). The influence of social media investment on relational outcomes: A relationship marketing perspective. *International Journal of Marketing Studies, 5*(4), 132–142.

Clein, E. (2019, June 28). Branding fake justice for Generation Z. *The Nation.* https://www.thenation.com/article/archive/social-justice-cgi-advertising-brud/

Cooley, D., & Parks-Yancy, R. (2019). The effect of social media on perceived information credibility and decision making. *Journal of Internet Commerce, 18*(3), 249–269.

Cowen, T. (2022). Miquela launches first PFP NFT project, gives fans glimpse at New Villa M Space. *Complex.* https://www.complex.com/pop-culture/miquela-launches-first-pfp-nft-project-gives-fans-glimpse-at-new-villa-m-space

da Silva Oliveira, A. B., & Chimenti, P. (2021). "Humanized robots": A proposition of categories to understand virtual influencers. *Australasian Journal of Information Systems, 25.*

Dang, T. (2023). The professional development of short videos: The case study of 'Liu Yexi' and the creation of virtual influencer IP 短视频专业化发展:虚拟偶像IP打造—以抖音'柳叶熙'为例；*河北画报. Hebei Image.* https://xueshu.baidu.com/usercenter/paper/show?paperid=192r0xj0uc6302g0mg4n08f0b2613013&site=xueshu_se

DeCordova, R. (2001). *Picture personalities: The emergence of the star system in America*. University of Illinois Press.

Djafarova, E., & Rushworth, C. (2017). Exploring the credibility of online celebrities' Instagram profiles in influencing the purchase decisions of young female users. *Computers in Human Behavior, 68*, 1–7.

Dwivedi, Y., Kapoor, K., & Chen, H. (2015). Social media marketing and advertising. *The Marketing Review, 15*(3), 289–309.

Feng, Y. (2022, December). The rise of virtual image endorsement in visual culture context. In *2022 4th international conference on economic management and cultural industry (ICEMCI 2022)* (pp. 1622–1629). Atlantis Press.

French, A. M. (2017). Let's meet offline: A mixed-methods approach exploring new trends in social networking. *Information Technology and People, 30*(4), 946–968.

Gammoh, B. S., Jiménez, F. R., & Wergin, R. (2018). Consumer attitudes toward human-like avatars in advertisements: The effect of category knowledge and imagery. *International Journal of Electronic Commerce, 22*(3), 325–348.

Genz, S. (2015). My job is me: Postfeminist celebrity culture and the gendering of authenticity. *Feminist Media Studies, 15*(4), 545–561.

Gifford, C. (2019, May 29). Indonesia is the world's fastest-growing e-commerce market [Review of Indonesia is the world's fastest-growing e-commerce market]. *The New Economy*. https://www.theneweconomy.com/business/indonesia-is-the-worlds-fastest-growing-e-commerce-market

Haclyakupoglu, G., & Zhang, W. (2015). Social media and trust during the Gezi protests in Turkey. *Journal of Computer-Mediated Communication, 20*(4), 450–466.

Hassan, S., & Shahzad, A. (2022). The impact of social media usage on small and micro social commerce enterprises in Malaysia. *Pakistan Journal of Commerce and Social Sciences, 16*(1), 141–166.

Hearn, A. (2008). Meat, mask, burden: Probing the contours of the branded self. *Journal of Consumer Culture, 8*(2), 197–217.

Huang, Z., & Benyoucef, M. (2013). From e-commerce to social commerce: A close look at design features. *Electronic Commerce Research and Applications, 12*(4), 246–259.

iiMedia. (2023). Research report on the development and trend of China's virtual human industry in 2023. 2023年中国虚拟人产业发展与商业趋势研究报告. https://www.iimedia.cn/c400/92538.html

Kim, D. Y., & Kim, H. Y. (2021). Trust me, trust me not: A nuanced view of influencer marketing on social media. *Journal of Business Research, 134*, 223–232.

Lazarsfeld, P. F., Berelson, B., & Gaudet, H. (1948). *The people's choice: How the voter makes up his mind in a presidential campaign*. Columbia University Press.

Lim, W. M. (2020). The sharing economy: A marketing perspective. *Australasian Marketing Journal (AMJ), 28*(3), 4–13.

Lin, X., & Wang, X. (2022). Towards a model of social commerce: Improving the effectiveness of e-commerce through leveraging social media tools based on consumers' dual role. *European Journal of Information Systems*.

Lin, X., Wang, X., & Hajli, N. (2019). Building e-commerce satisfaction and boosting sales: The role of social commerce trust and its antecedents. *International Journal of Electronic Commerce, 23*(3), 328–363.

Marwick, A. E. (2013). *Status update: Celebrity, publicity, and branding in the social media age*. Yale University Press.

Marwick, A. E., & Boyd, D. (2011). To see and be seen: Celebrity practice on Twitter. *Convergence: The International Journal of Research into New Media Technologies, 17*(2), 139–158. https://doi.org/10.1177/1354856510394539

McKinsey. (2018, November 12). *'True Gen': Generation Z and its implication for companies*. https://www.mckinsey.com/industries/consumer-packaged-goods/our-insights/true-gen-generation-z-and-its-implications-for-companies

McKinsey. (2020, June 29). *What makes Asia-Pacific's Gen Z different?* https://www.mckinsey.com/capabilities/growth-marketing-and-sales/our-insights/what-makes-asia-pacifics-generation-z-different

McKinsey. (2022, May 24). Marketing in the metaverse: An opportunity for innovation and experimentation. *McKinsey Quarterly*. https://www.mckinsey.com/capabilities/growth-marketing-and-sales/our-insights/marketing-in-the-metaverse-an-opportunity-for-innovation-and-experimentation

Mei, J. (2021). Virtual influencers: Walking around the boundary of real and virtual. In *International conference on educational innovation and philosophical inquiries (ICEIPI 2021)* (pp. 104–113).

Miyake, E. (2023). I am a virtual girl from Tokyo: Virtual influencers, digital-orientalism and the (Im)materiality of race and gender. *Journal of Consumer Culture, 23*(1), 209–228. https://doi.org/10.1177/14695405221117195

Molin, V., & Nordgren, S. (2019). *Robot or human? The marketing phenomenon of virtual influencers: A case study about virtual influencers' parasocial interaction on Instagram*. MSc thesis, Uppsala University. https://uu.diva-portal.org/smash/record.jsf?pid=diva2%3A1334486&dswid=-2763

Moustakas, E., Lamba, N., Mahmoud, D., & Ranganathan, C. (2020). Blurring lines between fiction and reality: Perspectives of experts on marketing effectiveness of virtual influencers. In *2020 international conference on cyber security and protection of digital services (cyber security)* (pp. 1–6). IEEE.

Mrad, M., Ramadan, Z., & Nasr, L. I. (2022). Computer-generated influencers: The rise of digital personalities. *Marketing Intelligence & Planning, 40*(5), 589–603.

Nouri, M. (2018). The power of influence: Traditional celebrity vs social media influencer. *Pop Culture Intersections, 32.*

Sands, S., Ferraro, C., Demsar, V., & Chandler, G. (2022). False idols: Unpacking the opportunities and challenges of falsity in the context of virtual influencers. *Business Horizons, 65*(6), 777–788.

Scolere, L., Pruchniewska, U., & Duffy, B. E. (2018). Constructing the platform-specific self-brand: The labor of social media promotion. *Social Media+ Society, 4*(3).

Shareef, M. A., Mukerji, B., Dwivedi, Y. K., Rana, N. P., & Islam, R. (2019). Social media marketing: Comparative effect of advertisement sources. *Journal of Retailing and Consumer Services, 46*, 58–69.

Shareef, M. A., Kapoor, K. K., Mukerhi, B., Dwivedi, R., & Dwivedi, Y. K. (2020). Group behavior in social media: Antecedents of initial trust formation. *Computers in Human Behavior, 105.*

Shin, D. H. (2010). The effects of trust, security and privacy in social networking: A security-based approach to understand the pattern of adoption. *Interacting with Computers, 22*(5), 138–428.

Statista. (2023). *Leading countries based on Facebook audience size as of January 2023.* https://www.statista.com/statistics/268136/top-15-countries-based-on-number-of-facebook-users/

Stephen, A. T., & Toubia, O. (2010). Deriving value from social commerce networks. *Journal of Marketing Research, 47*(2), 215–228.

Tajvidi, M., Richard, M. O., Wang, Y., & Hajli, N. (2020). Brand co-creation through social commerce information sharing: The role of social media. *Journal of Business Research, 121*, 476–486.

Tan, S. M., & Liew, T. W. (2020). Designing embodied virtual agents as product specialists in a multi-product category E-commerce: The roles of source credibility and social presence. *International Journal of Human Computer Interaction, 36*(12), 1136–1149.

The Influencer Marketing Factory. (2022, March 29). *Virtual influencers survey.* https://theinfluencermarketingfactory.com/virtual-influencers-survey-infographic/

Time. (2018). *The 25 most influential people on the internet.* https://time.com/5324130/most-influential-internet/

Wang, Y., & Yu, C. (2017). Social interaction-based consumer decision-making model in social commerce: The role of word of mouth and observational learning. *International Journal of Information Management, 37*(3), 179–189.

Wong, I. A., Sun, D., Xiong, X., & Li, X. (2023). Craving alterreal authenticity through the post-postmodern lens: An experimental inquiry. *Tourism Management, 94*, 104654.

Wu, Y., Nambisan, S., Xiao, J., & Xie, K. (2022). Consumer resource integration and service innovation in social commerce: The role of social media influencers. *Journal of the Academy of Marketing Science, 50*, 429–459.

Xinkedu. (2022). Will the internet giants win half of the game? The battle of virtual influencers. 这场虚拟人之战，互联网下场先赢一半？ http://news.sohu.com/a/622472990_116132

Zhang, H., Ju, Y., Gupta, S., & Zhang, L. (2014). What motivates customers to participate in social commerce? The impact of technological environments and virtual customer experiences. *Information Management, 51*(8), 1017–1030.

# 10

# Influencers, Materialism, Mental Health and Sustainability

### Qing Shan Ding and Saloomeh Tabari

## Materialism and Influencers

It is undeniable that social media influencers have amazing power and almost unparalleled reach in today's consumeristic society. Influencers can be very effective in terms of increasing brand awareness, enhancing customer engagement, changing consumer attitudes and reaching new customers. The negative impact of the dominance of influencers in our media landscape is often less mentioned. Perhaps one of the most damaging aspects of the obsession with influencers in our society is their active role in promoting materialistic values, especially among adolescents.

Belk (1985) suggested that materialism is a personality trait associated with possession, the lack of generosity and envy. Materialism can be

---

Q. S. Ding (✉)
Huddersfield Business School, University of Huddersfield, Huddersfield, UK
e-mail: Q.s.ding@hud.ac.uk

S. Tabari
Cardiff Business School, Cardiff University, Cardiff, UK
e-mail: tabaris@cardiff.ac.uk

© The Author(s), under exclusive license to Springer Nature Switzerland AG 2024
S. Tabari, Q. S. Ding (eds.), *Celebrity, Social Media Influencers and Brand Performance*,
https://doi.org/10.1007/978-3-031-63516-8_10

defined as personal values that pursue the acquisition and possession of material goods as a person's journey towards the fulfilment of life objectives (Richins, 2011; Richins & Dawson, 1992).

Kim et al. (2021) suggested that materialism is a term often loaded with multiple meanings. Although it is often associated with negative consequences such as experiencing lower subjective well-being (Christopher et al., 2009), materialistic values could have certain benefits, such as a determination for success and self-reliance (Richins & Dawson, 1992) and enhancement of positive mood (Hudders & Pandelaere, 2012), and could provide joy and security (Belk, 2010; Richins, 2017). The key characteristics of a materialistic lifestyle are the dominance of the acquisition of material goods, possession acquisition and ownership as central to one's life satisfaction and consideration of material goods as cues of success and self-evaluation (Kim et al., 2021). Materialistic individuals assess the success of others based on the quantity and quality of material possessions and normally evaluate life achievement by wealth, power, standard of living and status in society (Richins & Dawson, 1992). Materialistic individuals tend to admire the fortune, power, and status of other individuals; consumers in a materialistic society are especially drawn to individuals with high-quality material possessions (Agnihotri & Bhattacharya, 2021).

Materialism is not a modern phenomenon, and it dates back to very ancient civilisations (Rigby & Rigby, 1944). Kahle and Homer (1985) suggested that the attraction of celebrities often increases an individual's materialism level. However, one emergent facet of materialism is the effectiveness of traditional mass media and social media influencers in promoting materialist values (Seo & Hyun, 2018; Lou & Kim, 2019; Kim et al., 2021). The imitation of celebrity models and materialistic values has been established; this link is theorized under the lens of social comparison theory where consumers compare own accumulated goods with possessions of another to determine their own social rank (Chan & Prendergast, 2008; Kim et al., 2021). In terms of influencer advertising, the relationship could be similar to celebrities in that people may perceive the influencers as aspiring role models which positively affects purchase intention (Lou & Kim, 2019). It has been established that high materialistic values expressed in Instagram influencers' posts positively increase followers' consumption and purchase intentions; high-materialist individuals often experience hedonic excitement in anticipation of a purchase, resulting in greater buying intentions (Kim et al., 2021). This connection is particularly problematic for adolescents. Adolescents are often influenced by media celebrities in terms of brand choices, and they are more prone to use products that are disseminated by media-attractive celebrities (Goldsmith, 1999; Martin & Bush, 2000). Boon and Lomore (2001) concluded that adolescents have a unique connection with their favourite celebrities, and in today's context, celebrities are often social media influencers and vice versa, and adolescents are more prone to induce their choices. Furthermore, for adolescents in addition to the physical appearance, their idols also had some influence on their values of personal attitudes, such as ethical and moral values. High materialistic influencers promoting physical possessions such as luxury goods and sports cars are likely to encourage adolescents towards a materialistic lifestyle. The higher the attraction of adolescents to celebrities, the greater the degree of materialism exhibited by the respondents (Pinto et al., 2017). Furthermore, materialism has greater impact on adolescents with lower self-esteem. Adolescents with low self-esteem tend to have a higher degree of materialism (Yurchisin & Johnson, 2004; Chaplin & John, 2007; Pinto et al., 2017). It is claimed that materialists enjoy spending money to acquiring desirable possessions and frequently engaging in impulsive buying (Fitzmaurice, 2008). Materialism is a significant factor in terms of influencer popularity that it increases all the four key motivations of following influencers including authenticity, consumerism, creative inspiration and envy (Lee et al., 2022).

## Materialism and Mental Health

Influencers promote materialistic values and are welcoming sights for businesses, as undoubtedly it increases brand exposure, nurtures potential new customers and ultimately makes their products more desirable. However, the destructive power of materialism cannot be ignored, and it could be particularly damaging amongst adolescents. Materialism is widely established for its association with negative psychological distress including lower self-esteem, depression, loneliness and dissatisfaction with life (Mueller et al., 2011; Pieters, 2013; Tsang et al., 2014). To make matters worse, materialists tend to remedy such psychological deficiencies through further material acquisition, which creates a vicious circle (Reeves et al., 2012). A comprehensive analysis of toxic relationship between materialism and loneliness by Pieters (2013) revealed that they form a self-perpetuating cycle with vicious and virtuous sides. Materialism was associated with an increase in loneliness, and loneliness was associated with an increase in materialism over time. The three subtypes of materialism played qualitatively different roles in this unique cycle. Valuing material possessions as a measure of success and as a recipe for happiness was associated with increases in loneliness over time, and loneliness in return contributed to the growth of these subtypes of materialism. This forms the vicious side of the materialism-loneliness cycle, and it perpetuates once the relationship is created. Surprisingly by contrast, valuing possessions as a source of material joy in life was associated with decreases in loneliness over time, and loneliness was unrelated to the growth in this subtype of materialism. This models the virtuous side of the materialism-loneliness cycle. Materialism is a multidimensional phenomenon with subtle internal differences that have profound effects on psychological well-being.

A series of studies found that high materialists experienced fewer positive emotions and greater levels of depression, anxiety and substance abuse (Kasser & Ryan, 1993, 1996, 2001). Materialism has been consistently proven to lead to lower levels of life satisfaction. Tsang et al. (2014) suggest that high materialists find it harder to be grateful, and lower levels of trait gratitude could be explained by unmet psychological needs. Solberg et al. (2004) utilized gap theory to explain that materialists have unrealistically high expectations for the satisfaction that material goods could bring. Richins (2013) further suggests that materialists experience higher levels of expectation and anticipatory positive emotion than non-materialists before making a purchase. However, the acquisition of material goods could be ineffective in meeting expectations or sustaining these emotions, leading to a decline in positive emotions. To maintain positive emotions, materialists need to continually seek out new purchases, which lead to a chronic dissatisfaction and a decrease in psychological

## 10 Influencers, Materialism, Mental Health and Sustainability 201

well-being. Tsang et al. (2014) asserted that materialism may also impair need satisfaction because of decreased gratitude. Materialism and reduced life satisfaction could be explained by the decreased gratitude within high materialistic lifestyle, and the resultant declines in basic psychological needs. High materialists are less happy in life partially due to the fact that they find it more difficult to be grateful for what they have. This decrease in gratitude is associated with losses in basic psychological needs, which are essential for individuals to thrive.

Materialism was found to have negative consequences on not only personal but social well-being. Bauer et al. (2012) suggested that materialists value independence and therefore lead them to prefer greater social distance and to be less helpful towards others. Materialism leads to a broad range of psychological consequences that include not only lower preferences for social contact but also increased competitiveness, mistrust and diminished feelings of personal responsibility.

Adeyanju et al. (2021) revealed that Instagram and depression are interconnected. Instagram usage intensifies depressive and related symptoms compared to non-users and users of other social media platforms. Furthermore, the negative effects on psychological well-being could occur after immediate exposure to Instagram contents. Instagram also intensify negative effects through social comparison with strangers. As Instagram is full of image-perfect pictures and filtered photographs worldwide, some users, especially adolescents, might not feel good when comparing themselves to others. This is particularly susceptive to adolescents with low self-esteem. McCrory et al. (2022a, b) found that highly visual social media platforms, such as Snapchat, Instagram and TikTok, caused serious mental distress to adolescents. Social media features such as likes/comments on visuals and scrolling through a feed were associated with the role of 'viewer', instigating longer-lasting feelings of jealousy, inferiority and pressure to be accepted. To mitigate these negative feelings, young people switch to the role of 'contributor' by using filters and selecting highlights to their feeds and adjusting their personas, resulting in temporary feelings of higher self-esteem, better acceptance and greater popularity amongst peers. As social media users are constantly switching between the role of viewer and contributor, the emotions they experience are also constantly switching between instant inadequacy and instant gratification. These social media platforms trigger an unrelenting process of emotional roller coaster of highs and lows for their adolescent users. Young users of social media platforms also encourage the development of parasocial relationship with influencers, and it could adversely impact mental health through negative self-comparisons (Hoffner & Bond, 2022). A particular rising concern is the role of social media in adolescent girls' body image concerns and the development of depressive symptoms and eating disorders. Depressive symptoms increase considerably during adolescence, especially among young girls (Maughan et al., 2013), and rates of depression among adolescents were also on the rise (Geiger & Davis, 2019). Disordered eating is another potential problem during adolescence, especially among girls (Holm-Denoma et al., 2014; Neumark-Sztainer et al., 2011). The popularity of social media platforms caused additional challenges in tackling these problems. Choukas-Bradley et al. (2021) concluded that the features of social media intersect with adolescent developmental factors and societal over-emphasis on girls' and women's physical appearance, creating the 'perfect storm' to exacerbate girls' body image concerns. Ultimately, body image concerns served as a key mechanism underlying associations between adolescent girls' social media use and mental health. Social media could increase adolescent girls' body image concerns by heightening their focus on other people's physical appearance through frequent and repeated exposure to idealized images of peers, celebrities and social media influencers. This process created appearance-based social media consciousness, with exposure to idealized self-images actively encouraging the over-emphasis and over-valuing of physical appearance and peer approval of photos/videos. In the context of a new phenomenon—metaverse that proposes to combine teleworking, virtual reality and social media—the potential harm to mental health cannot be ignored. This naturally leads to consider questions such as how the users will be protected in metaverse and what regulatory mechanisms will be needed to ensure user safety and better protection of vulnerable groups (Benrimoh et al., 2022).

## A More Sustainability Future?

There is no doubt that fast fashion influencers, many with millions of online followers, played an important role in the increased consumption of cheap and trendy clothing. The fast fashion business model relies on quick reaction to changing consumer demands. This model deploys a fast production system to supply the inventory of hit styles and constantly introduce new ones. The quick fashion model became increasingly popular in the last two decades following the success of pioneering companies such as Zara and H&M, and the development of e-commerce platforms further accelerated its growth (Long & Nasiry, 2022). Fashion waste raises serious environmental concerns due to increases in fast fashion clothes consumption and a decrease in recycling. The fast fashion industry has yet to make sufficient efforts to achieve sustainability (Jang et al., 2012). Partially due to the growth of fast fashion, the fashion industry is experiencing increasing global scrutiny of its pollution on our environment. Its environmental impacts centred on textile and the entire fashion value chain, from production to consumption, including water use, chemical pollution, $CO_2$ emissions and textile waste. The environmental impacts from the fashion industry include over 92 million tonnes of waste produced and 79 trillion litres of water consumption during production process every year. The human and environmental health risks associated with inexpensive clothing and fast fashion are hidden throughout the lifecycle of every garment. It started with the growth of water-intensive cotton, then through the damaging release of untreated colouring dyes into local water systems, often associated with low wages and poor working conditions. Fundamental changes to the business model were suggested, from more sustainable manufacturing and supply chain, to shifts in consumer behaviour which means reduce clothing purchases and increased garment lifetimes. There is an urgent need for transition back to 'slow' fashion to mitigate the detrimental environmental consequences (Schlosberg, 2020; Niinimäki et al., 2020).

Influencers played an active role in promoting fast fashion consumption to their followers on various social media platforms. Many fast fashion companies such as Primark reduced their advertising budget and enlisted an army of nano influencers to engage and promote their brands on platforms such as YouTube. However, in recent years, there is a shift of social media influencers towards promotion of a more sustainable and environmentally friendly behaviour. Environmental influencers have amassed immense popularity in recent years on social media platforms, promoting a sustainable lifestyle by interweaving environmental topics with their everyday content (Dekoninck & Schmuck, 2023). Campaigners like Greta Thunberg inspired a new generation of influencers to expand their lifestyle-related social media operations (Sakib et al., 2020) for the promotion of positive societal causes (Allgaier, 2020) and environmental activism (Johnstone & Lindh, 2018). The environmental influencers are shrewd social media users who use their platform to champion environmental topics such as veganism, sustainable lifestyle and waste avoidance (Sakib et al., 2020). Gradually, they established themselves as credible trendsetters (De Jans et al., 2019) and online opinion leaders (Casaló et al., 2020). They hold considerable influence on their followers (Breves et al., 2021; Breves & Liebers, 2022), especially amongst young people, who are typically less politically active in the traditional spheres and adopt social media as a primary source for environmental or political information (Andersen et al., 2021). Environmental influencers acted as amplifiers in the electronic word of mouth of climate change debate, and the exceptional reach of highly active Twitter users played a very important role in promoting climate activism (Williams et al., 2015; Jung et al., 2020). Studies have shown that environmental influence not only is capable of changing attitudes but also instigates real change. Followers of influencers who champion environmental issues increased their political and caused oriented participation. There is a direct relationship between following influencers who actively discuss environmental concerns and participation behaviour among youth followers (Dekoninck & Schmuck, 2023), which is similar to the effects of following political influencers (Harff & Schmuck, 2023).

There is increasing awareness of the negative impact of social media on society's mental well-being; low levels of mental health literacy are an important contributor to low levels of help-seeking and increase poor mental health outcomes (Bonabi et al., 2016; Gorczynski et al., 2017). Social media and influencers have been identified as a resource to aid

## 10 Influencers, Materialism, Mental Health and Sustainability 205

mental health literacy and help-seeking (Naslund et al., 2020; Power et al., 2020). Mental health professionals working with social media influencers on TikTok and Instagram had great impact on increasing awareness, literacy and engagement of mental health issues, especially amongst young people (Pretorius et al., 2022). These platforms and influencers made mental health information more accessible and helped to overcome traditional barriers such as access, stigma and a preference for self-reliance. Young adults increasingly rely on social networking sites to seek help for their mental health problems; Instagram and influencer posts with pictures that tell stories which followers can connect to help the affected individuals to deal better with their experiences and increase the acceptance of mental health issues (Koinig, 2022).

Some have argued that Western society has started to witness the shifting from an overwhelming emphasis on material well-being and physical security towards greater emphasis on the quality of life for over 50 years ago (Inglehart, 1977, 1989). It is argued that modern states, with their welfare infrastructure and liberal development, could provide the environment and politics that citizens can express and achieve a wide range of values and lifestyles based on identity and non-economic interests (Inglehart & Welzel, 2005). Schlosberg (2020) asserted that there is a direct link between the shift in society's individual and cultural values and subsequent political change. When people get materially comfortable, they could develop post-materialist values and participate in representative democracies to demand the state to respond with new and improved public policies. It further suggests that sustainable consumption is the outcome of the lack of action on environmental and sustainability issues. It is based on the realization that we need more than simply environmental protection policies but also new collective functioning material practices that do not work against the sustainability and functioning of Earth systems (Schlosberg, 2020). Sustainable consumption integrates across industrial ecology, ecological design, ecological economics, sociology, psychology, science and consumer studies (Cohen et al., 2013). Community food, energy and other movements for sustainable products and integrated supply chains are embodiments of the shift from a postmaterial politics to sustainable materialism. It is argued that innovation is at the heart of sustainable materialism that involve the construction of new food systems, community energy and sustainable production. It moves on from a focus on individual values but should be seen in the context of a broader public and collective effort towards a new flow and circulation of material goods. In sustainable materialist societies, social and political change happens within an ecosystem that connects individual beliefs and actions with material, institutional and community processes and flows (Schlosberg, 2020).

# References

Adeyanju, G. C., Solfa, R. P., Tran, T. L., et al. (2021). Behavioural symptoms of mental health disorder such as depression among young people using Instagram: A systematic review. *Translational Medicine Communications, 6*(15). https://doi.org/10.1186/s41231-021-00092-3

Agnihotri, & Bhattacharya. (2021). Endorsement effectiveness of celebrities versus social media influencers in the materialistic cultural environment of India. *Journal of International Consumer Marketing, 33*(3), 280–302.

Allgaier, J. (2020). Rezo and German climate change policy: The influence of networked expertise on YouTube and beyond. *Media and Communication, 8*, 376–386.

Andersen K, Ohme J, Bjarnøe C, et al. (2021). Generational Gaps in Political Media Use and Civic Engagement: From Baby Boomers to Generation Z. London: Taylor & Francis.

Bailey, K., Basu, A., & Sharma, S. (2022). The environmental impacts of fast fashion on water quality: a systematic review. *Water, 14*(7), 1073.

Bauer, M. A., Wilkie, J. E. B., Kim, J. K., & Bodenhausen, G. V. (2012). Cuing consumerism: Situational materialism undermines personal and social well-being. *Psychological Science, 23*(5), 517–523.

Belk, R. W. (1985). Materialism: Trait aspects of living in the material world. *Journal of Consumer Research, 12*(4), 265–280.

Belk, R. (2010). *Possessions and self.* Wiley International Encyclopaedia of Marketing.

Benrimoh, D., Chheda, F., & Margolese, H. (2022). The best predictor of the future—The metaverse, mental health, and lessons learned from current technologies. *JMIR Mental Health, 9*(10), e40410. https://mental.jmir.org/2022/10/e40410

Bonabi, H., et al. (2016). Mental health literacy, attitudes to help seeking, and perceived need as predictors of mental health service use: A longitudinal study. *Journal of Nervous and Mental Disease, 204*(4), 321–324.

Boon, S. D., & Lomore, C. D. (2001). Admirer-celebrity relationships among young adults: Explaining perceptions of celebrity influence on identity. *Human Communication Research, 27*(3), 432–465.

Breves, P., & Liebers, N. (2022). #Greenfluencing. The impact of parasocial relationships with social media influencers on advertising effectiveness and followers' pro-environmental intentions. *Environmental Communication, 16*, 773–787.

Breves, P., Amrehn, J., Heidenreich, A., et al. (2021). Blind trust? The importance and interplay of parasocial relationships and advertising disclosures in explaining influencers' persuasive effects on their followers. *International Journal of Advertising, 40*(7), 1209–1229.

Casaló, L. V., Flavián, C., & Ibáñez-Sánchez, S. (2020). Influencers on Instagram: Antecedents and consequences of opinion leadership. *Journal of Business Research, 117*, 510–519.

Chan, K., & Prendergast, G. P. (2008). Social comparison, imitation of celebrity models and materialism among Chinese youth. *International Journal of Advertising, 27*(5), 799–826.

Chaplin, L. N., & John, D. R. (2007). Growing up in a material world: Age differences in materialism in children and adolescents. *Journal of Consumer Research, 34*(4), 480–493.

Choukas-Bradley, S., Roberts, S. R., Maheux, A. J., & Nesi, J. (2021). The perfect storm: A developmental–sociocultural framework for the role of social media in adolescent girls' body image concerns and mental health. *Clinical Child and Family Psychology Review, 25*, 681–701.

Christopher, A. N., Saliba, L., & Deadmarsh, E. J. (2009). Materialism and well-being: The mediating effect of locus of control. *Personality and Individual Differences, 46*(7), 682–686.

Cohen, M. J., Brown, H. S., & Vergragt, P. (2013). *Innovations in sustainable consumption: New economics, socio-technical transitions and social practices.* Edward Elgar.

De Jans, S., Cauberghe, V., & Hudders, L. (2019). How an advertising disclosure alerts young adolescents to sponsored vlogs: The moderating role of a peer-based advertising literacy intervention through an informational vlog. *Journal of Advertising, 47*, 1–17.

de Rezende Pinto, M., Mota, A. O., Leite, R. S., & Alves, R. C. (2017). Investigating the influencers of materialism in adolescence. *Tourism & Management Studies, 13*(1), 66–74.

Dekoninck, H., & Schmuck, D. (2023). The "greenfluence": Following environmental influencers, parasocial relationships, and youth's participation behavior. *New Media & Society, 0*(0). https://doi.org/10.1177/14614 448231156131

Fitzmaurice, J. (2008). Splurge purchases and materialism. *Journal of Consumer Marketing, 25*(6), 332–338.

Geiger, A. W., & Davis, L. (2019, July 12). *A growing number of American teenagers—Particularly girls—Are facing depression.* Pew Research Center. https://www.pewresearch.org/fact-tank/2019/07/12/

Goldsmith, R. E. (1999). The personalised marketplace: beyond the 4Ps. *Marketing Intelligence & Planning, 17*(4), 178–185.

Gorczynski, P., et al. (2017). Examining mental health literacy, help seeking behaviours, and mental health outcomes in UK university students. *The Journal of Mental Health Training, Education and Practice, 12*(2), 111–120.

Johnstone, L., & Lindh, C. (2018). The sustainability-age dilemma: A theory of (un) planned behaviour via influencers. *Journal of Consumer Behaviour, 17*(1), e127–e139.

Harff, D., & Schmuck, D. (2023). Influencers as empowering agents? Following political influencers, internal political efficacy and participation among youth. *Political Communication, 40*(2), 147–172.

Hoffner, C. A., & Bond, B. J. (2022). Parasocial relationships, social media, & well-being. *Current Opinion in Psychology, 45*, 101306.

Holm-Denoma, J. M., Hankin, B. L., & Young, J. F. (2014). Developmental trends of eating disorder symptoms and comorbid internalizing symptoms in children and adolescents. *Eating Behaviors, 15*(2), 275–279.

Hudders, L., & Pandelaere, M. (2012). The silver lining of materialism: The impact of luxury consumption on subjective well-being. *Journal of Happiness Studies, 13*, 411–437.

Inglehart, R. (1977). *The silent revolution.* Princeton University Press.

Inglehart, R. (1989). *Culture shift in advanced industrial society.* Princeton University Press.

Inglehart, R., & Welzel, C. (2005). *Modernization, cultural change, and democracy: The human development sequence.* Cambridge University Press.

## 10 Influencers, Materialism, Mental Health and Sustainability 209

Jang, J., Ko, E., Chun, E., & Lee, E. (2012). A study of a social content model for sustainable development in the fast fashion industry. *Journal of Global Fashion Marketing, 3*(2), 61–70.

Jung, J., Petkanic, P., Nan, D., et al. (2020). When a girl awakened the world: A user and social message analysis of Greta Thunberg. *Sustainability, 12*(7), 2707.

Kahle, L. R., & Homer, P. M. (1985). Physical attractiveness of the celebrity endorser: A social adaptation perspective. *Journal of Consumer Research, 11*(4), 954–961.

Kasser, T., & Ryan, R. M. (1993). A dark side of the American Dream: Correlates of financial success as a central life aspiration. *Journal of Personality and Social Psychology, 65*, 410–422.

Kasser, T., & Ryan, R. M. (1996). Further examining the American Dream: Differential correlates of intrinsic and extrinsic goals. *Personality and Social Psychology Bulletin, 22*, 280–287.

Kasser, T., & Ryan, R. M. (2001). Be careful what you wish for: Optimal functioning and the relative attainment of intrinsic and extrinsic goals. In P. Schmuck & K. M. Sheldon (Eds.), *Life goals and well-being: Towards a positive psychology of human striving* (pp. 116–131). Hogrefe & Huber.

Kim, E., Shoenberger, H., & Sun, Y. (2021). Living in a material world: Sponsored Instagram posts and the role of materialism, hedonic enjoyment, perceived trust, and need to belong. *Social Media + Society, 7*(3), 205630512110383. https://doi.org/10.1177/20563051211038306

Koinig, I. (2022). Picturing mental health on Instagram: Insights from a quantitative study using different content formats. *International Journal of Environmental Research and Public Health, 19*(3), 1608. https://doi.org/10.3390/ijerph19031608

Lee, J. A., Sudarshan, S., Sussman, K. L., Bright, L. F., & Eastin, M. S. (2022). Why are consumers following social media influencers on Instagram? Exploration of consumers' motives for following influencers and the role of materialism. *International Journal of Advertising, 41*(1), 78–100.

Long, X., & Nasiry, J. (2022). Sustainability in the fast fashion industry. *Manufacturing & Service Operations Management, 24*(3), 1276–1293.

Lou, C., & Kim, H. K. (2019). Fancying the new rich and famous? Explicating the roles of influencer content, credibility, and parental mediation in adolescents' parasocial relationship, materialism, and purchase intentions. *Frontiers in Psychology, 10*, 2567.

Martin, C. A., & Bush, A. J. (2000). Do role models influence teenagers purchase intentions and behavior? *Journal of Consumer Marketing, 17*(5), 441–454.

Maughan, B., Collishaw, S., & Stringaris, A. (2013). Depression in childhood and adolescence. *Journal of the Canadian Academy of Child and Adolescent Psychiatry, 22*(1), 35–40.

McCrory, E., Foulkes, L., & Viding, E. (2022a). Social thinning and stress generation after childhood maltreatment: A neurocognitive social transactional model of psychiatric vulnerability. *The Lancet Psychiatry, 9*(10), 828–837.

McCrory, A., Best, P., & Maddock, A. (2022b). 'It's just one big vicious circle': Young people's experiences of highly visual social media and their mental health. *Health Education Research, 37*(3), 167–184.

Mueller, A., Mitchell, J. E., Peterson, L. A., Faber, R. J., Steffen, K. J., Crosby, R. D., & Claes, L. (2011). Depression, materialism, and excessive internet use in relation to compulsive buying. *Comprehensive Psychiatry, 52*(4), 420–424.

Naslund, J. A., et al. (2020). Social media and mental health: Benefits, risks, and opportunities for research and practice. *Journal of Technology in Behavioral Science,* 245–257.

Neumark-Sztainer, D., Wall, M., Larson, N. I., Eisenberg, M. E., & Loth, K. (2011). Dieting and disordered eating behaviors from adolescence to young adulthood: Findings from a 10-year longitudinal study. *Journal of the American Dietetic Association, 111*(7), 1004–1011.

Niinimäki, K., Peters, G., Dahlbo, H., Perry, P., Rissanen, T., & Gwilt, A. (2020). The environmental price of fast fashion. *Nature Reviews Earth and Environment, 1,* 189–200.

Pieters, R. (2013). Bidirectional dynamics of materialism and loneliness: Not just a vicious cycle. *Journal of Consumer Research, 40*(4), 615–631.

Power, E., et al. (2020). Youth mental health in the time of COVID-19. *Irish Journal of Psychological Medicine, 37*(4), 301–305.

Pretorius, C., McCashin, D., & Coyle, D. (2022). Mental health professionals as influencers on TikTok and Instagram: What role do they play in mental health literacy and help-seeking? *Internet Interventions, 30,* 100591. https://doi.org/10.1016/j.invent.2022.100591

Reeves, R. A., Baker, G. A., & Truluck, C. S. (2012). Celebrity worship, materialism, compulsive buying, and the empty self. *Psychology & Marketing, 29*(9), 674–679.

Richins, M. L. (2011). Materialism, transformation expectations, and spending: Implications for credit use. *Journal of Public Policy & Marketing, 30*(2), 141–156.

Richins, M. L. (2013). When wanting is better than having: Materialism, transformation expectations, and product-evoked emotions in the purchase process. *Journal of Consumer Research, 40*(1), 1–18.

Richins, M. L. (2017). Materialism pathways: The processes that create and perpetuate materialism. *Journal of Consumer Psychology, 27*(4), 480–499. https://doi.org/10.1016/j.jcps.2017.07.006

Richins, M. L., & Dawson, S. (1992). A consumer values orientation for materialism and its measurement: Scale development and validation. *Journal of Consumer Research, 19*(3), 303–316.

Rigby, D., & Rigby, E. (1944). *Lock, stock and barrel: The story of collecting* (Vol. 692). J. B. Lippincott.

Sakib, M. D. N., Zolfagharian, M., & Yazdanparast, A. (2020). Does parasocial interaction with weight loss vloggers affect compliance? The role of vlogger characteristics, consumer readiness, and health consciousness. *Journal of Retailing and Consumer Services, 52*, 101733.

Schlosberg, D. (2020). *From postmaterialism to sustainable materialism: the environmental politics of practice-based movements.* Environmental Politics.

Seo, M., & Hyun, K. D. (2018). The effects of following celebrities' lives via SNSs on life satisfaction: The palliative function of system justification and the moderating role of materialism. *New Media & Society, 20*(9), 3479–3497.

Solberg, E. G., Diener, E., & Robinson, M. D. (2004). Why are materialists less satisfied? In T. Kasser & A. D. Kanner (Eds.), *Psychology and consumer culture: The struggle for a good life in a materialistic world* (pp. 29–48). American Psychological Association.

Tsang, J. A., Carpenter, T. P., Roberts, J. A., Frisch, M. B., & Carlisle, R. D. (2014). Why are materialists less happy? The role of gratitude and need satisfaction in the relationship between materialism and life satisfaction. *Personality and Individual Differences, 64*, 62–66.

Williams, H. T. P., McMurray, J. R., Kurz, T., et al. (2015). Network analysis reveals open forums and echo chambers in social media discussions of climate change. *Global Environmental Change, 32*, 126–138.

Yurchisin, J., & Johnson, K. K. P. (2004). Compulsive buying behavior and its relationship to perceived social status associated with buying, materialism, self-esteem, and apparel-product involvement. *Family and Consumer Sciences Research Journal, 32*(3), 291–314.

# Index

**A**

Adolescents, 197, 199, 201
Advertising Standards Authority
  (ASA), 18
AMOS, 121
Artificial intelligence (AI), 3, 94,
  106, 136, 189
Attitudes, 1, 2, 13, 27, 31, 43, 56,
  83, 107, 108, 110, 125, 142,
  197, 199, 204
Augmented reality (AR), 134
Average variance extracted (AVE),
  51, 117, 120

**B**

Behavioural intentions, 1, 2
Brand endorsements, 105

Brand identity, 86, 89, 93, 97,
  176, 182
Branding, 175–190
Brand loyalty, 1, 80, 178
Brands, vii, 1–5, 10, 13–17, 19, 21,
  26–29, 31, 44, 45, 56, 57, 66,
  70, 72, 73, 79–100, 106–108,
  124, 136, 137, 144, 159–163,
  165, 166, 175, 177–179,
  182–189, 204

**C**

Celebrities, vii, 1–3, 10, 13, 14, 16,
  18–20, 80–84, 86, 87, 90, 94,
  95, 105, 137, 160–162, 177,
  182, 198, 202
Celebrity endorsement, 1, 10, 80, 84

© The Author(s), under exclusive license to Springer Nature Switzerland AG 2024
S. Tabari, Q. S. Ding (eds.), *Celebrity, Social Media Influencers and Brand Performance*,
https://doi.org/10.1007/978-3-031-63516-8

**214    Index**

Chinese consumers, 115, 185
Composite reliability (CR), 52, 117
Consumer behaviour, vii, 67, 107, 145, 160, 161, 203
Consumer behavioural, 27, 31
Consumer brand experience, 13
Consumer culture, 19
Consumers' purchase intention, 105–126
Consumption behaviour, vii
Covid-19, 66, 180
Credibility, 13, 18, 45, 46, 57, 58, 65, 66, 68, 69, 88, 107, 108, 111, 112, 145, 162
Cultural background, 138, 183
Customers' purchasing decisions, 161

**D**

Digital, 3, 12, 14, 15, 39, 43, 68, 80–84, 86, 87, 94, 105, 124, 126, 134–137, 140–142, 144–150, 164, 165, 178, 181, 184, 186–190
Digital environment, 135, 140, 147, 178, 188–190
Digitalised, 134
Digital natives, 39, 68, 190
Dual-process mediation model, 27, 31

**E**

E-commerce, 86, 180, 181, 203
Endogenous constructs, 49
Estimates coefficients, 49
Ethics, 83, 137, 179

**F**

Fashion, 2, 3, 79, 80, 83, 85–87, 89–97, 99, 145, 162, 181, 186, 187, 203
Fashion industry, 89–90, 203
Fear of missing out (FOMO), 3, 4, 65, 159–167

**G**

Generational theory, 56
Generation X, 68, 73
Generation Z (Gen Z), 3, 4, 39–58, 82–83, 86, 175, 190
Gen Y, 83, 167
Gen Zers, 40, 42, 58, 83
Globalisation, 138
Global Village, 140

**H**

*Hyper-personal communication*, 143

**I**

Identity, 13, 14, 39, 108, 133–151, 161–164, 166, 177, 205
Immersive online environments, 146
Impulsive buying, 159–167, 199
Influencer marketing, 9, 70, 89, 92, 95, 98
Influencers, vii, 2–5, 9–31, 40, 43–48, 50–52, 56–58, 65–73, 79–100, 105–116, 118–120, 122–126, 133–151, 160–166, 175–179, 182–189, 197–206
Instafame, 20
Instafamous, 81

**Index**   **215**

Instagram, 15, 19, 29, 30, 39, 47,
    48, 68, 70, 72, 80–82, 84–86,
    89, 91, 92, 95, 97–100, 160,
    162, 176, 181, 183, 186, 198,
    201, 205

**M**

Marketing communications,
    9–18, 80
Marketing strategies, vii, 12, 57, 65,
    70–72, 80, 125, 126
Materialism, 4, 197–206
Mental health, 4, 185, 187, 197–206
Micro-influencers, 10, 11, 15–17,
    20, 42, 72, 88, 162
Millennials, 2, 58, 63–73, 82
Mobile-first, 9, 15

**O**

Online marketing platforms, 15
Online platforms, 11
Ordinary least squares (OLS), 49

**P**

Pandemic, 3, 66, 68, 70, 71, 86, 94,
    95, 160, 165, 180
Partial least squares structural
    equation modeling
    (PLS-SEM), 49
Perceived brand value, 44, 52
*Perceived reality*, 134
Perceived value, 44, 57, 106–110,
    112–114, 125, 126
Personal consumption, 14

Personalities, 2, 90, 137, 148,
    175, 179
Perspective, 133–151
Purchase behaviour, 56, 85, 126
Purchase intention, 4, 13, 15, 18,
    27, 39–58, 106–111,
    113–115, 120–126, 161, 163,
    164, 178, 198, 199

**Q**

Qualitative metrics, 29, 31
Questionnaire, 68, 115

**R**

Restaurant, 43

**S**

Snapchat, 39, 164, 201
Social Commerce (SC), 180
Social influence theory, 161–164
Social media, vii, 2–4, 9–31, 39, 40,
    42, 43, 45, 47, 48, 50–52,
    56–58, 65–73, 79–100, 108,
    115, 134, 136–138, 142–146,
    159–161, 163–165, 167,
    176–178, 181–184, 186–188,
    190, 197, 198, 201, 203, 204
Social media influencers (SMI), 2–5,
    10, 14, 15, 40, 43, 45, 46, 48,
    52, 56–58, 63–73, 81, 83, 84,
    137, 159–161, 163–167, 178,
    199, 202, 204, 205
Social media platforms, 9–31, 39,
    43, 45, 56–58, 70, 71, 82, 89,

**216   Index**

91, 108, 145, 164, 176, 182, 183, 201, 203
Social network service (SNS), 180
Stakeholders, 12, 20, 21
Stimulus-Organism-Response (S-O-R) paradigm, 106, 110
Sustainability, 4, 96, 166, 197–206

**T**

TikTok, 30, 39, 47, 48, 86, 88, 91, 94, 95, 99–100, 160, 162, 164, 165, 176, 201, 205
Traditional online marketing, 9
Travel destination, 63–73
Trustworthiness, 2, 4, 13, 30, 39–58, 65, 68, 69, 81, 82, 107, 147, 163

**U**

Unsustainable consumption, 3
Urge-to-buy (UTB), 3, 161, 163–166

**V**

Virtual influencers, 3–5, 85, 105–126, 133–151, 165, 175–190
Virtual reality (VR), 134
Virtual world, 3, 4, 133–151, 159–167, 185

**W**

Well-being, 4, 150, 200, 201
Word of mouth (WOM), 180

Printed by Libri Plureos GmbH
in Hamburg, Germany